The Structure of Conflict

Clyde H. Coombs
The University of Michigan

George S. Avrunin
The University of Massachusetts

LEA LAWRENCE ERLBAUM ASSOCIATES, PUBLISHERS
1988   Hillsdale, New Jersey   Hove and London

Lawrence Erlbaum Associates, Inc., Publishers
365 Broadway
Hillsdale, New Jersey 07642

Library of Congress Cataloging-in-Publication Data
Coombs, Clyde Hamilton, 1912-1988
The structure of conflict / Clyde H. Coombs, George S. Avrunin.
   p. cm.
Bibliography: p.
Includes index.
ISBN 0-8058-0011-5 : $29.95
1. Interpersonal conflict. 2. Conflict (psychology) 3. Conflict
management--Philosophy. I. Avrunin, George S. II. Title.
   BF637.I48C66 1988
   03.6--dc19   88-11154
                                      CIP

Printed in the United States of America
10 9 8 7 6 5 4 3 2 1

Preface

Conflict is ubiquitous, and this ubiquity is accompanied by unlimited variety. Literature on conflict ranges from historical descriptions and explanations of particular conflicts to attempts to introduce order into the variety by providing an overall structure. This book is in the latter category.

A theory that attempts to bring order to the chaotic variety of conflict usually begins by distinguishing types of conflict and formulating general explanatory principles that relate and integrate them. Such an approach is more familiar to the theoretician and academician than to the practicing negotiator, but a theory that neglects the practical problems of resolving conflict would be of little value.

In this book, we describe and explore some structural aspects of conflict. We believe that this framework points up some significant similarities between apparently unrelated conflicts and has important implications for both the choice of methods for resolving a conflict and the ease of achieving that resolution. We discuss some of these implications in detail, and we sketch proposals for empirical investigations of a few of them, but it is not our intention to give instructions on how to resolve any particular conflict. Instead, we hope that the framework we describe will provide useful insights for practitioners and stimulate further theoretical and empirical investigation.

Our introductory chapter discusses some of the classifications that have been proposed and introduces our own classification of conflict into three types. The remainder of the book is divided into three parts, one for each of the three types of conflict. Each part begins with an abstract that serves as a preview of the chapters in that part.

Part I is concerned with Type I conflict. This is conflict within an individual because he or she has to choose between options, each of which may be better than any other in some respect. An individual may be deciding which car to buy, where to go on a vacation, which university to apply to, or, indeed, whether to buy a new car, go on a trip, or help a relative go to a university. In each case, these are options and each option that is better than another in some respect satisfies some goal better than that other option. In making a choice, the individual resolves a conflict.

In the three chapters of Part I, we develop a theory of individual choice that describes a set of conditions under which an optimal choice is most easily arrived at. We present and discuss the behavioral principles and mathematical assumptions and make the important point that the simple case of "single peakedness" over a set of ordered options is sufficient for our purposes.

In Chapter 3, we discuss approach and avoidance processes and their use in the classification of Type I conflicts. We also consider the effects of framing (i.e., changes in the descriptions of formally equivalent options) on the difficulty of resolving conflicts within an individual or between individuals. Chapter 4 concludes Part I. It is wholly concerned with the relative difficulty of resolving different Type I conflicts, and contains a number of suggestions for empirical investigation.

Part II consists of eight chapters all concerned with conflict between individuals because they want different things but must settle for the same thing, what we call Type II conflict. Examples might include a husband and wife buying a house, labor and management negotiating an agreement, or two sovereign countries disputing a boundary.

These chapters proceed from the simplest possible conflict of this type, from a structural point of view, through increasingly more complex conflicts. From this point of view, complexity of a conflict increases with the complexity of the options and the number of parties involved in the dispute.

Although the structure of Type II conflict has much in common with Type I, problems arise which do not arise in Type I. The original intent of the Type I theory was descriptive but some aspects of the model, such as optimization, have a normative flavor, and when the theory is used to model the structure of Type II conflict, the normative flavor is intensified. Some of the normative issues lend themselves to convincing and generally acceptable rational solutions. In Chapter 9, for example, we show that there is a rational procedure for screening options of any complexity that will yield a set of options that are totally ordered and are optimal in a particular and precise sense of minimizing concession. We call this set the frontier of preference.

The normative principles on which procedures for choosing an option are based may be contradictory, and consensus does not provide an answer. We have made a point of making such considerations visible. Because of this lack of consensus, and because the actual choice of an option is highly dependent on the details of the particular case, we make no attempt to offer any general solution.

The eight chapters of Part II constitute the largest part of the book, and a variety of issues are discussed in them, including some pros and cons of debate in seeking a resolution to a Type II conflict, the negotiation process, and the relation of this structure of conflict to game theory. Other topics include the extension of the concept of the frontier of preference to Type I conflict and to Type II conflicts involving more than two parties, the relative difficulty of resolving the variety of Type II conflicts, and a measure of the distance between adversaries. Part II concludes with a chapter that relates Type II conflict to Type I, on the one hand, and to Type III, on the other.

Part III consists of two chapters. The first describes the nature of Type III conflict, which is defined as conflict between individuals because they want the same thing but must settle for different things. Such conflict is typified at one extreme by professional sports and by disputes between sovereign states at the other. From a structural point of view, these examples differ in the degree to which escalation is controlled. The matter of controlling escalation occupies much of our attention in Part III. Problems here are associated with the availability of courses of action and with the selection of a particular one. We discuss higher game theory in this context and then go into the matter of transformation of the type of conflict in some detail, emphasizing what is gained and the price paid.

The final chapter provides an integrative perspective on the three types of conflict and a final section concludes the book with some more personal observations on the subject of conflict, which are not intrinsic to the theory developed here.

In our study of conflict we have come to recognize that there are two facets that must be looked at independently, but whose interrelation must be understood. One facet is the individuals involved and the behavioral principles that govern them, and the other facet is the existence of options and their structural relation. In any particular instance the relative importance of either facet may range from negligible to decisive. Understanding their separate but interacting roles is a major goal of this book, and we suggest research problems along with discussing some findings already reported in the literature.

Where there is structure there is order, and where there is order there is mathematics. In most instances, the logical arguments are both elementary and helpful and so they are included in the text. Technical notes, used to pursue the exposition of some issues more deeply, are segregated in the text and may be skipped by the casual reader. More intensive mathematical developments are contained in iv

the appendices. A glossary of terms used with very particular meanings, more circumscribed than in ordinary discourse, is provided.

We have undoubtedly missed some important literature, but we have tracked down a good deal more than we have made use of here. If we have missed something particularly important, or not given credit to contributions that anticipated ours, we can only apologize and hope that we can remedy the oversight in the future. Needless to say, we have benefited from suggestions and criticisms over a number of years of many students, friends, and colleagues whom it is not feasible to list and acknowledge as they deserve. There are some, however, to whom we are especially indebted and we wish to express our appreciation for their comments and assistance. These include the following: Jack W. Atkinson, Robert Axelrod, Thom Bezimbinder, Edward Bordin, Bruce Carlson, Roger Cramton, Hubert Feger, Robben Fleming, Daniel Katz, Samuel Komorita, David Messick, John Miyamoto, John Palmer, Perry Shapiro, Karin M. Skadden, Barbara Smuts, and Eric Stein. None of these, of course, is responsible for the use we made of his or her suggestions.

In addition to the above, we owe a very special note of appreciation to Lolagene Coombs, Robyn Dawes, William Goldstein, and Alexander MacRae who argued, criticized, contributed, and endured draft after draft.

Finally, we wish to recognize the support by the National Science Foundation of part of the research on which this book is based through grants BNS 78-09101 and BNS 81-20299.

Contents

List of Figures

List of Tables

Chapter 1

Introduction

Choice and conflict are coexistent. It is our thesis that, under appropriate circumstances, there is an efficient and effective process by which an individual can arrive at an optimal choice when choosing among a variety of options. After an analysis of this mechanism and of the conditions which permit it to operate, we model the structure of conflict between individuals on it.

There is a vast literature on the subject of conflict, not because so much is known in a scientific sense but because it is so important a topic. Much of this literature is concerned with violent conflicts, particularly wars and revolutions. Neither time nor inclination permits us to review all of this literature, but, on a very selective basis, we will refer to some of the existing literature in which the ideas made use of here, or related ones, were introduced.

For our purposes a very general definition of conflict is the most appropriate: the opposition of response (behavioral) tendencies (English & English, 1958), which may be within an individual or in different individuals. Such a general definition includes conflicts such as that of an individual facing a choice between two job offers, or a conflict between the engineers and the stylists in planning a new car, or that between two sovereign states quarreling over fishing rights or one seeking hegemony over the other.

Some conflicts may not be very dramatic and are often resolved with little difficulty, but some have potential for escalation. We propose to show that there are systematic structural properties running through the spectrum of all conflicts and that these abstractions are relevant to the process of resolving conflict.

This is not a new idea. A good deal of scholarly literature has been directed at the problem of a theory of conflict. For example,

1

J. Bernard wrote critically in 1950 about sociological approaches to
conflict. She referred to invention and change on the dynamic side,
and class and caste on the structural side, as having become the
fashionable explanatory and analytic tools in sociology. She felt that
interactional processes had been neglected in sociological theory and
so the theory of conflict had been neglected in favor of the theory of
culture.

"The culture concept exonerates individuals as human beings.
The culture concept emphasizes nonpersonal processes. Human beings play the role almost of puppets. Cultural analysis, as a matter of
fact, could dispense with human beings entirely. Human will — free
or determined *n'importe* — can be ignored. Even more so the conflict
of human wills" (Bernard, 1950 p. 14).

Some theories and explanations are stated in terms of particular
sociological structures involving the distribution of power and authority between religious groups, or minorities, or some class structure (e.g., Dahrendorf, 1958). Some explanations are "hot-blooded"
— involving tension, sentiment, or frustration — or "cold-blooded"
— involving strategic considerations and self-interest (e.g., Bernard,
1957; Boasson, 1958).

Substantive descriptions and contextual explanations of particular
events may be insightful and satisfying, but their particularity may
at the same time interfere with detecting and recognizing the more
abstract features that are common to all of them. Conflicts between
spouses, between management and labor, or between two sovereign
states are enormously different on psychological, economic, sociological, and political levels, but on an abstract level, have, as we propose
to show, a common underlying structure.

The essence of social conflict is interaction. We propose that this
interaction has an abstract structure, and that concern for the peaceful resolution of social conflict may be more effectively implemented
when this structure is understood in a way independent of a specific
context. On an abstract structural level we will see similarities and
differences of a more formal nature which are simple conceptually
and valuable for adapting and transforming methods of resolution.
The process of abstraction is critical for developing new methods and
techniques and for the construction of general theory.

There are many different ways to organize and classify conflicts
and there need be nothing incompatible or contradictory among them.
Scholars with different purposes find it convenient to organize conflicts in terms most conducive to those purposes. Deutsch (1973), for
example, was interested in explicating social-psychological similarities and differences among conflicts, and classified them accordingly.

For example, one classification is in terms of the relationship between the objective state of affairs and the state of affairs as perceived by the conflicting parties while another distinguishes between destructive and constructive conflicts. Anatol Rapoport (1960), in contrast, took a more formal view of conflicts and classified them into three types: fights, games, and debates. Dahrendorf (1962) offered a very complex taxonomy which Angell (1965) reduced to six types.

These distinctions are structural in the sense of referring to social structure, but they are discrete taxonomies and do not clarify the continuity or relations between types. Conflicts of different types may be more or less difficult to resolve, and the continuity can be useful in understanding the implications of transforming one type of conflict into another.

We will propose a relatively formal logical structure into which one may map any particular conflict. The perspective taken in this analysis of the structure of conflict is what Schellenberg (1982) refers to as a social psychological one, a conflict of interest between individuals, motivated by self-interest and bounded by moral and ethical limits. This is an approach he identifies with Adam Smith's *Wealth of Nations* (1776) and is distinguished from a biological perspective and a sociological perspective; it is also distinguished from "hot-blooded" explanations of the origins of conflict.

The structure developed here provides a classification into types that are relevant to the selection of appropriate methods of conflict resolution. The interrelations of these types control the transfer and adaptability of methods of conflict resolution from one to another.

We are not primarily concerned here with the sequential programming of the interactions of the parties involved in the course of seeking to resolve a conflict. A very considerable literature already exists with this aspect as its main concern. Some of it is in a popular vein and some of it is serious scholarship (see, for example, Calero, 1979; Douglas, 1957; Oliva, Peters, & Murthy, 1981; Raiffa, 1982; and Schelling, 1960). Most of these provide descriptions of the bargaining or negotiation process and how to be effective at it. In Chapters 9 and 13 we will discuss the relation of some of this work, particularly game theory, to the structure developed here.

This monograph is directed at understanding conditions that ensure the selection of an optimal resolution and how these conditions might be approximated in the most complex conflict situations. Negotiation is perhaps the most familiar procedure for resolving conflict, but it is not equally successful in all conflicts. Other procedures are available, are used, and may be more or less effective. We are interested in the properties of conflict which make different procedures effective. We seek to characterize the varieties of conflict in ways most useful in the selection of a procedure for resolving particular conflicts and in identifying some of the problem areas most amenable to empirical study.

In the course of developing the structural relations that characterize and distinguish conflicts, some old and familiar concepts and problems arise which sometimes require elaboration, redefinition, and new interpretations. We will see that a given conflict may seem to be of one type, yet from another perspective appear to be of another type. Different categorizations may sometimes be a matter of framing, which is just as important in its effect on conflict between individuals as Tversky and Kahneman (1981) have shown it to be in individual decision making. We shall discuss the advantages and disadvantages of the transformation of a conflict from one type to another. We will see that something is gained and something is lost because such transformations involve a tradeoff between ease of finding a resolution and the power necessary to impose it.

As a first step we will distinguish between three types of conflict; the first is conflict within an individual, and the other two are types of social conflict. For lack of adequate descriptive terms we will simply call them Types I, II, and III.

Briefly, the three types of conflict are characterized as follows. Type I is conflict within an individual because he or she is torn between incompatible goals. An example is the individual faced with a choice between two vacation intervals, where one has more pleasurable activities available and the other is less expensive. Or consider a student choosing between two majors, one of which is less interesting but offers better job prospects. In each case the individual is pulled in conflicting directions by goals that are incompatible because no option exists which satisfies both goals maximally.

Types II and III are conflicts between individuals. Type II is conflict between individuals because they want different things and must settle for the same thing. An example would be a conflict between husband and wife who disagree on whether to buy a new house or a new car; or disagreement between labor and management on a wage scale; or two superpowers in disagreement over arms control. In each case a decision is sought that both parties will accept.

Type III is conflict between individuals because they want the same thing and must settle for different things. An example would be that of two men courting the same woman or two governments who want the same island. Only one, at most, can achieve the goal; the other party must settle for something different.

We shall use the Type I conflict as a paradigm because there is

some substantial theory about the optimal resolution of such a conflict. We will expand on that theory and examine the more complex
problems of social conflict, Types II and III, in that framework.

Part I

Type I Conflict

conflict that arises within individuals because they are torn between incompatible goals

Preview

In the case of a Type I conflict there is, under certain conditions an effective process that leads to an optimal resolution. The formal theory and a full exposition of it are contained in two papers (Coombs & Avrunin, 1977a, 1977b), which are summarized in Chapter 2. In Chapter 3 we elaborate on certain aspects of this theory that are sufficient and particularly relevant for its extension to conflict between individuals. These include the emphasis on an ordinal scale of options, the motivational processes involved, a discussion of framing and its effects, and the classification of Type I conflicts. Chapter 4 offers empirical suggestions for the study of the difficulty of resolving various Type I conflicts and for reducing that difficulty, and some concluding remarks relating to rational choice theory in economics and to the psychological considerations that emerge in alternative framing of options.

Chapter 2

The Theory of Individual Preference: Type I Conflict Resolution

2.1   Introduction

The conflict between incompatible goals felt by an individual who must make a difficult choice is usually regarded as something quite distinct from conflict between individuals, and it may seem unreasonable to expect such intraindividual conflict to serve as a model for understanding interindividual conflict. We will show, however, that a theory of individual preference that describes conditions under which an optimal decision is most easily reached has important applications to conflicts between individuals. Most of this book is devoted to exploring these applications.

Our purpose in this chapter is to introduce some ideas from the theory of individual preferential choice that underlie most of our subsequent development of the structure of conflict. These ideas are concerned with the very special situation in which the individual is choosing a single option from an ordered set and preference is described by a "single peaked" function.

Our interest in individual preference theory is restricted to such a special case because this case is all that is needed for modeling certain conflicts between individuals. The reason that this case is sufficient is not that the options and preferences in such conflicts between individuals are simple — on the contrary, they are at least as complex as those involved in individual choice. Rather, it is sufficient

11

because the options in a conflict between two parties may be screened to reduce them to an ordered set. Furthermore, this ordered set consists of the best options available, in the sense that any other choice would involve unnecessary concession by one or both of the parties, and the preference of each party is single peaked over this set.

This book is intended not just for academicians but also for experienced practitioners of conflict resolution whose formal mathematical training may be slight or far in the past. Our focus is on the ideas behind the formal theory and technical foundations. Detailed mathematical treatment is set apart in technical notes and the appendices and is not necessary for a working understanding of the structure we propose. This part of our discussion is, however, necessarily somewhat general and abstract. Our hope is that the generality will make previously unnoticed relationships visible and lead to increasing effectiveness in practice.

2.2 Single Peaked Functions

With simple stimuli as options — like the amount of sugar in coffee or the temperature of a shower — an individual's preference may often be described by a single peaked function (SPF) (J. Priestley, 1775; Wundt, 1874). That is, when simple options have a natural underlying ordering, preference generally increases up to some point in the ordering and then decreases. If the options are more complex, as in choosing a college or where to go for a vacation, preference is less often described by a single peaked function. This is true even when there is a natural ordering of the options based on some aspect such as cost. In general, preference functions over the ordering of these complex options may have several peaks with valleys between them.

The significance of SPFs is that they allow a simple search process that converges on the optimal decision. (The term "optimal" in this context means what is best for the individual from that individual's point of view.)

This search is illustrated in Figure 1(a) with an SPF over a scale of options, x. Starting at any point, moving in one direction decreases preference and moving in the other direction increases preference, except at the optimal point where a change in any direction decreases preference. With a preference function having several peaks, as illustrated in Figure 1(b), the search process can be trapped at a local maximum or be divergent. An exhaustive search is the only way to ensure that the optimal choice is found in such a situation, and

(a) Convergence

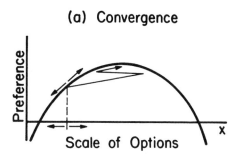

(b) Nonconvergence

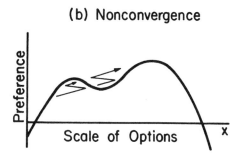

Figure 1: Search for optimality

such a search may be stressful, more costly than it's worth, or even impossible.

A homely example of such a search process is that of adjusting the temperature of a shower. If turning a handle one way increases the temperature of the water and turning it the other way decreases it, finding a particular temperature is a simple procedure. But if turning the handle changes the temperature inconsistently, it may be necessary to try all the possible positions of the handle to find the desired temperature.

We point out that the single peakedness of the preference function depends on the order in which the options are listed — there has to be a sense of "direction" in moving among the options. Indeed, given any set of options and any preference order, there are many ways in which the options might be ordered so that preference would be single peaked. When we say that preference is described by a single peaked function, then, we always mean with respect to some particular ordering of the options. The question of when there is a unique (or nearly unique) "natural" order is one that we will discuss in the next section, when we consider the conditions that might produce single peaked preference functions.

Here, however, we want to raise some issues concerning the measurement of options. In some cases, even when there is a natural ordering of the options, it may not be possible to assign numbers to them in a way that does more than reflect the ordering. It may be easy to say that one color is greener than another, or that one policy is more liberal than another, but not that one color is twice as green or one policy twice as liberal.

In other cases, however, the options may be easily characterized by a single number which does describe some important relationship between the options. Familiar examples might include the temperature of bowls of soup, the speed at which one drives on the highway, and the price of a commodity. In these cases, the numerical representation of the options has more significance than simple order: driving a certain distance at 60 miles per hour will take half the time that driving it at 30 miles per hour would.

When we represent an ordered set of options as points along a line, as we did in Figure 1, we are implicitly assigning numbers to the options as coordinates, or distances along the line. Such an assignment of numbers is called a "scale," and the distinction we have just drawn between different sorts of options corresponds to a distinction between different sorts of scales. This distinction between scales can be best phrased in terms of their degree of uniqueness: in what ways can the scale's numerical assignments be changed while still conveying exactly the same information about the options?

If the only information the scale conveys about the options is their order, the given scale values can be replaced by any other numbers in the same order. A scale with this degree of uniqueness is called an ordinal scale (see glossary). In the case of driving speed, however, the scale conveys information about ratios — we could change the numbers themselves by changing the units, but we must retain the information that one speed is twice as fast as another. In this case, we could replace the scale values by new ones obtained by multiplying by any positive constant. A scale with this degree of uniqueness is called a ratio scale. Scales with higher degrees of uniqueness, that is, scales whose information is preserved by fewer kinds of transformations, are said to be stronger. For example, a ratio scale is stronger than an interval scale, which allows addition of a constant as well as multiplication by a positive constant. Our familiar temperature scales are interval scales (see glossary).

Mathematically, the transformations that exactly preserve the information represented by a scale are used to characterize that information. So the types of scales that can be used to represent a collection of options depend on properties of the options. If it doesn't make sense to say that one color is twice as green as another, then it doesn't make sense to represent the "greenness" of colors with a ratio scale. There is a well-developed theory of measurement analyzing those properties of options that determine how they can be represented.

The type of the scale also controls the sorts of mathematical operations that can reasonably be performed on the scale values representing options. Suppose that "greenness" can only be represented on an ordinal scale. We could then replace the scale values representing a particular set of shades of green by any other numbers so long as we maintain their order, and this new scale would be just as valid a representation as the original one. But the sum or the ratio of the scale values corresponding to two colors will be different for the new scale, so the sum or ratio of scale values is not meaningful for ordinal scales. If our options are represented on a ratio scale, then, to preserve exactly the same information, the new scale values must be obtained from the old ones by multiplication by a constant. In this case, the sum of two scale values can change, but their ratio cannot, so dividing one scale value by another is a meaningful operation for ratio scales.

As a general principle, it is best to use the strongest scale that can be justified by the properties of the options being represented. But if there is reason to suspect that a substantial proportion of instances in a domain like conflict would not justify measurement at the level of a particular type of scale, such as a ratio scale, then theory based on such quantification is not appropriate to a large part of the domain. Such theory is either vacuous or wrong. If, on the other hand, a substantial proportion of instances in the domain would justify quantification at the level of, say, an ordinal scale, then theory based on that level of quantification will be appropriate for that portion of the domain, and also all instances in which stronger levels of measurement are also justified.

Throughout this book, we will assume that the options, and preference over them, are represented by ordinal scales (but further strengthened in one respect, discussed below and in more detail in Section 6.1). We believe that requiring a stronger scale will reduce the domain covered to trivial instances. Essentially, using the weaker measurement model results in saying less about more instances and the stronger model permits saying more about fewer instances. Although precisely what is meant here by "more" and "less" remains an open question in the absence of a great deal of new knowledge about the domain of conflict (see Coombs, 1983, for a more extended discussion of these issues), we hope to show here that significant things can be said about a large domain.

Even in cases where it would seem that options can be represented on a scale stronger than ordinal, we are not convinced that such a representation would be useful. Without an extended digression, we will say only that the apparent usefulness of many stronger scales is destroyed by a number of factors, and mention here only two of the most significant.

First, even when numbers can be objectively assigned to options, these numbers may not accurately represent an individual's assessment of them. The difference between having no children and having one child is not necessarily the same as the difference between having 3 children and 4 children.

Second, the existence of a numerical scale for options that is both stronger than ordinal and shared by adversaries in a conflict is extremely doubtful. Indeed, any attempt to determine an individual's scale in such a setting requires behavioral observations in a hostile environment in which it may benefit the parties to disguise their preferences. These objections, and others we will not discuss here, are sufficient to severely reduce the generality of any theory of conflict that depends on scales stronger than ordinal ones.

We will show that a common ordinal scale of options for two adversaries does exist, and that it consists of options which are best, in a certain precise sense. The algorithm for constructing such a scale is certainly dependent on knowledge of the preference orderings of each adversary over the available options, but only the orderings, not any additional information. Without knowledge of the preferences of adversaries in a conflict, there is little of substance to work with. One cannot hope to resolve a conflict to anyone's satisfaction when nothing is known of what anyone wants.

Even so, this aspect of a conflict — access to preference orderings — can be a serious obstacle to progress in resolving it. Preferences may be unclear to an individual, unstable, or just plain unknown. Furthermore, in conflict between individuals, what the parties want may be deliberately disguised or misrepresented, and preferences may be shaped by the options available. So volatility of expressed preference is a pervasive condition. However, this problem lies outside the scope of this book. We will assume that an individual has preferences and that knowledge of them exists.

We conclude this section with an account of certain implications of the existence of a single peaked preference function over an ordinal scale of options.

The peak of an SPF, representing the greatest level of preference, occurs over some point on the scale of options which we call the individual's ideal point. Because the options may be discrete, the ideal point may or may not correspond to an option. For example, consider a student seeking a course of a suitable level of difficulty in some particular subject. There may be several courses available, and none may be exactly what the student is looking for.

We assume that the courses are ordered in their level of difficulty, as assessed by the student. To say that the student's preference is represented by an SPF (with respect to the ordering by difficulty of the courses) is to say that the level of preference falls off steadily from that of an ideal course in both directions on the scale of difficulty. Thus, a course that is easier or more difficult than the ideal is less preferred, and the more the level of difficulty departs from the ideal, the less the course is preferred.

We assume that the difficulty of the courses may reach a level that is unacceptable to the individual, being too easy or too difficult. It is important to identify this level of preference as a zero point on the preference scale, and to say that options more preferred than this (courses having an acceptable level of difficulty) have positive preference, while those less preferred (courses having an unacceptable level of difficulty) have negative preference. The measurement properties of this type of scale are discussed in more detail in Section 6.1.

In Figure 2(a), we illustrate this hypothetical case. The scale of options is drawn as a continuous line for convenience and clarity, as will be the case in all subsequent figures, but we remind the reader that we do not require that it be more than an ordinal scale. The scale is shown with five options, drawn at equally spaced points and labeled a, b, c, d, and e in order of increasing difficulty. The order of preference, $c\,d\,b\,a\,e$, is given by the height of the preference function above the scale, and, for purposes of illustration, we have drawn the preference function as a continuous curve even though only preferences for the options might be known.

The preference function is seen to cross the scale, corresponding to the zero level of preference, at a point between a and b to the left of the ideal and at a point between d and e to the right of the ideal. This indicates that options a and e are unacceptable; a is too easy and e is too difficult. Because the scale of options is only ordinal, the shape of the preference function is arbitrary except for certain invariances. These are the locus of the peak, between c and d, the monotonicity (see glossary) of the descending branches on each side,

(a) An ordinal scale of options with preference order cdbae

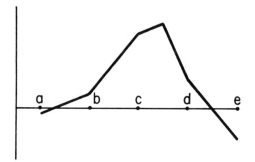

(b) Imposing a linearly symmetric SPF with same preference order

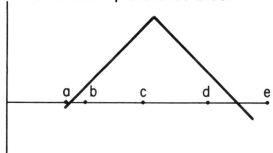

Figure 2: Relation beween shape of SPF and the measurement level of the scale of options

and the loci of the intersections with the scale, between a and b and between d and e.

We illustrate the arbitrariness of the shape of the SPF with Figure 2(b), in which the scale of options has been stretched so that the SPF descends linearly and symmetrically on both sides of the peak. The preference order again, of course, is $c\,d\,b\,a\,e$. This preference order may be obtained from Figure 2(b) by picking up the stretched scale at the ideal point and folding it, as shown in Figure 3. The rank order of the options on the folded scale is the preference order, the one nearest the ideal point being the most preferred and the one farthest from the ideal point being the least preferred. For obvious reasons, the name unfolding theory has been given to the analysis of

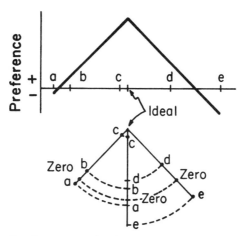

Figure 3: Preference order by folding a symmetric SPF

preferential choice data using this model (Coombs, 1964/1976).

Two points here are important for subsequent purposes. First, the preference order obtained by folding Figure 2(b) at the ideal would be the same if the SPF had any shape that was symmetric and preserved the loci of the ideal and the intercepts. This is obvious if we observe that the monotonicity of the two branches required for single peakedness necessarily preserves the rank order of all pairs of options on the same side of the ideal (unilateral pairs) and symmetry preserves the rank order of all pairs of options in which the members lie on opposite sides of the ideal (bilateral pairs). We assume only that the preference order, including the locus of the point with zero preference, is known. Our conclusions are therefore weaker than if the shape of the SPF were specified, but we can have more confidence that they will be confirmed empirically.

The second point is the following. When a preference order is unfolded, the zero point of preference unfolds to become two points on the scale of options, one to the left of the ideal point and the other to the right. The full significance of this will not be clear until we begin the study of interpersonal conflict of Type II in Chapter 5, but it is so important that a few preliminary words here are in order.

We will identify the zero point of preference with the status quo, when the status quo is an option, and assume that an individual is motivated both to improve it and to avoid worsening it. This will be the basis for identifying positive preference with approach processes and negative preference with avoidance processes in Section

3.1, and will then provide a framework for classifying varieties of conflict within Type I and, later, Type II. We will refer to these two zero points as initial positions in any negotiation, and now merely point out that their loci on the scale of options are affected by what are called "background" variables, variables that affect the preference values of all options. So we note that changing the status quo can change the loci of both initial positions.

For example, the initial positions for the student choosing a course may be changed by receiving a scholarship that frees up more time for studying. An easy course may become less attractive and a more difficult course may become more attractive. The ideal point may or may not change. The ordinal scale of options, based on their difficulty, remains unchanged, but the preference ordering, and especially the zero points, might change.

The initial positions, corresponding to the status quo and its unfolded image, are essentially reference points with respect to which the individual judges the acceptability of options. Of course, the status quo may itself be an option on the scale of options. For example, an individual may have an SPF for preference over number of children in a family, and the status quo would be the number of children the family already has. The individual's preference function will reflect background variables such as the health of the spouse, financial status, and so on. Such variables do not change the locus of the status quo on the scale of options, but may drastically affect the other initial position obtained by unfolding the preference order, and hence the acceptability of options.

2.2.1   Summary

These first two sections were intended to introduce a special case of individual preferential choice, that of an ordinal scale of options with a single peaked preference function over that scale, that has important implications for interindividual conflict. We have presented and illustrated these concepts in narrative form.

We have emphasized the generality of ordinal scales, pointing out that adversaries in a conflict may well share an ordinal scale of options, but not a stronger scale. A theory requiring a stronger scale would have a severely limited domain of application.

We have stressed the invariant properties of a single peaked preference function, the loci of the peak and intercepts (initial positions), and the monotonic decay of preference in both directions from the peak. These permit distinguishing between positive and negative preference and corresponding approach and avoidance processes, and will subsequently provide a basis for classifying varieties of Type I and Type II conflicts. We have also pointed out the distinctive roles of background variables and the status quo, and their relation to the initial positions on the scale of options.

Although we know that these brief notes cannot be completely adequate or convincing, we hope that they have provided a framework for discussing these aspects of individual preference. We therefore turn now to the problem of single peakedness of preferential choice and ask why it should occur and how it might come about.

2.3 A Behavioral Basis for Single Peaked Preference Functions

The roots of the notion of single peaked preference functions lie in Epicurean philosophy of the 4th century B.C. Epicurus identified seeking pleasure and avoiding pain as the primary impulses of living creatures and the foundations of ethics (Long, 1973). These primary impulses inevitably lead to conflict within an individual except in the circumstance that one of the available options is better than all the others in every respect.

More commonly, each option involves several aspects of pleasure and pain, or, in modern terms, benefit and cost, and no option is superior to all others in every aspect. A student, for example, may be offered a summer job or have the opportunity to travel abroad with friends. Tension is generated by the pull of the different options in the directions they favor, as perceived by the student. Choosing an option corresponds to deciding whether the gain in choosing *a* over *b* vis-à-vis the loss is more favorable than the gain in choosing *b* over *a* vis-à-vis its consequent loss. The choice resolves the conflict by accepting the tradeoff in one direction rather than the other.

When there are more than two options, and the options have a natural underlying order, then, as we have seen, a single peaked preference function describes an effective and efficient process for seeking an optimal resolution to the conflict within the individual. The emphasis in our discussion here will be placed on the conditions that ensure single peakedness because these conditions control the applicability of this notion to the process of resolving social conflict.

The theory of SPFs is a mathematical theory based on behavioral principles. In this section we introduce the theory by providing a brief narrative summary of its main characteristics. In the next section, we review the mathematical formulation of the theory.

It is important to distinguish two facets of the Type I decision problem, one consisting of what is brought to the decision situation by the individual and the other being the options from among which a choice is to be made. One facet has to do with the individual decision maker and the other has to do with the environment in which the decision is made.

We will think of options as possessing elemental components (see glossary), which are either increasingly desirable or increasingly undesirable. Consider, for example, choosing a new car. If increasing reliability is increasingly desirable and increasing cost is increasingly undesirable, then these may be two elemental components. The individual is assumed to perceive and assess the options in terms of these elemental components, and we will assume for our immediate purposes that each of these components can be measured on at least an interval scale. This last assumption, which is stronger than that which we require for the options themselves, is necessary in order to talk about the slope and acceleration of utility and preference functions.

We find it useful to think of the individual as associating a utility function to each of these components, and to think of preference as arising from a combination of these utility functions. These functions are useful fictions — they play no mathematical role in the theory and serve purely as heuristic devices — but they help illustrate and motivate some of the ideas.

The utility function associated with an increasingly desirable elemental component is an increasing function (i.e., more is better) and the utility function associated with an increasingly undesirable one is decreasing (i.e., more is worse). The shape of these utility functions is governed by two psychological principles: (a) good things satiate, and (b) bad things escalate. So we assume that the utility functions for the two kinds of components have positive or negative slope, respectively, and that in both cases they have negative acceleration and so are concave down (i.e., good things satiate increasingly slowly and bad things escalate increasingly rapidly). These are illustrated in Figure 4.

Consider, for example, foreign travel. At first, the strange sights and exotic foods are exciting and stimulating, but with repetition the novelty wears off. The good things satiate. At the same time costs are accumulating and affairs at home, both personal and professional, are deteriorating, slowly at first, but increasingly with increasing neglect. The bad things escalate. People like to travel but also like to return

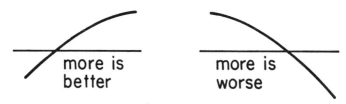

Figure 4: Two kinds of elemental utility functions

home.

We will assume nothing more about these utility functions than these general properties of positive or negative slope and negative acceleration, and we will refer to such functions as proper utility functions.

The fact that some attribute of options is increasingly desirable or increasingly undesirable does not ensure that it is an elemental component, but only that it is not immediately distinguishable from an elemental component over the observed range. However, monotonicity of preference over some range may be sufficient to justify regarding an attribute as elemental for some practical purposes such as experimentation or negotiation.

Options may have any number of perceived and relevant elemental components. For now, we will assume that an individual's preference function for options is obtained by aggregating the utility functions for the elemental components of the options. The most familiar and simplest way to combine the utility functions is simply to add them, and we will occasionally point out special aspects of this case. In the next section we will introduce a more general type of preference function, called a proper preference function, that is independent of the existence of utility functions for components.

We turn now to the second of the two broad facets of the Type I decision problem, the structure of the available options. In general, of course, there is no suitable natural ordering on the options if they have two or more elemental components and must be represented in a space of two or more dimensions. If an individual's preference over such a space of options has a maximum and diminishes in all directions like an umbrella, it would correctly be called a single peaked preference function over a multidimensional space. But, as we indicated earlier, it is sufficient for our purposes to deal only with single peaked functions over a one-dimensional set of options, such as those on an arc in a multidimensional space. We are concerned, then, with conditions that ensure that a preference function will be single peaked

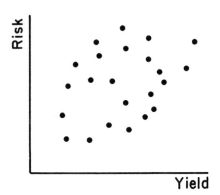

Figure 5: The domain of options

over a one-dimensional set of options, which may lie in a larger, multidimensional space.

In this connection, we introduce a third psychological principle. An option which is inferior in every respect to another option — it has less of the increasingly desirable elemental components and more of the increasingly undesirable ones — is said to be dominated by that other option. Our third principle is a rationality principle and asserts that dominated options are ignored. This ensures that the options actively considered are the best of those available, in at least the crude sense of not being worse in every respect than some other option, but this principle is not enough to ensure that the set of options actively considered will be totally ordered if there are more than two elemental components.

To illustrate this, consider an individual interested in investing and seeking to maximize yield and minimize risk. If there is no single option that is at least as good in all respects and better in at least one than all others, then the two goals are incompatible and the individual must make a tradeoff (i.e., resolve a conflict). In this case, the options available in the market place might appear to the individual as points in a two-dimensional space, as shown in Figure 5.

Any option that has less risk and at least as much yield as another or has more yield with no more risk than another, dominates the other and the latter is neglected. The process is illustrated in Figure 6. The option labeled *a*, for example, dominates all options to the left and above it, bounded by the vertical and horizontal dotted lines. There is a similar pair of lines for each of the options labeled *b* and *c*. Those are the only three options that survive. Every other option is dominated by one or more of these three options and none of them

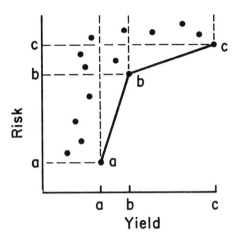

Figure 6: Construction of a Pareto optimal set

is dominated. Note that the line between a and b is the hypotenuse of a right triangle. If there were an option in that triangle it would not be dominated by either a or b and so would survive the screening also. There is a similar triangle with the line between b and c as its hypotenuse.

We call such a set of options, in which each is better than any other in some respect, *Pareto optimal* (see glossary); c, for example, has more yield than a but a has less risk. Note that the options that have survived the screening are ordered because they are ordered the same on both components.

If the options varied in three or more dimensions, then application of this rationality principle would not ensure that the options be ordered. For example, suppose in choosing a place to go for a vacation, the individual considered price, facilities, and location as the relevant components (not necessarily elemental), and suppose further that there were three options, d, e, and f. Let these three options be ordered on each component from most to least desirable as follows: price $d\,e\,f$; facilities $e\,f\,d$; location $f\,d\,e$. We see that d has the best price, e has the best facilities, and f has the best location, so they constitute a Pareto optimal set because each is better than any other in some respect. Note, however, that they are not ordered the same (or reversed) on each component. This is most easily seen by observing that more than two different options appear as the worst element in the preference orderings. This cannot occur if they are same ordered (or reversed) on the components of the option space.

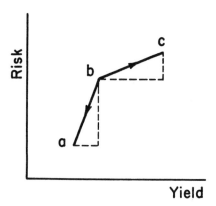

Figure 7: A set that is Pareto optimal but not efficient

Suppose instead that the orderings on the three components from most to least desirable were as follows: price $d\,e\,f$; location $f\,e\,d$; facilities $d\,e\,f$. Each is still better than any other in some respect: d has the best price (and the best facilities), f has the best location, and e is better than f in price and better than d in location. We note that they are now ordered the same (or reversed) on all three components; the three preference orderings end in either d or f and the ordering is $d\,e\,f$ (or reversed) and the preference functions are single peaked.

In general, a set of Pareto optimal options is ordered if and only if they are ordered the same (or reversed) on all relevant components. In particular, if the options have only two relevant components, then a Pareto optimal set is ordered, and is ordered the same (or reversed) on both components.

An ordered Pareto optimal set of options is a necessary condition for a single peaked preference function, but it is not sufficient. A stronger condition for the structure on the options is required to ensure that any and all proper preference functions will be single peaked. We can bring out the need for the stronger condition with the following illustration.

Consider an individual assessing the Pareto optimal set of investments in Figure 7. Individuals comparing options a and b observe that by giving up some yield a disproportionate amount of risk can be avoided, and they will be tempted to prefer a to b. Also, comparing options c and b, they observe that by taking a little more risk a disproportionate amount of yield can be obtained, and they will be tempted to prefer c to b.

The definition of a single peaked preference ordering is that the

Figure 8: An efficient set

intermediate option of an ordered triple cannot be least preferred. In this example, the ordered triple is abc and we have seen how the intermediate option, b, can come to be least preferred. We assure the reader that this may happen even if the preference function is proper.

The stronger condition required on the structure of the options is a property we call efficiency (see glossary) and is illustrated in Figure 8. An efficient set is Pareto optimal but is more than that. As one proceeds from one option to another in the ordering, some components get better and some get worse. To be an efficient set, those components that get worse must get worse faster than the others get better. This relation must hold between all appropriate pairs of components, which means that the component that gets worse the slowest must do so faster than the component that gets better the fastest. This relation must hold between all successive pairs of options in the ordering. It is easy to show that the condition that a set be efficient is both necessary and sufficient to ensure that all individuals with proper preference functions have single peaked preferences on that set (Appendix A).

There is, unfortunately, no obvious principle in behavioral science, within or external to the individual, to guarantee that the strong property of efficiency is satisfied, and this may explain why some individual's preference functions are not necessarily single peaked.

To review the critical points here, the first facet of the choice process, what the individual brings to the decision, may include a principle of rationality for screening the options to ensure Pareto optimality.

But this cannot ensure efficiency and, indeed, cannot ensure that the set be ordered unless the options have only two components, as we have seen. So the second facet of the choice process, the structure on the options, is not within the power of the individual to control except in rare circumstances.

It is, in our opinion, the failure of a set of options to satisfy efficiency that accounts for the relative infrequency of single peakedness in individual choice behavior.

It may be to the advantage of the reader if we look ahead, briefly, at this point, while this discussion is clearly in mind, and indicate its importance to resolving Type II conflict. It will be shown that among the options available in certain social conflicts there exists a subset we call the frontier of preference, over which negotiation and concession may take place in resolving a Type II conflict between two parties. It is Pareto optimal in two dimensions and so is totally ordered, regardless of the number of components or the qualitative complexity of the options. This is because the coordinates of the two dimensions are the respective preference rankings of the two parties. There is, however, no way in Type II conflict, either, to ensure that this set of options, constituting the frontier of preference, is efficient. But the preference functions of both parties are monotone, one with positive slope and one with negative slope. We will see, then, that it is possible to ensure a better structure on the options for Type II conflict resolution between individuals than it is for Type I conflict within an individual. This is why we made the point at the beginning of this chapter, that the simple case of single peakedness over a set of ordered options in Part I is sufficient for our purposes in Part II.

Single peakedness may occur, of course, for other reasons. For example, Aschenbrenner's work, discussed in Section 9.2, gives another set of conditions ensuring single peakedness. But there also, an efficient set of options is required. Single peakedness may occur even in the absence of an efficient set of options, of course, but that is merely a fortunate occurrence for the decision maker and not to be depended on. What we are seeking is sufficient understanding of these conditions so that, insofar as possible, we may take advantage of them in extending the structure to interpersonal conflict in ways that could ensure a better resolution and one easier to achieve.

This section is intended to provide an overall orientation to the more precise formulation of the structure of Type I conflict resolution presented in the next section. We would like to interpolate two parenthetical remarks here to assist the reader. First, the measurement-theoretic conditions provided to ensure the existence of SPFs are stronger than can always be assured, as has been pointed out in the preceding discussion, but on the behavioral level only ordinal preferences are needed. The theory is simple and, as descriptive theory, is falsifiable. We will at no point need to construct numerical representations of utilities from behavioral observations for purposes of experimentation or application. We do, however, from time to time construct numerical examples to simplify exposition and to construct figures that make the arguments easier to follow.

Secondly, and by way of explaining the need for the mathematical foundation given in the next section, we would add that the domain of all conflicts is not simple and for such a broad domain the theory is more complex, particularly in its extension to social conflict. Although conflicts may appear simple in particular instances and on a superficial level, the more deeply one probes the structure of conflict and the greater the variety of conflicts included in the domain that one seeks to understand and to encompass in a common framework, the more complexities appear. The analysis we make here of such a framework, although it may strain one's patience, is still only a dent in the surface. In the following section only definitions and results are presented and interpreted; mathematical details are contained in Appendix A.

2.4 Technical Note: A Mathematical Basis for Single Peaked Preference Functions

We now summarize the more technical aspects of the theory of Type I conflict. The less mathematically inclined reader may safely skip this section.

2.4.1 Proper Preference Functions

The proper utility functions we have introduced are the classical marginally decreasing utility functions of economics. But the utility of an elemental component may be a function of values of other components as well. The (negative) utility of the cost of a new car depends not only on the price but on the financial condition of the individual choosing the car. There is no way to isolate a component and get a single utility function for it, independent of the values of other components and what we have called background variables. Although we find it useful to discuss preference in terms of a simple (perhaps additive) combination of utility functions, a more general notion is necessary.

We assume that each elemental component of the options that is relevant to the decision can be represented on an interval scale. So each option may be regarded as a point in n-dimensional space, and we may regard a set S of options as a subset of n-dimensional Euclidean space, $\mathbb{R}^n$.

Definition. We say that a function $F\colon \mathbb{R}^n \to \mathbb{R}$ is a *proper preference function* for a set of options $S \subseteq \mathbb{R}^n$ if and only if

(*i*) all its first-order partial derivatives, F_i, exist,

(*ii*) if the i-th elemental component is increasingly desirable, $x_j \leq y_j$ for all j and $x_i < y_i$ implies that $F_i(x_1, \ldots, x_n) > F_i(y_1, \ldots, y_n) > 0$, and

(*iii*) if the i-th elemental component is increasingly undesirable, $x_j \leq y_j$ for all j and $x_i < y_i$ implies that $0 > F_i(x_1, \ldots, x_n) > F_i(y_1, \ldots, y_n)$.

The conditions on the partial derivatives correspond to our requirements that proper utility functions be monotone and negatively accelerated. An additive combination of proper utility functions, one for each elemental component, is a proper preference function, but the notion of proper preference function is more general. In particular, a proper preference function does not depend on the specification of a utility function for each component, independent of the values of the other components.

We also give a formal definition of single peakedness.

Definition. A function F is *single peaked* with respect to an ordering, $\prec$, if, for every ordered triple $a \prec b \prec c$, not both $F(b) < F(a)$ and $F(b) < F(c)$ are true.

A preference function is single peaked, then, if an intermediate option is never least preferred. This definition is a broad one, allowing ties in preference.

2.4.2   Pareto Optimal Sets and Efficient Sets

The second facet of Type II involves the set of available options. Here we discuss the notions of Pareto optimal sets and efficient sets.

Pareto optimal sets are those generated by an individual considering options according to our third psychological principle, that dominated options are neglected. A formal definition is

Definition. Let S be a set of options, regarded as a subset of $\mathbb{R}^n$ by scaling each elemental component. S is *Pareto optimal* if, for any pair of elements $(x_1, \ldots, x_n)$ and $(y_1, \ldots, y_n)$ of S, at least one of the following holds:

(i) there are two coordinates, i and i', corresponding to increasingly desirable components, with $x_i < y_i$ and $x_{i'} > y_{i'}$,

(ii) there are two coordinates, j and j', corresponding to increasingly undesirable components, with $x_j < y_j$ and $x_{j'} > y_{j'}$,

(iii) there are coordinates i and j, corresponding to an increasingly desirable component and an increasingly undesirable component, respectively, with $x_i > y_i$ and $x_j > y_j$ or with $x_i < y_i$ and $x_j < y_j$.

The definition says that, given any two options, each must be better than the other in some way, either by having more of an increasingly desirable component or less of an increasingly undesirable component. Thus, neither option dominates the other. With a Pareto optimal set of options, any choice between two options requires a tradeoff (i.e., the resolution of a conflict).

If there are only two elemental components and both are increasingly desirable or both are increasingly undesirable, the condition for Pareto optimality requires that the order of the options on one component be the reverse of the order on the other component. In this case, it is natural to consider the single peakedness of preference with respect to either of these orders, which are equivalent in the sense that preference is single peaked with respect to one if and only if it is single peaked with respect to the other. If there are only two elemental components, one being increasingly desirable and the other increasingly undesirable, the condition for Pareto optimality requires that the options be ordered the same on both components, and it is natural to consider single peakedness with respect to this order. If there are more than two elemental components, however, the orderings of options on different components need not be related and there may be no natural order to use.

We therefore introduce a stronger mathematical condition. The motivation for this definition has been presented in Section 2.3.

Definition. An *efficient set* in n dimensions $(n \geq 2)$ is a subset S of $\mathbb{R}^n$, together with a partition of the set $\{1, \ldots, n\}$ into two nonempty subsets I_1 and I_2 such that the following conditions are satisfied:

(i) for any pair $(x_1, \ldots, x_n)$ and $(y_1, \ldots, y_n)$ in S, $x_i < y_i$ for some i if and only if $x_j < y_j$ for all j, and $x_i < y_i$ for some i in I_1 if and only if $x_j < y_j$ for some j in I_2, and

(ii) for each triple $(x_1, \ldots, x_n)$, $(y_1, \ldots, y_n)$, $(z_1, \ldots, z_n)$ of points in S with $x_1 < y_1 < z_1$, there exists a $c > 0$ such that

$$c(y_i - x_i) \geq z_i - y_i \text{ for all } i \text{ in } I_1, \text{ and}$$
$$c(y_j - x_j) \leq z_j - y_j \text{ for all } j \text{ in } I_2.$$

The definition of an efficient set presented here is slightly modified from that in our original paper (Coombs & Avrunin, 1977b) to facilitate generalization to social conflict. The definition requires that an efficient set of options be ordered the same way on each elemental component, so there is a unique natural ordering on the options. In our applications, the set I_1 will consist of the dimensions corresponding to increasingly desirable components and I_2 will consist of those dimensions corresponding to increasingly undesirable ones. (The cases in which all components are increasingly desirable or all are increasingly undesirable will be discussed in the next chapter.)

The first condition in the definition of an efficient set ensures that every option in an efficient set will be nondominated (i.e., the set is Pareto optimal). If the options are Pareto optimal in two dimensions, they are ordered the same (or reversed) on both components and so either may be used to define the ordering on the options. Condition (i) goes further. It extends the concept of Pareto optimality to any number of dimensions in such a way as to ensure that the ordering on all components is the same (i.e., if one option is better than another option on some increasingly desirable component, then it is also worse than the other on any increasingly undesirable component).

The second condition of the definition of an efficient set ensures that the largest proportionate increment between two options on any increasingly desirable component will be no greater than the smallest proportionate increment on any increasingly undesirable component (i.e., the slopes of the line segments between successive options cannot decrease).

2.4.3   Existence of Single Peaked Functions

We state a theorem here on the existence of single peaked functions. A proof is given in Appendix A.

Theorem. *Suppose that $E = (S, I_1, I_2)$ is an efficient set in n dimensions with I_1 the set of components representing the increasingly* *desirable attributes of the options of S and with I_2 representing the increasingly undesirable attributes. If $G: \mathbb{R}^n \to \mathbb{R}$ is a function such that, for some strictly increasing $g: \mathbb{R} \to \mathbb{R}$, $F = g \circ G$ is a proper preference function for S, then G is single peaked on E with respect to the ordering by values on the components of either I_1 or I_2.*

This theorem summarizes our analysis of individual preferential choice behavior. An alternative theorem could be proven for the case in which utility functions with negative slope had positive acceleration instead of negative (or, more generally, for the case in which the partial derivatives of the preference function in directions corresponding to increasingly undesirable components were increasing rather than decreasing). This would be the case in which "bad things" adapted instead of escalated. However, proof of the theorem would further require that the positive acceleration be less than the absolute value of the negative acceleration of any proper utility function with positive slope. In psychological terms, these assumptions would be supported if bad things adapted instead of escalated and adapted more slowly than good things satiated. In the next section we summarize the cases that arise when bad things adapt rather than escalate.

2.5   If Bad Things Adapt

In the previous sections of this chapter we have considered conditions under which single peaked preference functions must occur if good components satiate and bad ones escalate. There is no question, however, that bad components exist to which the psychological response is adaptive. A case in point is the subjective response to catastrophes. The subjective response to 100 deaths in an accident is not 100 times that of the response to one, nor is the response to 1000 deaths an order of magnitude greater than that to 100.

There are only two cases to consider, depending on whether adaptation decelerates slower or faster than satiation over the set of options. Both cases may be quickly disposed of.

If the bad components adapt more slowly then the good components satiate, everything said in the earlier sections of the chapter, where the assumption was made that bad things escalate, goes through. The preference function will be single peaked on an efficient set.

If the bad components adapt more rapidly than the good satiate, nothing can be said in general about the shape of the preference function, even on an efficient set. The shape of the preference function depends on the particular values of the good and bad components of the options. Essentially, the bad components matter less and less; they just generate irregularities in the shape of the preference function.

An understanding of these factors that affect the shape of the preference function is desirable because the difficulty of the process of finding and accepting a resolution to a conflict, whether within or between individuals, is dependent on the structure on the options. Intelligent manipulation can control the difficulty of resolving a conflict in ways discussed in later chapters in Part I and Part II.

2.6   Summary

According to this theory of single peaked preference functions for resolving Type I conflict, the individual brings to the conflict situation proper utility functions (or, more generally, a proper preference function), supported by the psychological principles that good things satiate and bad things escalate. The environment contains the options. In order that a single peaked preference function always exists to ensure optimal resolution of the conflict, the options must constitute an efficient set. We are aware of no principle, behavioral or otherwise, that will ensure that this condition be met in a natural environment.

But the individual may also bring to the decision situation a rationality principle, that dominated options are neglected. Exercise of this principle ensures that the options form a Pareto optimal set. If there are exactly two dimensions then a Pareto optimal set is totally ordered with the options in reverse order on the components, in the sense that as they get better on one they get worse on the other. In the absence of an efficient set, individual preference functions may not all be single peaked.

The distinction between the two facets, that which the individual brings to the choice situation and that which is external, a part of the environment, has much in common with Simon's notion that behavioral systems are essentially simple but responding to a complex environment is what makes behavior look complicated:

> A man, viewed as a behaving system, is quite simple. The apparent complexity of his behavior over time is largely a reflection of the complexity of the environment in which he finds himself. (Simon, 1969, p. 52)

Parenthetically, we remark that single peaked functions tend to induce moderation in preferential choice in that as the desirable aspects of the ordered options increase, the undesirable aspects increase more rapidly and the cost will ultimately dominate the benefit.

Of course a single peaked preference function may exist even though all these conditions are not satisfied. For example, for any set of totally ordered options and any arbitrary utility function over them, there will exist another utility function such that their sum will be single peaked. Such a theory is so general that it is worthless. We have reduced the generality to a degree defensible by behavioral principles and, as we hope to show, increased the power to a level useful in the analysis of the structure of conflict.

This theory provides sufficient conditions but single peaked preference functions can arise in other ways. We remarked previously that Aschenbrenner (1981), for example, has shown that there is a class of models not involving proper preference functions which yield single peaked preferences on any efficient set. In Section 9.2.1 we review his contribution and examine some instances of this class of models as possible decision functions for resolving interpersonal conflicts.

We will refer to the theory presented in this chapter as the structure of Type I conflict and in the next chapter expand on this theory in order to introduce some concepts that are particularly important for understanding the structure of Type II conflict.

Chapter 3

Motivational Processes, Framing Effects, and the Classification of Type I Conflicts

In this chapter, we discuss the behavioral implications of the formal structure of Type I conflicts, particularly as they bear on the variety of such conflicts and the difficulty of resolving them.

3.1 Motivational Processes and the Concept of Ambience

In Section 2.3, we used investments differing in yield and risk to illustrate Pareto optimality. The individual is attracted by more yield but wishes to avoid more risk. This example is commonly regarded as an approach/avoidance conflict.

The terms approach and avoidance refer to motivational processes which are outgrowths of basic concepts in Kurt Lewin's field theory in social science (Deutsch, 1954; Lewin, 1931, 1935, 1951). Lewin observed that behavior in some circumstances could be described as either goal seeking or withdrawal and used the terms approach and avoidance processes to describe them. That such processes might play a significant role in the resolution of conflict seems inevitable. Consequently, we will need to give definitions of them in terms that will be transferable to the context of Type II conflict.

In Lewinian theory an approach/avoidance conflict is one in which there exist tendencies both to approach and to avoid some goal. An approach/approach conflict is one in which there exist tendencies to approach two different goals. An avoidance/avoidance conflict is one in which there exist tendencies to avoid two distinct goals. These concepts have been useful in a good deal of experimental research on decision making within organisms, animal and human. (See Miller, 1944, for an early review of this literature.)

We see that an approach/approach conflict, as Lewin used the term, is one in which an individual is faced with a choice between two options each of which is desired, presumably because any negative characteristics are outweighed by the positive ones. In the avoidance/avoidance conflict the avoidance tendencies for each option predominate. In either case, the conflict is resolved by comparing the aggregate tendency for each option.

The approach/avoidance conflict, as Lewin used the term, implies a different behavior mode from the other two. In this case there is only one proffered goal or option and it is regarded as having both kinds of tendencies, and these are in conflict. An example is the ambivalence of a squirrel approaching a peanut held out by a child. The resolution requires the aggregation of the approach and avoidance tendencies to determine which predominates. Thus, we may view the Lewinian approach/avoidance conflict as an accept/reject decision, a go/no-go, yes/no mode.

In contrast, the approach/approach and avoidance/avoidance conflicts are choices between options in which each option must first be processed as in an approach/avoidance conflict to determine its aggregate and then these total preferences must be compared to resolve the conflict, a comparative mode.

This difference in the mode of the approach/avoidance conflict compared to the approach/approach and the avoidance/avoidance conflicts gives rise to difficulties and complexities when we turn to conflict between individuals. These may be avoided, however, by conceptualizing the approach/avoidance conflict as a comparative choice, in the following manner.

We may regard the decision to accept or reject an option in Lewin's approach/avoidance conflict as a choice between the proffered option and the status quo. Both the proffered option and the status quo have approach and avoidance tendencies associated with them. We assign the value zero to the status quo; the aggregate for the proffered goal may then be positive or negative relative to this threshold for acceptance or rejection, approach or avoidance, respectively. The decision in the approach/avoidance conflict, then, becomes a comparative choice, the same mode as the approach/approach and avoidance/avoidance conflicts (see glossary).

What we have done here is to require that preference (utility) be measured on what we have called a signed ordinal scale (see glossary). A signed ordinal scale is an ordinal scale whose elements have positive or negative sign, and is subject to any arbitrary strictly monotone transformation which preserves sign. We have defined the status quo to have zero utility; all options preferred to the status quo are defined to have positive sign, and those to which the status quo is preferred are defined to have negative sign.

We have further assumed that an individual is motivated to improve the status quo and to avoid worsening it. This is a behavioral regularity we offer as our fourth behavioral principle and establishes the correspondence between the signed ordinal scale of the model and the behavioral (observable) concepts of approach and avoidance and of acceptance and rejection: positive sign is associated with approach processes, negative sign with avoidance processes. Furthermore, where individuals may be said to have preference, options will be said to have *ambience*. An option toward which an individual exhibits an approach process is said to have positive ambience and, correspondingly, an option toward which an individual exhibits an avoidance process is said to have negative ambience. The terms "good" and "bad", used with reference to options, reflect positive and negative ambience, respectively (see glossary).

3.2   The Effect of Framing

In the previous section, we have presented a classification of Type I conflicts as approach/approach, approach/avoidance, and avoidance/avoidance. As we will see later, there is a corresponding classification of the variety of Type II conflicts. This correspondence is important in part because it suggests that experimental research on the relative difficulty of resolving the different Type I conflicts may have implications for the difficulty of resolving those of Type II. The existence of such implications is, of course, an empirical question and remains to be investigated, but the conceptual correspondence provides a lead.

There are some things, however, that the formal modeling leaves unspecified but are demonstrably of great importance in partially explaining and predicting both the volatility and inconsistency of an individual's preferential choices and the vast range of individual differences. Among these is the freedom of the individual to determine which elemental components of an option will be considered to be relevant to the choice, or even what the elemental components might be.

The elemental components of an option relevant to a choice may well be different from one context to another. For example, a person's sex may be irrelevant when that person is being considered as a possible research assistant but not when he or she is being considered as a possible companion on an excursion. Furthermore, all the parameters of the utility function for such components are idiosyncratic, even the sign of the slope of the function. What one individual regards as a "good," or increasingly desirable, component may be regarded as a "bad," or increasingly undesirable, component by someone else. An example would be the price of a used car from the points of view of the seller and the buyer. So both the elemental components considered in making the decision and their roles in the decision will vary from individual to individual and from context to context.

These are rational factors in individual choice behavior. The work of Tversky and Kahneman (1986) on framing, however, has shown that the manner in which the options are described has effects that violate universally accepted principles of rational behavior. The term, framing, refers to changes in the descriptions of formally equivalent options that evoke quite different preferences. (Most of the studies have been on verbal descriptions, but changes in visual presentation can also produce the effects.) The following is an example of the effect, taken from an earlier study but reported again in the reference above (p. S260).

> Imagine that the U.S. is preparing for the outbreak of an unusual Asian disease, which is expected to kill 600 people. Two alternative programs to combat the disease have been proposed. Assume that the exact scientific estimates of the consequences of the programs are as follows:
> If Program A is adopted, 200 people will be saved.
> If Program B is adopted, there is a 1/3 probability that 600 people will be saved, and 2/3 probability that no people will be saved.

Out of 152 respondents, 72% preferred A and 28% preferred B. Tversky and Kahneman's report continues:

> In [this] problem, the outcomes are stated in positive terms (lives saved), and the majority choice is accordingly risk averse. The prospect of certainly saving 200 lives is

more attractive than a risky prospect of equal expected value. A second group of respondents was given the same cover story with the following descriptions of the alternative programs. ...

If Program C is adopted, 400 people will die.

If Program D is adopted, there is a 1/3 probability that nobody will die and a 2/3 probability that 600 people will die.

Out of 155 respondents, 22% preferred C and 78% preferred D. The report continues:

In [this] problem the outcomes are stated in negative terms (lives lost), and the majority choice is accordingly risk seeking. The certain death of 400 people is less acceptable than a two-thirds chance that 600 people will die. [These] problems, however, are essentially identical. They differ only in that the former is framed in terms of the number of lives saved (relative to an expected loss of 600 lives if no action is taken), whereas the latter is framed in terms of the number of lives lost.

These results, and many more that confirm them, suggest that interchanging positive and negative frames may generate contradictory preference orderings, an outcome that violates a basic consistency principle of rational decision making.

To seek some understanding of these effects, we explore conditions that reframing would have to meet to preserve the efficiency of a set of options and to preserve proper preference functions. A deeper understanding of the reasons for the effects of framing on preference could have significant implications for the resolution of conflict between individuals.

We briefly consider some of the consequences of a particularly simple kind of reframing. In Section 2.4, we gave definitions of proper preference functions, and we stated a theorem (proved in Appendix A) about the single peakedness of proper preference functions on efficient sets of options. That discussion depended on the representation of options as points in n-dimensional Euclidean space using interval scales for the elemental components of the options. Here, we consider the effects of a particular kind of transformation of those interval scales, corresponding to a simple sort of reframing of the options.

In the definition of a proper preference function, a distinction is made between those indices corresponding to increasingly desirable elemental components of the options and those corresponding to increasingly undesirable elemental components. Our definition of an efficient set involves an arbitrary partition of the indices into two classes, but the case of interest is where this partition also corresponds to the division between increasingly desirable and increasingly undesirable components. The theorem tells us that, in this case, any proper preference function will be single peaked on the efficient set.

We have assumed that each elemental component of the options can be measured on an interval scale. The information conveyed by such a scale is preserved by any transformation of the scale of the form $f(x) = ax + b$, where $a > 0$. A familiar example is the transformation between centigrade and fahrenheit temperature: $F = (9/5)C + 32$. Such a transformation preserves order, so if higher values of the original scale were more desirable, so are higher values of the transformed scale. Thus, rescaling of the sort allowed for interval scales cannot change an elemental component from increasingly desirable to increasingly undesirable, or vice versa.

Such a change can, however, be accomplished by reframing the options. Although the reframing used by Tversky and Kahneman in the examples discussed previously involves things that are probably too complex to be regarded as elemental components, it provides a good illustration of this process. In those examples, options are first characterized in terms of the number of lives saved from an expected death toll of 600, and higher numbers of lives saved are certainly preferred. The options are then reframed by presenting them in terms of the number of deaths due to the epidemic, and lower numbers of deaths are preferred. Mathematically, the transformation here is

$$\text{number of deaths} = (-1)(\text{number of lives saved}) + 600,$$

where we have chosen this slightly awkward form to indicate the connections with the allowed transformations of interval scales. The difference here, of course, is that the original scale value, number of lives saved, is multiplied by a negative number, and so the scale order is reversed.

We now examine some of the effects on efficient sets and proper preference functions of this sort of reframing of elemental components. Mathematically, such a reframing corresponds to a change of coordinates in which the original coordinate, say x_i, is replaced by $x_i' = -a_i x_i + b_i$, where a_i and b_i are real numbers with a_i positive. We note that this kind of transformation, which we call an affine reframing, is very special and that reframing can be enormously more complicated, but the effects of even this special sort of reframing indicate some of the issues involved.

Since such a change of coordinates reverses order (because $-a_i < 0$), reframing in this way converts an increasingly desirable component into an increasingly undesirable one, and vice versa. If the components are to be partitioned according to whether they are increasingly desirable or increasingly undesirable, such a reframing must move the affected component to the other part of the partition. We first consider the implications of this for efficiency.

Our definition of efficient set requires that the options be ordered the same way on each component. Since an affine reframing of a component reverses the order, an affine reframing of a single component necessarily destroys the efficiency of a set. However, if all the components of an efficient set are subjected to affine reframing, and the two parts of the associated partition are interchanged, the set remains efficient.

Affine reframing converts increasingly desirable components to increasingly undesirable ones, and increasingly undesirable components to increasingly desirable one. It therefore provides the mathematical framework necessary to handle options in which all the components are increasingly desirable or all the components are increasingly undesirable. By performing affine reframing of a subset of the components in such a case, we convert it to one in which some of the components are increasingly desirable and some are increasingly undesirable. Using this method, with affine reframings of the especially simple form $x_i' = -x_i$, we can give appropriate definitions of efficient sets and proper preference functions for these cases in terms of the definitions already discussed.

This raises some interesting and important, if somewhat technical, issues. If some of the elemental components of the options are increasingly desirable and some are increasingly undesirable, there is a natural partition of the components into two classes. But if all the components are, say, increasingly desirable, as could be achieved by reframing, there is no such natural partition and any given partition has a certain arbitrariness to it. We might ask for conditions under which a set is efficient or a preference function proper with respect to any partition, but it turns out that such conditions are extremely strong.

Consider a set of two-component options that is efficient with respect to either of the two possible non-trivial partitions. If we take $I_1 = \{1\}$ and $I_2 = \{2\}$, the definition of efficiency tells us that the ratio of change in component 2 to change in component 1 cannot decrease as we move from option to option in the direction in which the components increase. (This just says that the slopes of the line segments connecting successive options do not decrease.) On the other hand, if we take $I_1 = \{2\}$ and $I_2 = \{1\}$, the definition of efficiency says that the ratio of change in component 1 to change in component 2 does not decrease, so the slopes of the line segments do not increase. This argument extends to the case of options with more than two components, and tells us that a set that is efficient with respect to any partition consist of points lying on a straight line.

The case of proper preference functions is a little more complicated, because we need to use affine reframing and the machinery of the calculus, but the result is just as restrictive. If we are willing to slightly strengthen the differentiability condition and weaken a couple of inequalities in the definition of proper preference function, we can show that a preference function that is proper with respect to any partition is an additive combination of proper utility functions. (This can be seen by working in the case in which all the first-order partial derivatives are positive and looking at the information on second-order partial derivatives we get by switching a component from one partition to another. We need to assume that the second-order derivatives are continuous.)

Framing effects may thus be regarded as inevitable, particularly in view of the fact that the changes we have considered are of an especially simple form. Such considerations indicate some of the complexities involved in reframing, even of the extremely simple type discussed here.

Fortunately, these problems are not critical for our applications of the theory of individual preference to the structure of conflict, although the effects of reframing on individual preferences may be extremely important in resolving particular conflicts. As we will see later, our applications are mainly concerned with the case where there are only two components of the options, so that there are no serious problems with different partitions.

Before leaving the discussion of framing, we would like to highlight another subtlety of the empirical example just cited, and another aspect of the complexity of framing. In that example, each outcome of the programs to combat the disease may be characterized by a single number, the number of lives saved out of the 600 expected deaths. The reframing in the example consists of replacing this number by the number of deaths, or 600 minus the number of lives saved. As we have indicated, even this kind of simple change of coordinates can have significant implications for many aspects of preference.

But we suggest that what actually happens in this case is even more complicated. As we noted before, we believe that "the number of lives saved out of 600 expected deaths" is not an elemental component. It seems reasonable that there are at least two elemental components here, number of lives saved and number of deaths caused by the disease, and that the options can be characterized by a single number only because there is an expectation of a fixed number of deaths. When the options are framed positively or negatively, in terms of lives saved or deaths due to the disease, only one of these components is used to label the options. If this change in the salience of the components affects the relative influence of the two components on preference, then the effect of framing is to change the preference function in ways very much more complicated than a simple change of coordinates. It would have been interesting to compare the A and D options and, especially, the B and C options. The problem is probably not sufficiently well-defined to draw any general conclusions.

Since it may not be obvious why we dwell on the interpretation of these mathematical results on individual decision making when we are concerned with the structure of conflict, particularly between individuals, a word of explanation is called for here. It should already be apparent that what individuals bring to the problem of making a choice (e.g., a proper preference function and some rationality) is only one side of the coin; the other side is the structure that exists on the options: (e.g., order, Pareto optimality, efficiency). When we get to the problem of resolving conflict between individuals, in Part II in particular, this facet of the problem is just as relevant, and the framing of options can play a very significant role. An understanding of some abstract considerations that affect the acceptability of options can be of help in creatively meeting the challenge of constructing options over which adversaries can reach agreement. This is an area of research in individual decision making that has potential significance for the resolution of certain social conflicts.

3.3   The Classification of Type I Conflicts

Under single peakedness, the preference ordering is obtained by folding the scale of options (cf. Section 2.2). When the preference ordering is unfolded, the individual's indifference point becomes two points on the scale of options. The status quo is at one of these points and the other point is another (possibly hypothetical) option, one that is equivalent in preference to the status quo (see Section 2.1).

As mentioned in Chapter 2, we will use the term initial positions to refer to the points on the scale of options which correspond to the status quo or, more generally, correspond to the intersections of the SPF with the scale of options (see the points labeled *ip* in Figure 9).

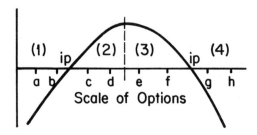

Figure 9: Effect of peak and initial positions on approach and avoidance processes

Figure 9 displays an SPF intersecting a scale of options at two points, both labeled *ip*. The vertical dotted line in the figure bisects the SPF at its peak, dividing it into right and left branches, and bisects the scale of options. Each branch is monotone over its portion of the scale of options. The bisection of the SPF together with the initial positions partitions the scale of options into four segments labeled (1) to (4). There are eight options shown, labeled *a* to *h*, two in each segment.

The options in segments (1) and (4) have negative ambience and hence induce avoidance processes; the options in segments (2) and (3) all have positive ambience and hence induce approach processes.

Any option in segment (2) or (3) represents an improvement on the status quo and would be accepted, by definition, if it were the only one available. Any option in segments (1) and (4) represents a worsening of the status quo and is unacceptable in the absence of coercion from some external source.

It seems likely that differences in the ambience of options would be reflected in differences in the difficulty of choosing between them. We speculate briefly on this topic here, and in detail in Section 4.1, because it merits empirical investigation; the particular outcome of such empirical research, although not at all central to our discussion here, may be significant for understanding differences in the difficulty of resolving Type II conflicts.

One might anticipate that the decision to accept or reject an isolated option should be one of the simplest decisions to make. What is required in principle is the relative assessment of the advantages and disadvantages (i.e., the improvement versus the worsening of the individual's status quo) and, according to whichever dominates, the effect is to accept or reject, respectively.

The proffered option may represent an improvement on the status quo in certain respects and a decrement in other respects. The conflict, then, in an accept/reject decision is an approach/avoidance conflict, whether the gain is worth the cost.

The conflict engendered by a choice between a pair of options may be classified by the corresponding pair of ambiences. If the options are from segments (2) and/or (3), the conflict is an approach/approach conflict. Both options have positive ambience, both represent an improvement on the status quo. But they represent different improvements in that each exceeds the other in qualitatively different ways; the conflict is essentially a tradeoff as to which is the greater good.

If the options are from segments (1) and/or (4), the conflict is an avoidance/avoidance conflict. Both options have negative ambience, both represent a worsening of the status quo. But they represent a worsening in qualitatively different ways; the conflict is essentially a tradeoff as to which is the lesser evil. If the pair of options includes one with positive ambience and one with negative ambience, or if either of them is the status quo, it is an approach/avoidance conflict.

The logical simplicity and psychological meaningfulness of the definitions of the motivational processes, approach and avoidance, based on the sign of the preference function are particularly well adapted to the classification of Type II conflicts as we shall see later and again in detail in Chapter 10.

Different Type I conflicts may be expected to differ in the difficulty of resolving them, some hardly deserving the name of conflict, others perhaps requiring outside intervention to resolve.

In the next chapter we discuss the possible implications that the structure of Type I conflicts may have for the relative difficulty of resolving them and suggest lines of research on Type I which could be fruitful in resolving Type II conflicts.

Chapter 4

The Difficulty of Resolving Type I Conflicts: Research Suggestions and Conjectures

An individual, in making a choice between options, is resolving a conflict. When there is some structure on the options — an ordering — and some structure on the preference function — a single peaked function — then we may anticipate that some of the structural characteristics will affect the difficulty of making the decision that resolves a conflict, quite aside from substantive considerations. Some of these structural characteristics are the ambience of the options and the slope and intercepts of the preference function. The ambience of the options distinguishes the three varieties of Type I conflict, approach/approach, approach/avoidance, and avoidance/avoidance.

If the role of these structural factors in determining the relative difficulty of resolving these varieties of Type I conflict was understood, then further research could be intelligently directed at controlling such factors with the intent of reducing the difficulty of resolving serious Type I conflicts. Furthermore, the possibility that such results would generalize to certain conflicts between individuals increases their importance. Structural effects on the difficulty of resolving conflict are of interest only if there are invariances in these effects from one context to another. For example, it would be interesting to know that an individual choosing where to go for a vacation finds an approach/approach conflict easier to resolve than an approach/avoidance conflict. But it would be far more interesting if this were also true when deciding what car to buy. In the face of the infinite variety of such contexts in which conflicts may arise, it is only invariances that permit abstraction, the construction of theory, and the emergence of a science. To carry this a step further, looking ahead, the most important invariances are those that would transfer from Type I to Type II and hold for a conflict between husband and wife and also between labor and management.

In brief, our remarks that follow about possible structural effects on the difficulty of resolving Type I conflicts are intended to be independent of context (the absence of any formal well-defined structure on the infinite variety of contexts precludes our consideration of it).

In the following two sections we propose such research. In the first section, the role of ambience and its possible relation to other structural aspects is discussed, and, in the second section, the research is directed at controlling ambience. Research is sometimes more interesting when results are anticipated and even more interesting when such expectations fail to materialize. Partly for that reason and partly because we find it irresistible, we anticipate some results and provide the reasons for expecting them. These conjectures are not logical consequences of this theory of the structure of conflict but must stand or fall on their own. They add spice. We offer them here in the hope of stimulating the empirical research that will sustain or reject them.

The objective of such research is to seek systematic effects on the difficulty of resolving Type I conflicts that are attributable to the sign of the preference function and the sign of its slope at the locus of the option, and the interaction of these factors on the difficulty of choosing between pairs of options.

4.1   The Effect of Ambience

This discussion will be abstract and general, but we shall parallel it with a concrete example. For this purpose we shall let the eight options labeled a to h in Figure 9 from the previous chapter represent an efficient set of gambles ordered from left to right on two components, one with a proper utility function with positive slope and one with a proper utility function with negative slope. For simplicity let these be the only components on which the options differ. For example, let the options be monetary gambles and let the amount to win be increasing from a to h and the amount to lose worsening from a to h, with probabilities fixed.

Any other two components could be chosen, for example amount to win as before and probability of winning decreasing from a to h. This could be done experimentally by fixing the probability of losing and the amount to lose and having a third outcome of zero which absorbed the residual probability.

Clearly, there are many experimental manipulations possible involving good things getting better and bad things getting worse or good things getting worse and bad things getting better. Good and bad options are essentially changes relative to the reference point of zero (i.e., the status quo) and so are not only relative but also variable due to the volatility of the status quo.

For concreteness and rhetorical convenience in the examples to follow we will refer to the two components as yield and risk, or, as appropriate, gain and loss, both increasing from a to h, and with utility functions having positive slope and negative slope, respectively. Neither is elemental as each may be compounded of outcomes and their probabilities in this context; but preference for each will be assumed to be monotone over the relevant interval for illustrative purposes. There is no loss of generality and the terms are simple and convenient.

As mentioned earlier, we are going to discuss the relative difficulty of making a choice between pairs of options with same and different ambience. For convenience, we will designate the various kinds of pairs with lower case Roman numerals, which will also identify the paragraphs in which each is discussed.

(i) Consider a pair of options under the same branch of the SPF but from different segments, for example, one from segment (1) and one from segment (2), or one from segment (3) and one from segment (4). We call such a pair of options a unilateral pair in that both options are under the same branch of the SPF (i.e., on the same side of the peak).

An option with positive ambience will dominate (in preference) an option with negative ambience. These choices might even be easier than those of whether to accept or reject an isolated option because the latter require comparison with the status quo, set at zero, whereas one option with positive ambience and one with negative ambience are more different from each other than either is from the status quo, making discrimination easier. There may also be some inertia making it difficult to abandon the status quo, further reinforced by the uncertainty usually associated with change.

An example of such a conflict would be the choice between options a and c (see Figure 9). Option a is one in which the low yield does not justify even the low risk, so a has negative ambience. Option c is one in which the greater yield does justify taking the somewhat larger risk than in a. So c has positive ambience. In a the risk is dominant and in c the yield is dominant. (It is understood, of course, that this is all in the mind of the individual according to the assessment and aggregation of the components as reflected in the SPF.)

A parallel scenario could be written for options e and g as another example of this class *(i)*.

(ii) Consider a unilateral pair of options drawn from the same segment, and with positive ambience, for example c and d from segment (2) or e and f from segment (3).

In general, choice between options drawn from the same segment essentially requires discrimination in the sense that the tradeoff between the components is dominated by one of them, and it is the same one in both options. In this case the yield has dominated the risk because the ambience is positive for both options, more so for d than for c and more so for e than for f. The decision requires discriminating the relative dominance in the two options. We have here in c and d a pair of two acceptable options and one dominates the other in preference, so it would seem that the conflict would be a pleasure to face and resolve. The same would hold, of course, for the pair of options e and f from segment (3).

(iii) Consider a unilateral pair of options drawn from the same segment, but a segment with negative ambience, for example a and b from segment (1) or g and h from segment (4). Here again these are unilateral pairs from the same segment but the risk component dominates the yield component because they have negative ambience, so neither member of a pair is acceptable.

We might anticipate that choice between options in such segments will be made with resistance and accepted with reluctance compared with choice between options in segment (2) or (3).

(iv) We turn now to consider bilateral pairs of options in which one member of the pair is under one branch of the SPF and the other member is under the other branch. We would anticipate that the simplest of these is that in which the ambience of the two options is different, one positive and one negative.

This is a situation much like that of class *(i)* except that a complication has been added in that the options are under different branches of the SPF instead of the same branch. The example used in class *(i)* was between a and c. Now we will replace c with f.

As pointed out before, a is an option with negative ambience because the low yield does not justify even its low level of risk. In the case of option f we have an option with high yield and high risk, somewhat beyond the individual's preferred level of exchange but still one in which the positive contribution of the high yield justifies the high risk. In a the risk is dominant. In f the yield is dominant, just as it was in c, but in c the individual is willing to take more risk to obtain more yield. In f the individual would prefer to take less yield in order to be exposed to less risk.

We anticipate that bilaterality in general would be a more difficult conflict to resolve than its corresponding unilateral match. There is some experimental evidence which supports such an inference in that bilateral choices tend to have a longer latency (Greenberg, 1961), and tend to be more inconsistent (Coombs, 1958).

(v) Consider next a bilateral pair of options with positive ambience, for example, one option from segment (2) and one from segment (3). We would anticipate a significant degree of conflict here compared with *(iv)*. The conflict, for example could involve the choice between c and e, or between c and f, or d and e, or d and f. In each case the yield is sufficient to overcome the risk, as all options have positive ambience.

But from c to e, for example, there is a comparatively large increment in yield and a large increment in risk. In the case of c the individual is motivated to take more risk for more yield if such an option were available, and in the case of e, the individual is motivated to take less yield if the risk were diminished sufficiently. So from c the individual is driven toward e and from e the individual is driven toward c. We would classify this as an approach/approach conflict because both options have positive ambience.

We anticipate that this conflict would be more difficult to resolve than case *(ii)* because in the latter case, in the options c and d, yield dominates risk in both and the comparison requires judging whether the increment in yield from c to d is worth the increment in risk. Indeed, because the peak is to the right of d in the figure, the individual would have preferred more yield with more risk, if not disproportionate (i.e., if not past the peak). The monotonicity makes this decision easier.

But in the case of c versus e the increment in yield and the increment in risk bracket the ideal level and the conflict is between whether to go too far, e, or whether to not go far enough, c. Of course, c and e are more discriminable than c and d on the scale of options but not necessarily more discriminable in preference.

All in all, however, it is a happy situation, no choice is bad, it's just a matter of which is best among desirable options (i.e., all options are good).

(vi) In contrast to case *(v)* consider a bilateral pair of options in which both options have negative ambience, for example, one from segment (1) and one from segment (4), say options b and h. In option b the very low level of risk is still too high for the very low level of yield and the option is unacceptable. In the case of option h the very high level of risk dominates the very high level of yield and h also is unacceptable.

The increments in yield and in risk from b to h also bracket the ideal level of tradeoff in this efficient set. So one has non-monotonicity and negative ambience. This conflict is an avoidance/avoidance conflict. Like case *(iii)*, such a choice is apt to be made with resistance and accepted with reluctance but not necessarily; consider a parent faced with a demand for a ransom to free a kidnapped child.

In summary, our anticipations reflect the effect of three factors on the difficulty of resolving a Type I conflict. Difficulty is expected to increase with:

1. options from the same segment rather than different segments

2. negative ambience rather than positive

3. nonmonotonicity rather than monotonicity.

So cases *(i)*, *(ii)*, and *(iii)* should be increasingly difficult to resolve; cases *(iv)*, *(v)*, and *(vi)* should be increasingly difficult to resolve. Also, *(iv)* should be more difficult than *(i)*, *(v)* more than

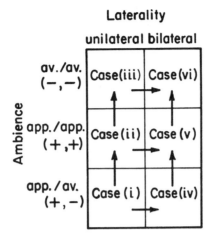

Figure 10: Conjoint design for testing power requirements

(ii), and *(vi)* more than *(iii)*. All of these speculations are in need of experimental research.

These three factors may be viewed as being generated by two general factors, the sign of the ambience and the laterality of the pair of options. These relations are portrayed in Figure 10 in a 3 × 2 experimental design. There are three levels of ambience as indicated and two levels of laterality. Each of the six cells corresponds to one of the six cases and the arrows indicate the direction of increasing difficulty according to our speculations.

The figure reveals that the expectations are based on the hypothesis that under an SPF the difficulty of resolving Type I conflict, other things being equal or irrelevant, can be decomposed into two independent factors, ambience and laterality, because all parallel arrows point in the same direction (Krantz, Luce, Suppes & Tversky, 1971).

Whether these two factors have additive effects or interact can only be partially tested from these ordinal relations alone. A 3 × 3 design would be better. This is possible if we go beyond SPFs and include multipeaked preference functions. The latter are the rule in Type I conflict resolution and would introduce another column in Figure 10 that might be expected to be more difficult to resolve from the point of view of structure. This column would be generated by the dip between two successive peaks and would have pairs in all three rows of the figure. It would be generated by deliberately constructing a Pareto optimal but inefficient set of options such as illustrated in Figure 7. Speculation on the relative difficulty among these pairs is even more hazardous and will not be discussed further here.

There are other comparisons between the cells of Figure 10 that are possible; these would reflect tradeoffs between the two factors that would be interesting. Another question of interest is whether these relations are context bound and, if so, what characteristics distinguish the contexts.

An unanswered question, of course, is what response measure should be used to indicate difficulty of decision: decision time, choice probabilities, ratings, galvanic skin responses, etc. That these might not agree is to be expected, an approach/approach conflict may be a pleasure to prolong compared with an avoidance/avoidance conflict and yet be rated easier.

All of these considerations are empirical issues and not crucial to the theory of the structure of conflict as developed here, so we refrain from further speculation. Hopefully, these expectations will prove to be wrong when tested because they seem commonsensical and so don't become interesting unless they are wrong. Another way of putting it is that if common sense is sustained empirically then any theory must satisfy it. And then the theories don't do any work. Theories are only discriminable when they go beyond common sense or when common sense is contradicted.

4.2   On Changing Ambience

If it is correct that ambience is related to the difficulty of resolving Type I conflicts, then it would be useful to know not only what this relation might be but how to take advantage of it by changing the ambience. Our expectation is that such knowledge will be at least as useful in reducing the difficulty of resolving Type II conflicts as well.

There are two obvious points of attack to change the ambience of a conflict. These two points of attack are a consequence of the relation between the locus of the options on the scale of options, on the one hand, and certain characteristics of the preference function on the other, as illustrated in Figure 9. One point of attack is to manipulate the locus of the options vis-à-vis the SPF, the other is to change the "shape" of the preference function.

The most important characteristics of a preference function, given that it is single peaked, are the location of the peak and the location of the zero points (initial positions) on the scale of options. The fact that the scale of options is only ordinal means that the shape of the SPF between peak and initial positions is arbitrary within the limits of preserving monotonicity.

BLOOM COUNTY

Figure 11: Effect of background variables

All the options between the initial positions represent an improvement on the status quo, and the peak indicates the best option. There are an unknown number of factors that enter into determining the locus of the peak and the initial positions. The status quo, for example, may include not only an option as part of one of the initial positions but also the effect of many other variables that are not, strictly speaking, unique to any option. We will call such variables background variables.

As an example, consider an individual's utility functions for the yield and risk of a prospective investment. The individual's financial status and family responsibilities are background variables. An inheritance could change the parameters of the component utility functions, or, more precisely, the preference function, and hence the acceptability of a prospective investment.

As another illustration consider an individual contemplating having a child or having another child. The individual has a status quo which includes not only the current number of children but background variables like health and attitudes of the spouse, economic status and prospects, etc. A change in health or financial position could change the locus of the peak but not the initial position that includes the status quo, the current number of children. Changes in the background variables could, however, change the locus of the other initial position, the unfolded image of the status quo, because such changes might also alter the assessment of the zero point. The important thing about background variables is that they are susceptible to outside intervention independently of any option. The cartoon strip reproduced in Figure 11 is very apropos.

Another lever by which the preference functions can be changed is by modifying or creating options. In principle, many efficient sets are possible in a domain and changing the set has the effect of changing the shape of the SPF without any change in the background variables.

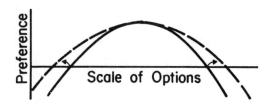

Figure 12: Tampering with the status quo

For example, introducing a new option that dominates one or more existing options, changes the apparent shape of the SPF. We will illustrate, shortly, how some of these effects have been or may be studied experimentally.

In any specific instance the effect of a particular manipulation on an individual's preference function is a matter of that individual's taste and only someone intimately acquainted with the individual may hope to predict it accurately. For example, the effect of an inheritance may cause some individuals to become more conservative in their choice of investments and others to become more aggressive. Consequently, we discuss certain manipulations in abstract terms and the reader is warned that our illustrations, though hopefully reasonable, are precarious and not part of our central argument.

A builder may choose to bid or not to bid on a contract but as his status quo deteriorates, almost any proposition is increasingly attractive. In general, it seems reasonable to anticipate that as the status quo degenerates, the initial positions become farther apart on the scale of options in the sense that options which had previously been unacceptable because of negative ambience may now find favor. We have illustrated such a possible effect with Figure 12.

Two SPFs are shown in the figure, the dotted one suggesting the effect of a deterioration of the status quo that had no effect on the locus of the peak. In such a case the preference ordering could remain unchanged but the accept/reject threshold for the options would have shifted. If the change in the status quo affected one of the component utility functions more than the other, then the locus of the peak and the preference order would also be changed.

Uncertainties about these effects reflect the lack of sufficient experimental study directed at isolating empirical regularities. There has been some related experimental work comparing unpaid volunteer subjects with subjects paid to participate in a gambling experiment. This might be interpreted as a manipulation of the status quo but the experiments don't analyze individual preference orderings and

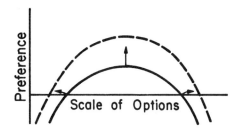

Figure 13: Tampering with the options

accept/reject data under the two conditions.

An alternative manipulation is a change in the options instead of the status quo of the individual. The experimenter could add a positive increment to the outcomes in every gamble (i.e., "sweeten" the options). A possible effect of such a tampering is illustrated in Figure 13. Here the figure describes the effect as a vertical translation of the preference function.

If this were the effect, the preference ordering would remain unchanged over the transformed options but every original option would be dominated by its transform, and the initial positions would be further apart. If the effect of the increment were relative to the amount to win then the shape of the SPF would be changed systematically with respect to any fixed scale of options.

Different experimental treatments like, perhaps, manipulating the status quo and manipulating the options, can be designed to be mathematically identical in final outcomes, for example, by paying the subject to play a gamble instead of sweetening the outcomes, but their effect on behavior may not be identical. If they are not the same in their effects on preference and acceptability, then regularities in their differences could lead to a theoretical understanding that would be important for effective outside intervention. These manipulations are tools in the hands of a third party seeking a resolution to a Type II conflict, and predictability of their different effects can be advanced by experimental study of Type I conflict.

Tversky and Kahneman (1986) refer to studies in which changes in prices may be framed as discounts or as surcharges. While rational economic considerations would consider them equivalent, psychological tendencies would not. Referring to work by Thaler (1980), they make the point that it is easier to forego a discount than to accept a surcharge because the same price difference is valued as a gain in the former case and as a loss in the latter. The credit card lobby is said to insist that any price difference between cash and credit card purchases should be labeled a cash discount rather than a credit surcharge.

The empirical study of preference reversals is an example of research in individual decision making which directly attacks issues potentially relevant to conflict resolution between individuals. It is not clear whether the empirical manipulations change the locus of the peak or the initial positions or whether there is some other explanation. But theoretical understanding of behavioral regularities are of importance because peaceful conflict resolution is dependent upon preference reversals.

In this section on Type I conflict we have tried to make three points: one, that not a great deal is known about the shaping of preference functions beyond a phenomenological level, two, that there is sufficient structure and understanding of preferential choice to support systematic experimental study, and three, that such study would be of value to those social scientists, statesmen, and professionals concerned with conflict resolution.

4.3   Concluding Remarks on Type I Theory

The impetus for building this theory of single peaked preference functions was to provide a descriptive theory of a phenomenon that is sometimes characteristic of individual choice behavior. The behavioral system we describe is compatible with prevailing views of such behavior and is well supported empirically; the mystery, then, is why is the phenomenon, single peakedness, so rare?

Somewhat to our surprise, the answer we obtained was that the difficulty lay in the structure on the options. To ensure that *all* preference functions were single peaked, given this very simple description of a behavioral system, requires that the options satisfy certain conditions that in general can only be said to be unreasonable.

Although the applicability of single peaked functions as a descriptive theory of individual preferential choice is limited, it is very suitable as normative theory for a certain type of conflict between individuals, as will shortly become apparent. This remark does not imply that the environment of conflicts between individuals is less complex than that within individuals. Rather, as will be seen, it is easy in principle to approximate, in certain essential respects, the conditions required for single peakedness in a conflict between two parties, an approximation that may be much more difficult to achieve in a Type I conflict.

The best known normative model for preferential choice is the economic model for maximizing expected utility developed by von Neumann and Morgenstern (1947). This preference function does not satisfy the conditions for a proper preference function, and so would not necessarily yield a single peaked preference function in the presence of an efficient set.

This is illustrated by the following example. Let p be the probability of winning and $1 - p$ be the probability of losing in a two-outcome gamble. Let w be the amount to win and l be the amount to lose. So p and w are attractive components, and l is an unattractive component. Let $I_1 = \{p, w\}$ and let $I_2 = \{l\}$. Consider the following points in pwl-space: $x = (0,0,0)$, $y = (1/3,3,3)$, $z = (2/3,6,8)$.

The set $\{x, y, z\}$ is efficient with respect to the given partition, so a proper preference function would be single peaked on it. But $E(x) = 0$, $E(y) = 1 - 2 < 0$, and $E(z) = 4 - 8/3 > 0$. So y has the smallest expected value of the three points and single peakedness is violated. This is not to say, of course that the existence of an SPF over an efficient set of risky options implies that maximizing an expectation is not the preference function.

Maximizing an expectation, however, is unacceptable as a descriptive theory of individual preferential choice (see Schoemaker, 1982, for an extensive review of literature and, more recently, Tversky & Kahneman, 1986). Tversky and Kahneman demonstrate, with representative instances from a substantial body of research, that all the basic principles on which expectation maximization theories are based are violated by experiments on the formatting of options, for example, between positive and negative framing, (see Section 3.2.1 for an example). They make the point that their theory is "unabashedly" descriptive.

It is clear from research on framing that the preferences of individuals for options that are formulated verbally can be biased in direction, such as risk averse versus risk seeking. Differential visual framing, sometimes called display effects, can also effect choice, but this has not been systematized as well as Tversky and Kahneman have done for verbal framing. A deeper understanding of these psychological considerations, and the factors that favor and inhibit their occurrence, would be very useful to those involved in seeking resolution of Type II conflicts.

A suggested experimental paradigm for the study of such effects would be to construct an efficient set in one frame, say positive, and its corresponding set in a negative frame. Peaks and intercepts for an individual's SPF are readily parameterized (ordinally) and the effects of differential framing could be quantified without making questionable and untestable assumptions. The extension of Type I theory to Type II conflict involves screening for an optimal set of options and the outcome of the algorithm might depend on the framing of the options. Understanding of the factors inducing biases is of immense value in the construction of options in the first place and in the conduct of the negotiation itself.

Part II

Type II Conflict

conflict that arises between individuals because they want different things and have to settle for the same thing

Preview

We begin in Chapter 5 with an example of the simplest case of a Type II conflict from the point of view of structure: the case in which a husband and wife are in conflict over the number of children they will have. This example is used to bring out the essential correspondence between Type I and Type II conflict in that the opposing utility functions in a Type I conflict are in one head and in a Type II conflict they are in different heads. Then in Chapter 6 we discuss some of the problems that arise because the opposing utility functions are in different heads.

We turn in Chapter 7 to a more complex Type II conflict, Edgeworth's economical calculus where the options can differ on two independent variables, and we use wages and amount of work as an example, as he did. In Chapter 8 very complex options are discussed and some literature on the problem of contriving them is surveyed.

In Chapter 9 the construction of a totally ordered scale of options called the frontier of preference is described for any two-party Type II conflict. The procedure is based on the theory of single peaked functions and minimizing compromise in a certain precise sense. We treat two problems separately: screening options to isolate an optimal set and selecting an option from that set. The first lends itself to a rational solution; the second is for the most part a normative problem sensitive to judgment and opinion. Three aspects of the second problem, selecting an option, are discussed: the effect of multipeakedness on negotiation, some of the pros and cons of debate as a means of reaching a decision, and the process of negotiation itself.

The frontier of preference is shown to converge on Edgeworth's contract curve and is a generalization of that notion to more complex options. We offer an ad hoc procedure for the extension and application of the frontier of preference to Type I conflict that might be useful in complex and difficult decision problems faced by an individual. We compare this structural approach to conflict resolution through the construction of the frontier of preference with the approach of classical game theory.

Chapter 10 takes up the classification of Type II conflicts based only on ordinal structural characteristics, extends the classification to as many as nine varieties, and discusses the relative difficulty of resolving them. In that chapter, we introduce a metric for the distance between adversaries in a Type II conflict.

In Chapter 11, we discuss multiparty Type II conflicts in the context of election systems, one of the principal methods for resolving such conflicts. We review the jury system as a special form of an election system and explore empirically an ad hoc extension of the frontier of preference to elections.

Chapter 12 summarizes Part II, reviews the correspondences between Type I and Type II conflicts, and discusses the basic characteristic that distinguishes Type II and Type III conflict.

Chapter 5

Basic Concepts

5.1 Introduction to Type II Conflict

Some conflicts arise between individuals because they want different things but must settle for the same thing, for example, a conflict between husband and wife over where to go for a vacation, between business partners over a new product, between tenant and landlord, between an employee and the boss, between heads of state at a summit meeting. The latter particularly captures attention.

The early history of summit meetings and how they are distinguished from ordinary meetings between heads of state is offered by Wernick (1986) in an account that begins with the summit between Richard the Lion Hearted, King of England, and Saladin, the Sultan of Egypt, ending with a treaty sworn to by both, in 1192, concluding the Third Crusade. Wernick characterizes a summit as

> ... a meeting between the leaders of two or more rival or enemy Great Powers trying to satisfy their mutual demands and head off future conflict. ... rulers who are capable of making major decisions on the spot and have the authority to carry them out. ... In addition, summitteers must have a practical agenda, something agreed upon on which they can compromise. (p. 58)

Wernick continues

> Richard and Saladin had separate missions, and the missions were irreconcilable. Richard's was to reconquer Palestine, Saladin's was to rid it of invaders. ... But they were realistic politicians, capable of a realistic assessment

67

of the situation. "Men of ours and yours have died," declared Richard, "the country is in ruins and events have entirely escaped anyone's control. Do you not believe that it is enough?... There must be an end to all this."

The fact was, as both leaders had come to see, that neither side could win a decisive victory. (p. 60)

It may seem lèse majesté to put such a conflict in the same class as that between a tenant and landlord or that between a husband and wife, but stripped of personalities, historical context, and the social milieu, the abstract structure is the same. And that is what we propose to show, along with the kinship of this type of conflict to that of Type I and the implications of that structure for the resolution of such conflicts.

In general, so long as the parties to a conflict want different things but seek a single option among the possibilities, one that is to hold for both of them, then the conflict is Type II. If, instead, they choose to go their own ways, then it either ceases to be a conflict or becomes a conflict of Type III. But that is another story, one we take up in Part III. In this chapter, we begin the analysis of Type II conflict by relating its structure to that of Type I.

Understanding the structure of a Type I conflict within an individual gives us a grasp on the structure of conflict between individuals. The definition of a Type I conflict is one in which an individual is torn between incompatible goals. This definition expresses the conception of an individual faced with a totally ordered set of options and having two kinds of utility functions over them, one with positive slopes and one with negative slopes, and both types concave down. The individual's preference is driven in one direction by one of the kinds of utility functions and in the other direction by the other kind of utility function. The individual is torn between incompatible goals because there is no single option that maximizes both kinds of utility functions and yet a single option must be chosen.

The translation of this conception to the case of conflict between individuals who want different things and have to settle for the same thing is simple and obvious. We put the two kinds of utility functions in different heads and require that a single option from the totally ordered set of options be chosen for both of them.

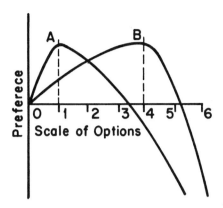

Figure 14: Family conflict over number of children

5.2 An Example: A Conflict Between Husband and Wife Over Number of Children

We shall begin the discussion of Type II conflict with an example that is simple from a structural point of view, permitting the introduction of basic concepts with few complications. Consider the conflict that may occur between a husband and wife on the issue of how many children they will have. The options are the natural numbers on the scale of options. In general, individuals have a single peaked preference function over that scale when the number of children is not confounded with a sex bias (Coombs, Coombs, & McClelland, 1975). Two such functions are shown in Figure 14, for our example, with a current state of no children as the status quo, set at zero utility for both parties. For abstract purposes it matters not which party is the husband and which is the wife so we have labeled them A and B.

The preference functions of the two parties include all background variables such as health, housing, finances, etc., as assessed by each party.

Note that the SPFs have been drawn to the same scale. There is a subtle and complex problem arising here that has never been solved, the problem of interpersonal comparability of utility. We will postpone discussion of this problem to the next chapter.

We see from the figure that A has a peak preference for 1 child and B a peak preference for 4 children. A's right-hand branch crosses the option scale between options 3 and 4 so that is the initial position equivalent in preference to the status quo for A. A, then, has positive ambience for from 1 to 3 children and negative ambience for 4 or more. B's right-hand branch crosses the option scale between options 5 and 6 and so has positive ambience for 1 to 5 children.

Both parties prefer 1 child to none and both prefer 4 children to more; hence the conflict is only over the options 1, 2, 3, or 4 children. Note that these are the options between the two peaks.

We will call the segment of the scale of options that is bounded by the two peaks the *viable options*. The "inner" branches of the two SPFs, and only the inner branches, are in conflict over the viable options. A's right-hand branch has a negative slope and hence is a decreasing preference function over the options from 1 to 4; and B's left-hand branch has positive slope and hence is an increasing preference function. The preference orderings of the two parties are in agreement over all options on each side of the viable options. To the left of A's peak both preference functions have positive slope and to the right of B's peak both preference functions have negative slope.

Over the options from 1 to 3, then, the conflict is an approach/approach conflict and over option 4 it is an approach/avoidance conflict in accordance with the classification of conflicts discussed in Section 3.3. The conflict over 1 to 3 children will be the likely focus of negotiation, perhaps, being an approach/approach conflict, rather than the conflict over 4 children, an approach/avoidance conflict.

Consider a possible later development. The family has had its first child so the status quo is changed from zero to one child and, of course, the shapes of the SPFs may also have been changed by virtue of background variables. We suppose the situation to be that displayed in Figure 15.

We see that A wants no more children — the status quo is ideal for A and any departure from it has negative ambience — and that B would now most prefer 2 but also regards 3 as an improvement on the status quo (i.e., B has positive ambience for 3 children).

Both parties prefer 2 to more than 2, so the only viable options are the status quo or 2 children (i.e., one more child). We see that the ambience is positive for B but negative for A, and so the conflict is an approach/avoidance conflict.

We don't presume to resolve the conflict. Such a presumption, to know what is best for others, requires answers to such general questions as those raised in the next chapter and other issues outside the scope of this analysis. We wish merely to use these examples to reveal the basic underlying structure of a Type II conflict.

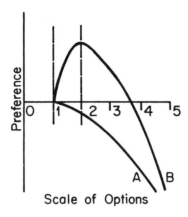

Figure 15: Shall we have another?

5.3 Structural Differences Between Type I and Type II Conflict

The example we have been discussing brings out clearly the fundamental difference between the structures of Type I and Type II conflicts. In the Type II case, there exists a common totally ordered scale of options over which each adversary has an SPF. One branch from each of the two adversarial SPFs is taken to form the Type II conflict. If the peak of one party, say A, is to the left of the peak of party B, then only the right-hand branch of A's SPF and the left-hand branch of B's SPF are relevant, since both parties prefer the nearest peak to any option under an "outer" branch. It is convenient to refer to these as the inner branches of the adversarial SPFs. These branches, the one from A with negative slope, and the one from B with positive slope, characterize the Type II conflict in that the individuals want different things and must settle for the same thing. We see that the inner branch of each party's preference function in a Type II conflict plays the role of one of the opposing utility functions in a Type I conflict.

Each inner branch has associated with it an approach or an avoidance tendency depending on the locus of the option. If for example, the left-hand branch of the SPF shown in Figure 9 were the inside branch, then the options in segment (1) would induce an avoidance process and the options in segment (2) an approach process because of their negative and positive ambience, respectively. If the right-hand branch of the SPF shown in Figure 9 were the inside branch, then the

options in segment (3) would induce an approach process and those
in segment (4) an avoidance process.

Each viable option has two inner branches covering it, with an
approach or an avoidance tendency associated with each. So each option may be classified as approach/approach, approach/avoidance, or
avoidance/avoidance corresponding to whether its ambience is positive for both parties, positive for one only, or negative for both.

We shall classify a Type II conflict over a pair of options each
of which has approach/approach tendencies associated with it as an
approach/approach Type II conflict. A Type II conflict over a pair of
options each of which has avoidance/avoidance tendencies associated
with it is an avoidance/avoidance Type II conflict. Any Type II conflict involving an option with an approach tendency associated with it
from one adversary and an avoidance tendency associated with it from
the other adversary will be classified as an approach/avoidance conflict, regardless of whether the other option is an approach/approach,
an approach/avoidance, or an avoidance/avoidance option. Further
refinement of the classification of Type II conflicts is possible and
discussed in Chapter 10.

In Type II we may not have proper utility functions but just ordinal versions of them given by the inner branches. The problem
of combining these preference functions is more complicated because
they are not comparable, as they are when they are in the same head,
and the combination rule that is available in one head is absent in
Type II. In brief, the things to be combined are harder to work with
and the rule of combination is harder to determine. These are the
root differences between Type I and Type II and from them other,
deeper problems emerge which significantly affect the resolution of a
Type II conflict.

These emergent problems are of two general types, one consisting
of technical problems that lend themselves to acceptable rational answers and the other of normative problems, the answers to which are
in part matters of opinion and judgment and consensus. These two
types of problems will emerge repeatedly in Part II.

One example of the technical problems is that of approximating
an efficient set. In any particular conflict of either Type II or Type
I, there need be no efficient set, but, as we shall see in Chapter 9,
it is much easier to approximate one in Type II than in Type I.
Another technical problem is due to the status quo in a Type II
conflict being in two heads in contrast to Type I where it is only in
one head. In our example of a conflict between husband and wife
over number of children (Figure 14) we set the initial status quo at
zero children for each party. But each party has background variables

such as health, financial status, and family pressures which each party assesses independently. Hence the status quo of each SPF, unfolded, gives rise to initial positions which reflect these assessments.

What is important about this is that initial positions of the two parties may be subject to independent manipulation, in that a change in a background variable, for example, may have a positive effect on one party and a negative effect on the other. In a Type I conflict the two initial positions are almost impossible to manipulate independently.

An example of normative problems that arise is that of the equitable distribution of gains and/or losses in the absence of unambiguous measures of contribution and/or blame. Fundamentally, there are abstract issues of fairness and justice which are almost inevitable in a Type II conflict where sharing of gains and losses is inevitable, and resisted.

These distinctions between Type I and Type II structure are reflected in their relative status as descriptive and normative theory. Type I theory, the theory of individual preferential choice, is intended as descriptive theory, a theory of how single peakedness may come about, and hence is falsifiable. It makes very strong predictions, which have been upheld empirically. It is not unreasonable that a good descriptive theory of human behavior should also have potential as normative theory, on the grounds that it has evolved under the principle that the fitter did survive. In this respect, Type I theory also has some easily recognizable normative characteristics such as those discussed in Chapter 2.

When we seek to transfer the Type I model to Type II conflict, the structure appears to transfer only in certain respects. A critical problem is that of the lack of a suitable analogue for the proper preference function in Type I theory. The question in Type II theory is how to aggregate the two adversarial arms of SPFs from different heads to determine an optimal decision. A solution involves considerations that do not arise in the resolution of Type I, such as equity, fairness, justice, and power. Because some of these considerations are normative in character, we will distinguish between the rational analysis of the structure of Type II conflicts and what we offer as normative principles and procedures. The latter are matters of individual taste, consensus, or policy, are in the public domain, and hence are subject to change.

We turn, now, to a discussion of some of these normative aspects. We regard these problems as unsolvable, in the near future, at least in any universally acceptable way. However, as a point of fact, they are solved implicitly, in every instance in which a Type II conflict is resolved. Inasmuch as these are normative questions, answered by what society does in these instances, their study may reveal emerging principles for social ethics.

Chapter 6

Utility, Power, and Fairness

6.1 Utility

In the case of a Type I conflict, we can think of the individual as having two or more proper utility functions which are aggregated into a total preference. If they are aggregated by a proper preference function and the scale of options is an efficient set, a single peaked preference function results. An SPF makes possible an effective converging search mechanism for selecting the most preferred option, an optimum decision.

In formally modeling this process, the utility for each component attribute is usually assumed to be measured on an interval scale, a numerical representation in which the zero point and the unit of measurement may be changed. The aggregation of these utilities is then accomplished by some arithmetic operations, such as addition. (The measurement status of the more general proper preference functions is similar.)

When we try to transfer this mechanism to the Type II conflict, two separate problems emerge. One is the problem of interpersonal comparability of preference (utility) and the other is the problem of fairness. The first problem is the comparability of the opposing preference scales; the second is the problem of aggregating these opposing preference scales (i.e., what to optimize). We will refer to this aggregation rule in a Type II conflict as a *decision function*. It plays the role of the preference function in a Type I conflict, that which aggregates the individual's component utility functions, a rule which is the individual's answer to the question of what to optimize.

Given our heuristic of imagining proper utility functions for elemental components, all other utility functions are composites or aggregates of elemental utility functions, and are the formal equivalent of empirically observed preferences. So the term "preference" is used when emphasis is on the empirical event and the term "utility" is used when the emphasis is on the numerical representation based on formal principles. No commitment is implied to any particular empirical procedure for observing preferences nor to any particular representational model for measuring utility.

In the case of Type I conflict we assume that neither problem exists. The first problem requires that preference be measured on a "difference scale." This is one in which an individual's scales may have different origins but the unit of measurement is the same (see Suppes & Zinnes, 1963). Such a scale permits the comparison of differences within an individual so that it may be said that an individual prefers a over b twice as much as he or she dislikes c more than d. In the case of a Type I conflict, the opposing scales are assumed to be the same because they are in one head and so comparability of units of measurement across attributes is a given, though in fact the difficulty of such comparisons undoubtedly contributes to the difficulty of making many choices. In a Type I conflict the second problem is the individual's aggregation function, which is unknown but is often assumed, for simplicity and in the absence of any evidence to the contrary, to be a weighted additive function of the individual's utilities for the components. The individual is presumed to be able to decide for himself or herself what is a "fair" weighting of the opposing components in the weighted additive model.

A psychological quantity like utility or preference may seem intuitively compelling but its logical basis is not transparent. Logical justification is a matter of constructing a representation theorem from a set of axioms. Then, if the axioms are not contradicted empirically and are otherwise acceptable, the numerical representation may be regarded as justified.

No completely satisfactory justification for the measurement of an individual's utility exists. Von Neumann and Morgenstern (1947) provide a representation theorem that justifies measurement on an interval scale if its premises hold. Empirical support for the system is lacking; there are systematic failures in testing the implications of the theorem and, indeed, in testing the individual principles on which the theorem depends (see Section 4.3).

The trouble is well hidden. We first make the argument, which is somewhat technical, and then illustrate it with an example. The measurement of preference (i.e., utility) is on an interval scale so the zero point of the preference scale is arbitrary (and is usually assigned to the status quo). The transformations that preserve the meaning of an interval scale are the affine transformations (see glossary) so, if a change occurs in the status quo an affine transformation is assumed to accommodate it. If preference and, of course, its formal image, utility, are monotone with an ordered scale of options, then a change in the status quo with an affine transformation of the utility function preserves monotonicity between the utility function and the preference function and such transformations are justified, at least ordinally.

If, however, preference is not monotone with an ordinal scale of options but, for example, is properly single peaked, then a change in the status quo and/or background variables may change the locus of the peak of the preference function and the loci of the points on the scale of options that correspond in preference to the status quo. If the loci of the peak and/or the intercepts of the preference function change, then the preference ordering may be changed nonmonotonically, some pairs of options may remain ordered the same in preference and some may become reversed in preference. These changes may occur with either unilateral or bilateral pairs; there is no simple correspondence.

We illustrate this argument with Figure 16. There are two SPFs shown, each linear and symmetric over the same scale of options. The SPF on the left is the same as that in Figure 2(b) and the one on the right is obtained by a simple translation to the right, as if an improvement in the status quo had changed the preferences for all options as indicated in the figure. The preference order is changed from $c\,d\,b\,a\,e$ to $d\,c\,e\,b\,a$, a change involving three transpositions (i.e., three interchanges of two options).

Options d and e have risen in the preference order and options c, b, and a have been reduced in the ordering. These nonmonotone changes in the preference order mean that the change in the status quo cannot be represented by any monotone transformation of the utility measures.

We will note here that not only is the preference order substantially changed but some other strange things appear to have happened. The most preferred option, d, is less preferred than the previous most preferred option, c, and the range of utility is changed. In view of the fact that all these changes take place in one head, it is tempting to infer that the increase in the status quo has made the individual less happy with the set of options as a whole, although two, d and e, have improved in preference.

Such an inference is unsupported by the data however. To make such an inference, one would need, among other things, preferences

(a) Translation of an SPF

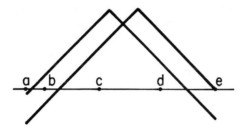

(b) Nonmonotone change in the preference order

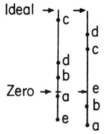

Figure 16: Illustrating nonmonotonicity of utility with change in status quo

across the two I scales. (One would need to know, for example, whether option *e* under the new status quo is preferred to option *a* under the old status quo.) Whether this would be a useful question to ask, however, depends on how rapidly the individual adapts to a change in the status quo and the reliability of memory traces for preferences. Furthermore, it is of course doubtful that a change in the status quo would translate an SPF so systematically as in this example. In any real case, a change in the status quo could be more disruptive, for example, the SPF could lose its symmetry and its linearity with respect to that cardinal scale of options (a different cardinal scaling of the options would be required to restore symmetry and linearity, but the ordinal scale of options would be preserved if single peakedness is preserved by the change in the status quo).

So in the presence of proper SPFs (or any preference function that is nonmonotone with a scale of options, or if no total ordering of the options exists), an affine transformation of the utility function is inadmissible in response to a change in the status quo and/or any relevant background variables. The utility function needs to be reconstructed empirically.

To summarize the conclusion, if preference is not monotone with a totally ordered scale of options, then an affine transformation of the utility function in response to any change in the status quo or background variables need not preserve monotonicity between preference and utility.

This criticism and consequent limitation of utility theory loses much of its force where the preference function is monotone with a total ordering of the options, as in the case of elemental components but also in the case of a few other more complex attributes. Money is the most common example, and, interestingly enough, it is the most common variable used in empirical tests of the theory. If, furthermore, the utility of money is linear, exponential, or a power function, each of which finds support (Pfanzagl, 1959; but see also, Krantz & Tversky, 1965; Krantz et. al., 1971), then the ratio of the intervals would be preserved under translation or changes in unit, and there would be no evidence of the lack of generality of the theory.

Preference is made up of a bundle of (elemental) utility functions, and if the composite utility (i.e., the preference function) is monotone with the components, all of which are isotonic (same ordered or reversed) with each other, then the approximation is close enough to be neglected in most practical cases, and difficult to assess experimentally. But if the composite is not isotonic with all components then tradeoffs must occur, and preference may be properly single peaked. Then a change in the status quo can shift the peak and destroy monotonicity between preference and utility, as we have shown.

This is the reason we have abandoned the use of cardinal utility scales in Type I conflict, although we admit to their practical usefulness in certain special cases (e.g., where preference is monotone with the independent variable and where the status quo and background variables are stable over the relevant time span). But for theoretical purposes such as analyzing the structure of conflict and generalizing to conflict between individuals, an exceedingly dynamic domain, we find the assumption of cardinal utility (preference) scales indefensible.

In place of cardinal utility (preference) we use ordinal utility (preference) which is very general and sufficiently strong for our purposes after we have strengthened it to a signed ordinal scale. Such a scale, incidentally, is an important kind of interpersonally comparable utility, discussed next.

6.1.1   Interpersonal Comparability of Utility

In the Type II conflict, the seriousness of the first problem, the problem of individual utility scales, escalates (like bad things generally) into the problem of interpersonal comparability of utility. That problem has been with us at least since the utilitarianism of Jeremy Bentham in the 18th century. His proposal for optimizing social decisions required measuring the utility of each member of the society for each alternative decision, and then aggregating them for each alternative to determine its social utility.

This is the second problem, that of the aggregation rule. He proposed to sum up the individual utilities for each possible decision over the members of the society, then to choose that decision which would maximize the total welfare, on the principle that everyone should contribute equally to the total and on the principle that society should maximize the average (total) return.

It was Bentham's intent to weight each individual equally in the aggregation rule, but that is somewhat ambiguous in that there are at least two meanings. It could mean requiring the same unit of measurement for the difference scales of all individuals or it could mean that individuals are to contribute equally to the total variance of the social values of the options.

This distinction is clarified here for readers not familiar with the statistical and measurement concepts that are involved because these are important for understanding the level of utility measurement we introduce. It is intuitively evident that the greater the differences an individual perceives among a set of options the greater the range of that individual's utility scale would tend to be. If an individual saw little reason to prefer one option over another the corresponding scale of utility would tend to have a shorter range than if the individual saw greater reasons to prefer one option over another.

But the range is not a very good measure of differences for most purposes. A more useful measure is the variance (see glossary), largely because of its algebraic properties. For example one can add the variances of individuals' scales to obtain the variance of the sum of their scales but you cannot add their ranges to get a total range. Furthermore, if an individual's scale were multiplied by 10, the variance of the scale would be multiplied by 10 and that individual would contribute 10 times as much variance to the total variance; that individual would, in effect, be weighted 10 times as much as an individual who had one tenth the variance.

Note that the variance of an individual's scale (like its range) is independent of the origin, the zero point, that is, adding a constant (positive or negative) to a scale changes the origin correspondingly, but has no effect on the variance of the scale. But multiplying a scale is equivalent to changing the unit of measurement, as in the familiar transformation from kilometers to miles, the numbers get smaller because the unit is larger.

If weighting individuals equally means that they should contribute equally to the total variance, the distinctions made between options, then their scales can easily be transformed to the same variance before adding them. If weighting individuals equally means having the same unit of measurement, then we must have interpersonal comparability of utility for which there is no justification.

There is no acceptable way known for individuals to communicate to others their utility for an option in the unit of measurement used by another individual. Indeed, the context of a Type II conflict is such that, even if one could, it is not in one's interests to do so. In a Type I conflict, any misrepresentation of either utility function could only lead to a less than optimal decision, never a better one. Individuals could hurt themselves because the peaks of their SPFs would be displaced. So individuals are induced to be truthful to themselves in resolving the conflict between their own adversarial utility functions.

In contrast, in a Type II conflict, if either party truthfully reveals its utility function (the inner branch of the preference function), that party is vulnerable to exploitation by the other party. In a bargaining situation between buyers and sellers, a typical Type II conflict, it is well known how much of a disadvantage it is to the buyers to reveal to the seller how interested they are in a purchase or, vice versa in a sale (i.e., the maximally acceptable buying price or minimally acceptable selling price).

The second interpretation of Bentham's intent to weight each individual equally by contributing equally to the total variance of the social values, requires measurement of each individual's utility function on a difference scale but does not require interpersonal comparability of utility in the sense of a common unit of measurement—quite the contrary.

In this second sense, what is called for is multiplying the difference scale of each individual by an appropriate constant so that the variance of each individual's scale of preferences over the options is the same. This is equivalent, of course, to changing the unit of measurement of each individual and hence differential weighting of individuals in the first sense. For example, individuals who did not differentiate between options, who said, in effect, they didn't care which option was chosen, are neglected in the social welfare because they have zero variance under any unit of measurement.

This social welfare function has the advantage of not requiring an interpersonally comparable unit of measurement, which an additive rule would. Incidentally, we are not proposing this or any other social welfare function but illustrating some of the issues and some pros and cons. A partisan position on a social welfare function, aside from technical aspects, is a political issue and not within the province of this book.

In general, the utilitarian principle of the greatest good for the greatest number may be effective as political rhetoric, but it is nearly vacuous as a guide to a social welfare function. This issue is discussed by Rescher (1966), who shows just how complex it is.

In the absence of any empirical support for the logical requirements of interpersonal comparability of utility, a decision function dependent on it is not tenable. Hence, we conclude that interpersonal comparability of utility is not useful in a conflict situation and in this context it is a mythical problem, a "snare and a delusion," although an interesting academic exercise.

One's everyday experience would seem to run counter to this conclusion; consider, for example, the agreement of huband and wife on their interpersonal comparisons of relative likes and dislikes. Narens and Luce (1983) examined this intuition formally and demonstrated "the existence of mechanisms that lead to total agreement about comparative preference without forcing any true intercomparability of utility" (p. 249).

They show that mechanisms can exist that, under suitable social conditions, would satisfy the intuition of ordinal intercomparability of utility without justifying cardinal intercomparability. Narens and Luce illustrate the sort of empirical constraint on ordinal intercomparability that would be required for the existence of true intercomparability. This constraint would require that an individual be able to predict the ordinal intercomparability of two other individuals who have never met but with each of whom the first individual has ordinal intercomparability. They suggest, with good grounds, that the predicted comparability of our friends' preferences is violated.

We have added to the ordinal scale of an individual's utility, an origin, a zero point, which we assign to the individual's status quo and which we identify behaviorally as a threshold between acceptance and rejection (see Section 3.1). We equate this threshold across individuals (i.e., we assume comparability of the zero point). The behavioral principle we invoked in support of this critical and strong assumption is that individuals are motivated to improve on their status quo and motivated to avoid worsening it (i.e., this is the distinction between approach and avoidance motivational processes).

This is not, perhaps, intuitively compelling because we all know that individuals may like or dislike their status quo and it would seem that the utility measure assigned should be positive or negative, correspondingly. Unfortunately, this is inaccessible in any meaningful and useful way. So we have abandoned it but adopted a common zero point defined behaviorally, and recognize and accept its volatility in response to the status quo, background variables, and strategic usefulness. This is interpersonal comparability of utility not in the sense of a common unit of measurement but in the sense of a common origin distinguishing positively and negatively signed preference, approach and avoidance behavioral processes, respectively.

6.2 Power

Of course Type II conflicts are resolved all the time, and one might wonder how comparability of utility can be avoided. From even casual observation, however, it would seem that decisions reflect the relative influence of the two parties, which has little to do with a mythical interpersonal comparability of utility but a great deal to do with the relative exercise of power. From the courtroom, to the legislature, to a family decision as to where to go for a picnic, persuasiveness and willingness to yield are important factors influencing the resolution of the conflict.

To illustrate the difference between comparability of utility and comparability of power, take two examples. First, consider the simple Type I conflict of an individual deciding whether to accept an investment opportunity. The individual is attracted by the potential yield and repelled by the potential loss. The individual has a positive and increasing utility function for yield, which is satiating, and a negative and decreasing utility function for loss, which is escalating. Their relative magnitude on the respective utility scales, both in one head, leads to a judgment, pro or con the investment. We assume this conflict is resolved on the basis of comparability of the utility scales and their relative importance (weights) in the individual's mind.

Now consider the parallel conflict in a Type II context. Individual A works for B and asks for a raise. Individual A has a positive and increasing utility function for the amount of the raise, and it is satiating. Individual B has a negative and decreasing utility for a raise, and it is escalating. Comparison of their respective utility functions is not the path to resolving this conflict. A is the weaker as B has the power of decision unless A can exercise some power, for example, by threatening to quit. The effectiveness of that depends on how seriously B takes the threat and its consequences.

The process of negotiating a raise is the process by which the participants exercise their power to influence the decision. When the process is stalemated or threatening to escalate, it is common to turn to a third party, chosen to be disinterested and fair, among other attributes. The presumption is that the different utility functions of the disputants can be put into the head of one individual (i.e., transforming the conflict from Type II to Type I) and that the individual's judgment can be optimal.

But even here, the problem of a proper preference function still emerges. In a pure Type I conflict, the individual is motivated to do the best for himself or herself, a single entity. A Type II conflict transformed into a Type I involves a different problem, not necessarily to maximize the total utility of the adversaries combined, but to achieve a "fair" distribution of utility between them. Even if interpersonal comparability of utility were conceptually acceptable and practically available (i.e., operationalizable), this problem would remain.

To reveal some of the depth and complexity of the problem, we discuss in the next section two simple models that might seem at first as reasonable attempts at fairness and yet are quite different in their consequences.

6.3   Fairness

It is evident from even a cursory review of the literature that the heart of the problem of fairness may be formulated in terms of how to determine the disparity in distribution if it seems called for. Certainly, if two parties are equal in all respects, such as in contribution, need, wealth, power, etc., the consensus is that an equal share seems inherently fair. It is when parties differ in these components that differences in shares may appear defensible, to one if not the other.

Fairness is a human concept in the sense that it does not exist in nature. There are no observations that can be made of natural phenomena that imply fairness or justice. It is a human concept just like the concept of risk. It is in the mind of the beholder, and what is in the mind of one is not necessarily in the mind of another. Fairness can be defined in any way one chooses, to mean whatever one wants it to mean. This point of view is illustrated in the papers by Pazner (1977) and Daniel (1978) in which a division is considered fair if the people involved agree that it is fair.

One way to approach such a problem is to lay down some basic principles intended to be more or less acceptable and to derive a rule or model which follows as a logical consequence of the principles. This was the pattern in which information theory, signal detectability theory, game theory, and social choice theory were all developed; they are all normative theories that have been of immense importance in behavioral and social science.

Unfortunately, this approach may run into difficulties in that desirable principles may be found to be incompatible (as in social choice theory, Arrow, 1963). Consider the following scenarios in the context of fairness as examples. It may be argued that a man and a woman doing the same job should get the same salary because their contributions are the same: the principle of equal pay for equal work. It may also be argued that an individual who is the sole support of a family should get a higher salary than one whose responsibility is less. But we see that the principle of equal pay for equal work is violated by this principle of more pay for the same work if responsible for others.

This approach, from the top down or the general to the specific, proceeding from fundamental principles to a solution, is particularly congenial to economists, mathematicians, and legal philosophers; see, for example, Raiffa (1982), Varian (1974, 1976), Rawls (1971), Rescher (1966), Nash (1950), and Daniel (1978). As just illustrated, the problem is difficult if principles which are acceptable in isolation are incompatible. Consequently, any solution must favor some principles and require others to yield. Thus, there can be different solutions to the same conflict, all defensible by acceptable principles, but incompatible and in violation of other acceptable principles. It is easier to agree on principles where the consequences are not all evident than it is to agree on solutions when it is clear whose ox is being gored.

Another approach, which we will refer to as being built from the bottom up, is more pragmatic, and that is to study the consensus of fairness judgments on distributions varying in a controlled and systematic manner and using subjects with no vested interest. This approach is congenial to psychologists, who are more oriented toward descriptive theory than normative, generally speaking, (there are, of course, many exceptions). In this approach the experimenter seeks regularities in the data which may, with some insight, suggest general principles. (See Walster, Walster, & Berscheid, 1978, for a review of empirical literature on equity and an attempt in this direction.)

Nontrivial regularities in the tradeoffs are important for theoretical purposes, and they are usually obscured by monotonic effects, which are of little interest for that purpose; thus, it helps to anticipate them and know where to look. A priori descriptive models are frequently used for this purpose, and we describe two possibilities.

Let there be two parties, A and B, each of whom can claim a share of some positive outcome or share responsibility for some deficit. We consider the case in which there are two factors for claiming a share, and for convenience we will refer to them as contribution and need. Let A's relative contribution be p_1 and relative need be p_2 where $0 \leq p_i \leq 1$. So the corresponding parameters for B are $1 - p_1$ and $1 - p_2$.

The basic problem in fairness may be formulated in terms of how to handle disparity in distribution (and/or concession) if it seems called for. There are two obvious simple models, one basically additive and the other multiplicative.

Model 1 is an additive model. The individual gets a share equal to the average of the inputs. This model is one possible extension to two factors of the equity principle proposed by Aristotle: the shares of two parties should be in the same ratio as their contributions (Ross, 1966).

Letting $S(A)$ represent A's proportionate share,

$$S(A) = \frac{1}{2}(p_1 + p_2).$$

In this model one's share is proportional to the sum of one's inputs. It is also equivalent to getting a share equal to the product of the inputs and splitting the remainder equally,

$$S(A) = p_1 p_2 + \frac{1}{2}\left(1 - p_1 p_2 - (1 - p_1)(1 - p_2)\right).$$

Instead of getting a share equal to the product of one's inputs and then splitting the remainder equally, an obvious alternative is to split the remainder in the same proportion. In this case one's share is equal to the product of one's inputs rescaled, and we have Model 2.

Model 2 is a multiplicative model. The individual's share is a function of the product of the inputs.

$$S(A) = \frac{p_1 p_2}{p_1 p_2 + (1 - p_1)(1 - p_2)}.$$

Table 1 contains $S(A)$ according to Model 1 for various values of p_1 and p_2. $S(B)$, of course, is $1 - S(A)$. The table is symmetric about the diagonal because of the symmetric treatment of the variables.

p_2 = Need	p_1 = Contribution										
	0.0	.10	.20	.30	.40	.50	.60	.70	.80	.90	1.00
0.0	0.0	.05	.10	.15	.20	.25	.30	.35	.40	.45	.50
.1		.10	.15	.20	.25	.30	.35	.40	.45	.50	.55
.2			.20	.25	.30	.35	.40	.45	.50	.55	.60
.3				.30	.35	.40	.45	.50	.55	.60	.65
.4					.40	.45	.50	.55	.60	.65	.70
.5						.50	.55	.60	.65	.70	.75
.6							.60	.65	.70	.75	.80
.7								.70	.75	.80	.85
.8									.80	.85	.90
.9										.90	.95
1.0											1.00

Table 1: A's fair share under model 1

A's share under this model is also displayed in Figure 17. The abscissa is A's relative contribution and the ordinate is A's share according to the line representing A's need.

We see from Table 1 and Figure 17 that the model is linear. Each parameter, p_1 and p_2, contributes half its value to the share. Thus, if individuals make no contribution, they get a share equal to half their relative need. And in the absence of any need, the share is half the relative contribution. If only one parameter were relevant, say p_1, as in a business venture in which need is disregarded or if the two parameters were equal, $p_1 = p_2 = p$, then A's share is equal to p. If contribution and need are complementary the two parties share equally.

Table 2 and Figure 18 present $S(A)$ for Model 2 as a function of p_1 and p_2. Figure 18 shows that this model is nonlinear in its treatment of disparity in distribution. It is much more sensitive to departures from a norm of "equal shares for equal inputs" compared with Model 1.

Being below .5 has a disproportionately depressing effect and being above .5 has a disproportionately rewarding effect; these effects are symmetric. If the departures from .5 are complementary, they balance out and the shares are equal.

As in Model 1, if an individual's contribution and need are complementary, then so are those of the other party and they share equally. If only one parameter were relevant, then the share is equal to that parameter, as in Model 1.

Both models are readily generalized to more than two parties and more than two parameters, and more general forms could include monotone transformations or weights on the parameters. The param-

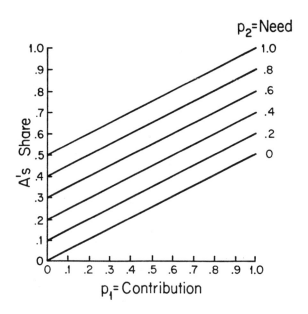

Figure 17: A's share under model 1

eters were identified here as contribution and need, but they could be given other interpretations. Need, for example, could be interpreted as wealth or power. Deutsch (1974) lists nine different inputs to fairness, each of which has been used by one or more societies at one time or another, and Reis (1984) offers 17.

These models are discussed, not in the expectation that either will reflect consensus, but rather to dramatize the differences that can appear from rather modest changes in the conceptualization. This makes the bottom-up approach, when it seeks a meaningful conceptualization from empirical curve fitting, very difficult and precarious.

Much psychological research has already been done in this area under the rubric of equity theory (Adams, 1965; Anderson, 1976; Harris & Joyce, 1980; Mellars, 1982; Messick & Cook, 1983; Walster et al., 1978). Consensus among subjects as to what is a fair distribution is not as high when there is more than one factor affecting fairness. For example, what is judged as a fair proportionate share not only

Need p_2	Contribution p_1										
	0.0	.10	.20	.30	.40	.50	.60	.70	.80	.90	1.00
0.0	0.0	0.0	0.1	0.0	0.0	0.0	0.0	0.0	0.0	0.0	.50
.1		.0122	.0270	.0455	.0690	.1000	.1429	.2059	.3077	.50	1.0
.2			.0588	.0968	.1429	.20	.2727	.3684	.50	.6923	1.0
.3				.1552	.2222	.30	.3913	.50	.6316	.7941	1.0
.4					.3077	.40	.50	.6087	.7273	.8571	1.0
.5						.50	.60	.70	.80	.90	1.0
.6							.6923	.7778	.8571	.9310	1.0
.7								.8448	.9032	.9545	1.0
.8									.9412	.9730	1.0
.9										.9878	1.0
1.0											1.0

Table 2: A's fair share under model 2

depends on inputs but on how much there is to divide up (Mellars, 1982). Such results are incompatible with models that are formulated only in terms of proportions, such as Models I and II, and do not take absolute quantities into account.

There is a metatheoretic principle lurking in the background here which may have relevance to the concept of fairness. There are instances in which human judgment is better represented by a "rotation" of variables. The simplest example is seen in adjusting the two faucets of a shower, one for cold water and one for hot water. The individual manipulates these control variables to achieve a satisfactory volume and temperature, essentially a rotation to a sum and a "difference."

A more complex example is that of a preference for a family of some number of sons and some number of daughters. A model based on an SPF over the number of boys plus an SPF over the number of girls *rarely* accounted for the preference order over family composites in studies in numerous countries around the world. An alternative model based on an SPF over the total number of children plus an SPF over the algebraic difference between the number of boys and girls was overwhelmingly superior to it and to a number of other alternative models, and was very satisfactory (Coombs, L.C., 1976). This, again, is an instance in which the relevant psychological variables are obtained by something like a rotation to a sum and difference, a size of family preference and a sex bias (see Coombs, Coombs, & McClelland, 1975).

When the rotational principle is at work, an experiment which focuses on one (unrotated) variable with the other fixed may yield results which are highly context bound. In such a case, interpretation of the experimental results is limited to a special case and of no general

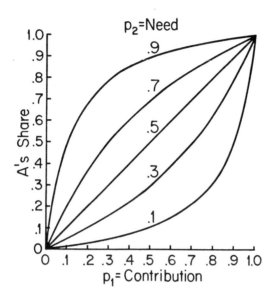

Figure 18: A's share under model 2

theoretical import.

Rescher (1966), in his book on distributive justice, makes a similar point, as do Walton and McKersie (1965) in their analysis of the behavioral processes involved in bargaining.

All of this discussion is relevant to the problem of fairness and justice, both of which are human concepts. Justice, in the narrow sense, is identified with fairness and, in the wider sense, with the general good. The former is related to the pattern of distribution and the latter to the total amount to be distributed.

Rawls treats fairness as the more fundamental conception, and Rescher regards justice as the more fundamental. These matters are important to a society if there is a trade-off between them or a cause and effect relation between inputs and outputs. The distinction is illustrated in Figure 19.

The illustration is greatly simplified to bring out the critical distinction they make. We consider only one factor, the contribution

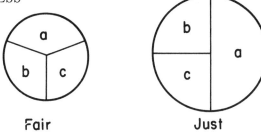

Figure 19: The distinction between fairness and justice

of each party, and neglect how qualitatively different contributions are to be measured on a common scale, as well as all other factors like need, power, etc., that might be regarded as relevant. Almost everyone agrees in such a case that it is fair for individuals who make equal contributions to share equally, and this is illustrated on the left side of the figure. On the right side of the figure we have a situation in which the total is increased by an unequal distribution, perhaps by encouraging invention, which brings advantages to all as everyone gets more than before. A preference for the society portrayed on the right may be seen as preferring to swim in a bigger pond in which one loses relatively but gains in absolute terms (i.e., subordinating envy to cupidity). Again, the suggestion is that the relevant variables may be a sum and difference mediating attitudes toward fairness.

A related framing of this same problem is that of the distribution of wealth in a society if there is a relation between the mean and the variance. This relation, of course, may not be monotone but single peaked in the sense that at any given level of the total wealth there is an optimum level of variance that encourages growth and development or whatever the society values. When put in these terms, other parameters of the distribution such as bounds and skewness come to mind.

Empirical research on fairness is oriented toward seeking regularities in the judgments of people about fairness, with a view to formulating descriptive laws. For our immediate purposes, we used models 1 and 2 merely to show how reasonable principles can be quite different in their effects. The empirical approach, from the bottom up, reveals the sensitivity of the data to context and hence the narrowness of the domain to which any empirical generalization applies. An excellent discussion of the limitations of most of the empirical research on equity and fairness, one which exposes their conceptual complexity, is contained in Camerer and MacCrimmon (1983).

With (empirical) consensus low and with principles in conflict, convergence of research on fairness from the top down and from the bottom up may be a long time coming.

The concept of fairness, being a human conception, could emerge from consensus based on observation, experience, and abstraction. For this reason empirical descriptive research such as that just described has value. However, psychological research on the concept of equity has been mostly confined to the problem of distributing or sharing a divisible product like profit or loss. The concept of fairness (and justice) goes beyond that, as we have just seen, and this is one of the reasons why research on normative principles is so important.

Consider, for example, Type II conflicts such as those between environmentalists and developers, tenants and landlords, or refugees and host countries. In such cases the concept of equity may not apply in the sense of sharing a product. Instead, as we shall see in Chapter 9, such conflicts may be reduced to a set of options ordered in one direction by one party and in the reverse direction by the other party.

Suppose, for example, that there are three options, x, y, z, and the status quo, sq. Suppose that party A has the preference order x, sq, y, z and party B has the preference order z, sq, y, x. The option y has negative ambience for both because the status quo is set at zero, but the conflict between x and z is severe as each is the first choice of one and the last choice of the other. Obtaining consensus on what is fair, or on whose rights are greater or less, or which principles to accede to and which to violate, is not likely. But if the status quo of both parties deteriorates enough to give y positive ambience for both parties it becomes an acceptable resolution. This is why the study of reshaping preference functions was introduced (see Section 4.2).

Conflicts between principles occur in Type I as well as Type II and are, perhaps, the most difficult of all to resolve as there is usually no compromise or tradeoff possible. For example, a surgeon may be faced with saving the life of a mother or an unborn child. Consensus on conventions in such cases can immeasurably reduce the pain of such conflicts and make it bearable.

The problem of distributive justice has been introduced here because of its relevance to the selection of the option that resolves a conflict, the subject of Section 9.2. Any simple formula, such as one finds in equity theory, is only possible when contributions entitling a party to a share are in the same "coinage" as the outcomes, as in the case of profits and loss in a business venture. But in the case of different inputs, as when one partner contributes money and the other partner management, the assessment of relative contribution is itself an issue.

An instance of the empirical work on this problem is a study of van Avermaet (1975) in which subject A works, for example, 90 minutes and accomplishes three units; and subject B works 45 minutes and accomplishes six units. A (or B) is asked to distribute (divide) the payment. Each does it "equitably" — but with an egocentric bias, emphasizing the dimension that benefits him or her. A number of studies of biases in fairness judgments are reviewed in Messick and Sentis (1983).

When, and if, the problem of measuring relative contributions is resolved, the formula for disbursements is still an open question, as we have tried to suggest with models 1 and 2. Broader issues arise in this decision, such as the motivational implications and the impact on society. A disproportionate distribution is increasingly motivating to venture capital, innovation, and entrepreneurship, but it encourages competition, exploitation, and potential unrest. A tradeoff is inevitable and what is best for a society in the short or long run is an open question. The human relations, the economics, the politics, and the ideology of a society are shaped by and reflected in such decisions.

Furby (1986) discusses these same issues and much relevant literature, pointing out that there are two orientations to the issues of justice or fairness that have been recognized. One is a view of justice or fairness from an impersonal, impartial orientation, and the other is from a more personalized one in terms of an ethic of care and responsibility for others.

These two orientations might also be recognizable when formulated as a social or public orientation on the one hand versus a private or self-interest orientation on the other. The first is the greater good of the whole at greater cost to one; the second is the greater good of one at slight cost to the whole. Dawes points out (personal communication) that these two orientations are polarized in such games as the N-person Prisoner's Dilemma.

Our own point of view is that this entire domain is rampant with semantic uncertainty and ambiguity; that this state reflects the fact that one's concept of justice is an outgrowth of social interaction, a product of experience, and whether one is the actor or the observer. Because the social milieu is not static but constantly changing, as what is new and valued becomes commonplace, criteria and standards of distributive justice may be expected to change, more rapidly, perhaps, in their particularities, more slowly in their universalities.

We may put the problem of fairness in perspective in another way. When two individuals disagree on which of two tones is louder or which of two lights is brighter, one of them is wrong; nature provides an independent measure. When two individuals disagree on their preference between two colors or between two musical compositions, we can believe that neither is wrong. Nature does not tell us which color or which musical composition should be preferred.

Judgments of fairness are of the same kind. A split or division no more has a "fairness" attached to it than a color has a "preference" attached to it.

From such a perspective, a universal measure of fairness is not the problem. Sometimes, in such cases, the difficulty should be circumvented rather than met head on. N. R. F. Maier (1952), in his work with employee dissatisfaction, emphasized the importance of employees' participation in the decision process to their acceptability of the decision. The recognition that an important part of the determinant of how "just" the resolution of a conflict is, actually lies in the control of the process by which a conflict is resolved, has important implications for the peaceful resolution of conflicts (Lind, Lessik, & Conlon, 1983; Rescher, 1966; Thibaut & Walker, 1975, 1978). A distinction is made between process control and decision control. In negotiation, for example, both the procedure by which a decision is reached and the decision itself are under the control of the disputants. Binding arbitration, in contrast, puts the decision in the hands of a third party, but the procedure which controls the input of information and evidence is in the hands of the disputants and affects the acceptability of the decision.

This distinction suggests that research on the role of process control and its effect on the perception of justice would have more immediate and useful implications than seeking a formula for selecting a just or equitable decision. Our interest in the problem of justice and fairness may be profitably directed toward what makes a decision, a compromise, more acceptable.

Chapter 7

Edgeworth's Economical Calculus

We introduced some basic concepts of Type II conflict with the example of a husband and wife in conflict over number of children, an example in which a totally ordered set of options is naturally available. This permitted us to direct attention exclusively to the antagonists and contrast what they bring to the Type II conflict situation to what the individual brings to Type I conflict. We then discussed in the last chapter some special problems that arise which do not arise in a Type I conflict.

We direct our attention now to the other aspect of the Type II conflict, the structure on the alternatives or options. It is, of course, not to be expected that a totally ordered set of options will be naturally available. A first and simple step toward increased complexity is that of a two-dimensional space of options. Edgeworth, part of whose work we shall shortly review, made a major contribution over 100 years ago by showing that, under certain plausible conditions in this two-dimensional case, there is a one-dimensional, totally ordered subset of options from which the final choice should be made. Any option not in this one-dimensional set is worse for at least one party, and no better for the other, than another option in the set.

Edgeworth, an English barrister and economist, introduced in 1882 what he called "economical calculus" using the problem of drawing up a contract between two parties exchanging commodities, such as work and wages. We will summarize his analysis and draw the parallel between it and Type I conflict within an individual.

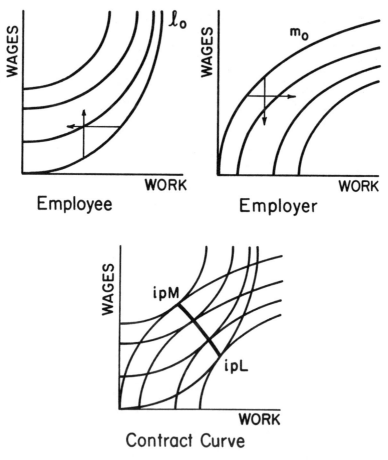

Figure 20: Edgeworth's economical calculus

7.1   Edgeworth's Scale of Options for Negotiation

Edgeworth proposed two laws, one he called a law of decreasing utility, and the other a law of increasing labor. How these come together in an exchange situation is illustrated by the sequence of panels in Figure 20.

In the panel at the upper left, the exchange situation is portrayed from the point of view of the prospective employee. The curves represent indifference curves of the employee. Their shape reflects the assumptions that the employee would always prefer to work less for a given wage and would always prefer higher wages for a given amount of work, as indicated by the horizontal and vertical arrows, respectively. The law of decreasing utility and the law of increasing labor result in the indifference curves being positively accelerated. The indifference curve labeled l_0 is the curve through "no contract" and all other contracts equivalent to no contract in the view of the employee. It is the employee's boundary for making a contract. Any contract to the right of that indifference curve would be tantamount to working for nothing.

In the panel at the upper right, the exchange situation is portrayed from the point of view of the prospective employer. For the employer, the situation is reversed, work is "good" and wages are "bad." At any fixed wage the employer would always prefer more work to less, and for any fixed amount of work, would prefer to pay less rather than more, as indicated by the horizontal and vertical arrows, respectively. The indifference curve labeled m_0 is the employer's boundary for making a contract. Any contract to the left of that curve would be tantamount to paying wages for no work.

When these two sets of indifference curves are superimposed, as in the lower panel, each indifference curve of one party is tangent to a unique indifference curve of the other party, and the curve consisting of the points of tangency Edgeworth called the *contract curve.*

The point where two indifference curves are tangent represents, for each party, the option it prefers among those on the other party's indifference curve. This follows from the shapes of the curves and the directions of increasing preference, as determined by the laws of decreasing utility and increasing labor. A point not on the contract curve, therefore, corresponds to a contract that could be improved for one party without worsening it for the other (i.e., it could be replaced by a contract that is on the same indifference curve of one of the parties but that is preferred by the other party). Edgeworth concluded that the final contract agreed upon should correspond to a point on the contract curve.

The initial positions of the employer and employee on this contract curve are labeled *ipM* and *ipL*, respectively. The point *ipM* is, for the employer, a contract equivalent in utility to no work, no pay, so the employer would prefer any contract on the contract curve to the right of that point. The point *ipL* is, for the employee, a contract equivalent in utility to no work, no pay, so the worker would prefer any contract on the contract curve to the left of that point. Note that both parties' preferences are monotone on the contract curve, but in opposite directions. Any point on this contract curve between these initial positions would make both parties better off, but each party prefers to be nearer the other's initial position.

The space of options is two-dimensional and the contract curve is a one-dimensional piece of it. There are an infinite number of one-dimensional pieces and the contract curve is the optimal one. It is optimal because, for the reasons just indicated, the contract at a point of tangency is the most preferred contract by one party from among all the contracts on the indifference curve of the other party through it. The contract curve intersects each indifference curve of one party at the option the other party likes best.

Although the contract curve is the optimal set of options, it is not an efficient set. It is not hard to see that the laws of decreasing utility and increasing labor imply that the contract curve runs from high-wages/low-work to low-wages/high-work, with wages decreasing with increasing work along the curve. The employee's preference decreases and the employer's preference increases as wages decrease and work increases. This implies that for each party there is one option on the contract curve that dominates all the others, in the sense that it is better in both wages and work. Hence, the contract curve is not even a Pareto optimal set for either party, and so it cannot be an efficient set either.

For the contract curve to be a Pareto optimal set, it would have to be ordered the same (not reversed) on work and wages. If both were increasing, then for each party the set would be Pareto optimal in that, for any pair of options each is better than the other in some respect.

There is another view of the structure, however, and that is to regard the preference orderings of the two parties over the contract curve as the two components, and not the amounts of work and wages. Then, from the point of view of a third party, the set is Pareto optimal because of any two options, one favors one party while the other favors the other party.

But, even from this point of view the set cannot be efficient in general because this would require that the contract curve be convex in the coordinates of Labor's and Management's preference functions. It would only be a happy coincidence for the successive ratios of increments and decrements in preference to be monotone in the direction required, and this would require some interpersonal comparability of utility. Hence, there is nothing to ensure that the decision function will be single peaked.

Each party's preference function over the contract curve is monotone and they have slopes of opposite sign (i.e., Management has increasing preference for any option to the right, Labor has increasing preference for any option to the left). As drawn, all options have positive ambience, so the situation is an approach/approach conflict. Such conflicts between management and labor are usually resolved by negotiation, an exercise in relative power. For an interesting analysis of the course of such negotiation, see Douglas (1957), and for some interesting examples of the dynamic interaction of technological development and occupational and geographical mobility with the contract curve, see Boulding (1965).

7.2   Type II Representation

Let us reformulate Edgeworth's problem as a Type II conflict. Each party, Labor and Management, has a utility function for work and for money. If Management, for example, has an increasing utility function for amount of work which satiates and a decreasing utility function for wages which escalates, the result is a single peaked function over any efficient set of options. The same is true for Labor except that Labor's utility function for wages is increasing and for amount of work decreasing. These were Edgeworth's assumptions and are instances of the more general principles that good things satiate and bad things escalate.

Although the contract curve cannot be an efficient set for both parties, each party's preference function is monotone and that is the way they are displayed in Figure 21. The preference function labeled L is that of Labor and the one labeled M is that of Management. Their intercepts with the scale of options are labeled ipL and ipM, which are their respective initial positions. The segment of the ordinal scale of options between the initial positions are the optimal options that form the contract curve.

Negotiation would take place as an approach/approach conflict over the options between ipM and ipL, and when a contract is agreed upon the conflict is resolved and a new status quo obtains.

We see that this conflict between Labor and Management has much the same structure as that between husband and wife over number of children, but is somewhat more complicated in ways we may summarize as follows.

The problem of efficient decision making has two phases: the first is to restrict options to a totally ordered scale of viable options and the second is to select an option from that set. In the case of preference for number of children, the first step is easy; a one-dimensional scale of options exists naturally. The second step may or may not be easy depending on considerations, some of which are normative, see Section 6.3, and some of which are structural, see Section 9.2.2.

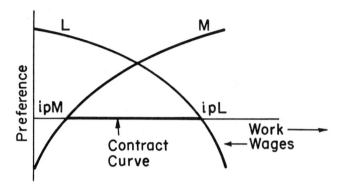

Figure 21: Edgeworth's contract curve: Type II representation

In the case of Labor versus Management over amount of work and wages, both problems are difficult. We naturally have a two-dimensional set of options and there are many possible one-dimensional subsets. We know that there is a best one-dimensional piece, Edgeworth's contract curve, but we don't know where it is. Then, given the contract curve, which we don't have, the problem of selecting an option faces the same difficulties, structural and normative, as in the previous example.

Of course, besides these differences, there are great differences in the psychological and social factors in which these conflicts are embedded. But such aspects are of infinite variety, specific to each conflict, and beyond the scope of this monograph. It is our intent to examine only abstract characteristics so that parallels between structure and procedures can be recognized and made use of.

7.3 Application of Edgeworth's Model to Changes in Economic Conditions

Let us first suppose, for clarity of illustration, that a recession has occurred and Management wants to abandon the old contract and feels the need for renegotiation before Labor does. We will assume that Management's marginal utility for work has decreased but Labor's remains unchanged in this first phase of a dynamic process.

In such a case the points of tangency of Management's new indifference curves with those of Labor's old indifference curves will be shifted nearer the origin, generating a new contract curve as is illustrated in Figure 22. The (hypothetical) old contract is shown in the

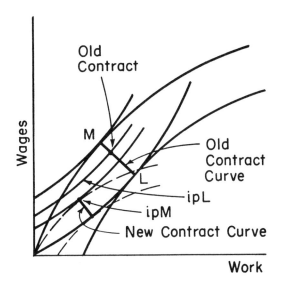

Figure 22: Phase 1 of renegotiation in a recession: An Edgeworth representation

figure as a point on the old contract curve between the old admissible bounds provided by Management on the left and by Labor on the right.

Management wants cheaper labor, represented by a new indifference curve through "no contract" and shown as a dotted line in Figure 22. The new contract curve is shown bounded on the left by ipM.

As Labor's indifference curves have not yet changed, the old contract is still Labor's initial position for any renegotiation. We see that Labor's indifference curve through the old contract, labeled ipL, does not intersect the new contract curve to the right of ipM. Hence all contracts between ipM and Labor's initial position, ipL, have negative ambience for both parties and would constitute avoidance/avoidance conflicts.

Of course Labor's indifference curves change also in response to the recession, albeit more reluctantly, and in the same direction as Management's, toward cheaper labor. The slope of Labor's indifference curve through any point is decreased and a new contract curve is generated and the situation approaches that displayed in Figure 21, an approach/ approach conflict.

A Type II schematic representation of the first phase of the same conflict is shown in Figure 23. The scale of options is ordered from left to right, increasing in work and decreasing in wages. The two

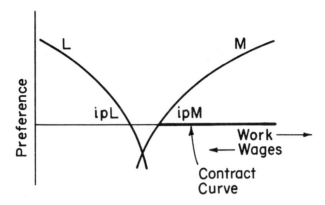

Figure 23: Phase 1 of renegotiation in a recession: Type II representation

inner branches labeled L and M are from the respective preference functions of Labor and Management under the assumption that only Management's indifference curves have changed up to this point.

Management's preference function has shifted to the right relative to Labor's, so much so that contracts between the initial positions are all avoidance/avoidance conflicts, in contrast to Figure 21. The new contract curve from Management's point of view should be to the right of ipM and these are all approach/avoidance conflicts in which Labor's avoidance processes are stronger than for any other segment of the scale of options.

We are describing renegotiation as a dynamic process involving changes in both parties' indifference curves generating new sets of options, and seeking an optimal set that would constitute an approach/approach conflict. Certain obvious implications of this description follow. The rapidity of the response of Management's and Labor's indifference curves to changes in the economy and the rate of change in the economy control the ambience of the options on the contract curve. The greater the lag between Management and Labor's response, or between renegotiations, relative to the change in the economy, the more difficult the resolution process.

The application to a booming economy provides another scenario which should help to clarify this process. Let us assume that in this circumstance Labor wants to abandon the old contract and feels the need for renegotiation before Management does. Labor's marginal utility for work has increased, and Labor wants higher wages.

In this case, Labor's new indifference curves are steeper and will generate a new contract curve as illustrated in Figure 24. Labor's

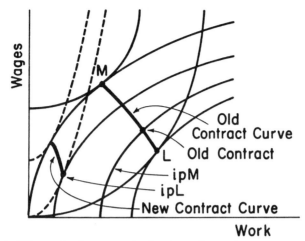

Figure 24: Phase 1 of renegotiation in a booming economy: An Edgeworth representation

new indifference curve through "no contract" (shown as a dotted line in Figure 24) is tangent to an indifference curve of Management at *ipL* and forms the right boundary of a new contract curve.

Since Management's indifference curves have not changed yet, the old contract defines the status quo, the initial position, for Management, and the indifference curve through the old contract is labeled *ipM*. All contracts between *ipL* and *ipM* have negative ambience for both parties and would constitute avoidance/avoidance conflicts.

In the case of a booming economy one might anticipate that Management's need for increased labor would lead to rapid adjustment of Management's indifference curves, the lag between Labor's and Management's adjustments would be reduced, and the time of transition from the condition displayed in Figure 25 to that displayed in Figure 20 would be relatively short.

Some of these comparisons are brought out more clearly in the simpler Type II representation of the first phase of a booming economy, shown in Figure 25. Note that the only change from Figure 23 is the location of the contract curve in this phase. If the conflict over the contract curve in Figure 23 is called an approach/avoidance conflict, that in Figure 25 is an avoidance/approach conflict — a distinction that is very important substantively, but structurally insignificant.

In Figure 25 the initial step in this dynamic process shows Labor's SPF shifted to the left relative to Management's, so much so that the segment of the option scale between their initial positions is a set of avoidance/avoidance conflicts.

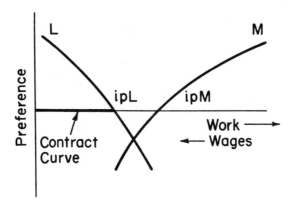

Figure 25: Phase 1 of renegotiation in a booming economy: Type II representation

As Management's indifference curves change in response to the change in the economy and with a need for more labor, a new contract curve is generated and the situation would rapidly approach that shown in Figure 20.

The reader is again reminded that the scale of options is an ordinal scale and the only characteristics of the shape of SPFs that are important are the location of the peaks and the intercepts of the inner branches with the scale of options.

7.3.1 Summary on Renegotiation

In renegotiation, if one party's indifference curves have changed more than the other's, it may be expected to more readily abandon an existing contract as a point of departure for renegotiation. Its new initial position may exclude the old contract as an acceptable option. In our examples we assumed that in a recession Management would more readily abandon the old contract and Labor more reluctantly; and in a booming economy we assumed the reverse. These are not meant as serious substantive assumptions but are merely plausible enough to serve our purpose of describing a continually changing process. In general, one party would regard the current contract more favorably than the other would.

There would appear to be two possible routes to avoid the emergence of negative ambience for contracts between initial positions. One would be to schedule renegotiation sufficiently often so that a segment of the contract curve would consist of approach/approach options. The other would be to clearly abandon the old contract as a point of departure for either adversary. In the latter case the situation is restored to that displayed in Figures 20 and 21. Then the entire contract curve consists of approach/approach conflicts.

In all of this discussion, no procedure has been provided for constructing the contract curve and the discussion has been confined to an atypical limiting case of two dimensions, work and wages. The more typical instance involves many dimensions of concern to both parties and the generalization of Edgeworth's formal model to more complex conflicts is justified only by making unrealistic and unsupportable measurement assumptions. In the next chapter we introduce the most structurally complex of two party conflicts, and we will see that the structural complexity is due to the options. In Chapter 9 we provide a rational and practical procedure for screening a set of options of any complexity to produce a totally ordered subset which converges on the contract curve.

Chapter 8

On Constructing Options

The conflicts discussed in Chapters 5 and 7 were characterized by options that were relatively simple and numerically precise. Most of the serious and important Type II conflicts are not over such simple options but over vastly more complex ones. Examples include the conflict between environmentalists and developers on the use of park land, between the proponents of nuclear power and those for the development of renewable resources, between tenants and landlords on improvements, responsibility, and rent, between administration and faculty on elimination of a department, and between sides in almost any civil protest. In all these cases each party holds an ideal position, but there is no natural or readily available set of options neatly ordered between them, and resolution of the conflict still requires that one option be settled on.

It is clearly desirable that options be constructed between the ideal positions of the parties to serve as candidates for compromise. If these options do not naturally exist, and they usually do not, options need to be constructed and then screened to form a totally ordered set.

In most such conflicts the options will be complex, each option an entire portfolio of piecemeal decisions, a different subset of interdependent tradeoffs. For example a nuclear freeze agreement needs to specify *which systems* are covered (there are over 100 nuclear systems deployed in the world), *how much verification* there is to be, and *when* the agreement is to be effective. Tradeoffs are necessary. Agreement becomes unattainable if too much verification is demanded, and it is vacuous if too little is required; an earlier effective date is made possible if fewer systems are covered or less verification is required. Clearly, many different agreements are possible, each one a package of tradeoffs and each more or less preferred by each party to other packages.

The construction of options is not the main concern of this monograph, but their existence affects the difficulty of resolving a conflict in a particular way that is discussed in Section 10.2. Contriving options is one of the most important problems in decision theory, so we wish to enhance its visibility.

The actual construction of options is context bound and is the proper job of experts, statesmen, politicians, and academicians intimately knowledgeable about the origins of the conflict, its history, the current antagonists and the surrounding circumstances. We briefly describe one of the processes by which options are created in complex conflicts. This process, used effectively by President Carter at Camp David with Premier Begin of Israel and President Sadat of Egypt, is known as the *single negotiable text* (Raiffa, 1982). A third party, acting as negotiator, formulates a proposal and discusses it with one of the adversarial parties, seeking out the areas in which willingness to concede may be greater or less and revising the proposal accordingly. The negotiator then discusses the revised proposal with the other party and, pursuing the same strategy, adapts the proposal further, and then returns to the first party. This is a process of adaptive search for agreement.

The initial proposal, of course, is not unique. The adaptive process is creative and agreement is not guaranteed. Hence, it is possible to construct more than one option as a consequence of beginning with different initial proposals or following a different sequence of revisions. The process could lead to a set of options, no one of which is preferred by both parties to all the others. Indeed, this is almost inevitably the case. What one party concedes on one issue it will seek to make up on another, and this balancing of tradeoffs can usually be accomplished many ways.

An analogy from Type I conflict is that of seeking a portfolio of stocks and bonds for an investor. There are many factors that bear on yield and risk in the selection of a stock or bond. One could begin with any meritorious stock or bond and add additional prospects to the portfolio, reaching a final portfolio in many different ways. Imagine, for example, the different portfolios that different stockbrokers would build for the same customer. For the customer, the resulting set of options forms a Type I conflict.

Pruitt (1983), writing on achieving integrative agreements, has suggestions for the creative development of options and Bazerman and Neale (1983) discuss biases that affect negotiators. The latter paper, for example, discusses the framing of options to shift biases from risk averse to risk seeking on the grounds that individuals treat the prospect of gain differently from the prospect of loss (see Section 3.2 also).

Lockhart (1979) offers some useful suggestions in the search for a strategy for bargaining in international conflicts. The suggestions are equally useful for contriving options, which is at the core of resolving conflict. He points out, for example, that the adversary is not usually a homogeneous entity but a composite of conflicting interests, a mixture of personalities with different perceptions and interpretations. Such differences mark areas of tradeoff that can be turned to good account in the construction of options. Putnam (see Cooper, 1985, pp. 28-29) in a study of annual economic summit meetings of the EEC, from 1975 on, found the most successful summits occurred when there were substantial disagreements within governments — not just between — on what ought to be done. Ingroup/outgroup effects are such, however, that a member of one group tends to view another group as a single homogeneous entity, which obscures cues to its internal differences and tensions, and hence to different possible options.

Now we turn to the problem of screening options to choose a subset from among which one will be chosen to resolve the conflict. Each option may be a multiattribute bundle of great complexity, and the problem is to construct a total ordering of a subset of options that will be optimal in a precise sense.

Chapter 9

The Frontier of Preference

Given a set of options from whatever source, the process of conflict resolution may be conveniently divided into two problems, screening them to select a subset that is optimal in some sense and then selecting one to resolve the conflict. The first problem has a simple rational solution, which we call the frontier of preference, and the other involves normative issues requiring agreement on matters of policy and principle. We discuss these two problems in turn, including some aspects of the process of negotiation. We then show that the frontier of preference converges on the contract curve and we discuss its extension to Type I conflict. The chapter concludes with a comparison of this approach to conflict with that of game theory.

9.1 The First Problem: An Optimal Scale of Options

We propose a procedure for screening any number of multiattribute options in a two-party Type II conflict to arrive at a totally ordered subset that is optimal in a particular sense. We have already seen that the resolution of a Type II conflict is a compromise involving concessions from an ideal position on the part of at least one but usually both parties. The procedure developed here is optimal in minimizing the concessions of the parties by placing a sort of least upper bound on the concession from each. The distribution of the concessions within those bounds, is then determined by the exercise of power and/or rules for fairness or justice.

Let the two parties be A and B and let S be the set of all options, designated $a, b, c \ldots$. We assume that there exist two binary preference relations, $\succ_A$ and $\succ_B$, associated with the two parties, A and B, respectively, and the options a and b are the ideals of the respective parties. The idea is that an option is eliminated if both parties agree that some other option is at least as good and one of them prefers it.

Definition. An option x in S is an element of the *frontier of prefer-ence* if and only if there does not exist a y in S such that $y \succ_A x$ and $y \succeq_B x$ or $y \succeq_A x$ and $y \succ_B x$, where $\succ$ and $\succeq$ are strong and weak binary preference relations, respectively, of one of the two parties, A or B, as indicated by the subscript.

What remain are only the hard choices, in which what is better for one is worse for the other, the essence of all conflict. When an option is on the frontier, there are no options that dominate it, in the sense of making both parties at least as well off and one of them better off.

The definition provides a necessary and sufficient condition for the frontier of preference to be totally ordered between the most preferred options of the two parties.

This definition is constructive in that only a qualitative testable relation is required. Suppose, for example, that the set S contains the following options:

$$S = \{a, b, p, q, r, s, v, w, x, y, z\}$$

and the respective preference orders of A and B are as follows:

$$\succ_A: \; arsxyvzwbpq$$

$$\succ_B: \; bpqzyvwxasr.$$

The options below b in A's preference order, p and q, may be eliminated because A agrees with B that b is better. Similarly, the options below a in B's preference order, s and r, may be eliminated because B agrees with A that a is better.

This leaves:

$$\succ_A: \; axyvzwb$$

$$\succ_B: \; bzyvwxa$$

It is readily seen that v and w must be deleted because both parties prefer y to these two options. What remains, then, is the frontier of

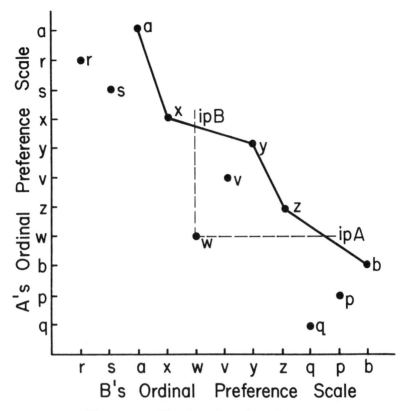

Figure 26: The frontier of preference

preference with the options ordered between the two most preferred options as follows: $a\,x\,y\,z\,b$. Preference decreases for A from a to b and increases for B from a to b.

This ordering, $a\,x\,y\,z\,b$, is the ordering under the inner branches of the preference functions between the two peaks (i.e., the two preference orderings, $\succ_A$ and $\succ_B$, are monotone but exactly reversed over the frontier of preference).

In Figure 26 we illustrate the example just discussed and introduce approach and avoidance processes. In this figure, A's and B's preference orderings define the vertical and horizontal axis, respectively, with the options equally spaced on an ordinal scale (i.e., distance between options is arbitrary and meaningless in the absence of cardinal interpersonally comparable utility).

The frontier of preference is indicated by the line connecting the options a, x, y, z, and b. A's preference is monotone decreasing from upper left to lower right and B's is the exact reverse.

Note that if the option a were not included in S, options r and s would become part of the frontier, which would be a loss to both parties; and if option b were not included in S, option p would become part of the frontier and this would also be a loss to both parties. Knowing the ideal options, a and b, defines the peaks and restricts the viable options to minimize concessions in a sense defined later.

Given the two-dimensional representation of the options, and the frontier of preference, in Figure 26, it is tempting to ask whether the frontier might be an efficient set. But this representation has coordinates given by the purely ordinal and incomparable preference scales of the two parties, so the definition of efficient set makes no sense in this context. One could still ask whether the options on the frontier form an efficient set (in what may be many more than two dimensions) for either party alone. However, we already know that each party's preference is monotone along the frontier, so preference is single peaked in any case.

The conflict over the options on the frontier may involve approach or avoidance processes depending on initial positions derived from the status quo and/or background variables. Suppose, for example, that the issue is the extent to which recently incorporated land is to be commercially developed or made into a park and its initial state is the point w in Figure 26. The projections of the point w on the frontier, labeled ipA and ipB, give the initial positions of the antagonists A and B.

A increasingly prefers all options on the frontier to the left of ipA and B increasingly prefers all options to the right of ipB. Clearly, the options y and z, and only these options, constitute an approach/approach conflict because both parties are driven toward each other from their respective initial positions. These options represent an opportunity for both parties to improve on the status quo. This instance corresponds to what Stagner and Rosen (1965) call the bargaining zone and would be part of what Bishop (1963) calls the utility frontier.

Initial positions may be more or less subject to strategic manipulation, perhaps more so than the preference order itself. When an option is part of the status quo, however, as in the example discussed in Chapter 5 on preference for number of children, strategic misrepresentation is more difficult than if there is nothing to anchor one of the initial positions on the ordinal scale of options.

If the option w, representing the status quo in Figure 26, were not dominated it would be on the frontier, in which case the conflict would be an approach/avoidance conflict in both directions. For both parties the status quo would be better than any change desired by the other party, the same situation as a worker asking the boss for a raise.

This situation also conveniently illustrates how the ambience of the conflict changes with the status quo. In this case, the more the status quo deteriorates in the view of one of the parties, the lower it drops in that party's preference ordering, further separating the two initial positions and thereby making acceptable some previously unacceptable options. For example, in the case of newly incorporated land delay may be crucial. A lengthy delay could convert an approach/avoidance conflict into an approach/approach if the status quo deteriorates with time. Rising costs could have that effect on the developers, and soil erosion could have that effect on the environmentalists.

It is not necessary, of course, that a particular change in the status quo will have the effect on the ambience we illustrate in this example. In general it can only be said that a change in the status quo may affect the ambience of the options for either party independently of the other. Substantive changes like this may change the parameters of the conflict, and so are likely to affect the difficulty of resolving it. The relation between these parameters of a conflict and the difficulty of its resolution is the subject of the next chapter.

A principal advantage of the frontier of preference is that it reduces the complexity of any two party Type II conflict to a total ordering of options between the two parties by using the two preference orderings as the coordinates. No matter what the dimensionality of the options or the space in which they are embedded, it is transformed into a two-dimensional preference space and the frontier of preference is a one-dimensional piece of that space.

A counterargument to the use of the frontier of preference might be made on the following grounds, illustrated with Figure 27. In the figure, we see that A's ordering is $x\,y\,z$ and B's ordering is $y\,x\,z$. The option z would be eliminated from the frontier because both parties prefer x to z (and also y to z). The choice would lie between x and y.

However, party A might argue against the choice of y because B would be getting what B wants and A would be doing all the conceding. A's argument could be that z is a better choice because then B would be making about as much concession as A and this would be more fair.

Let us examine A's argument. The validity of A's argument is dependent upon all of the following conditions holding: (a) that measures of utility, and its concession, are interpersonally comparable by

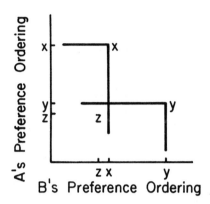

Figure 27: A counter argument to the use of the frontier of preference

a demonstrably valid procedure, (b) that the concession already made from A's ideal that would be made by A in accepting x is exactly equal to the concession already made from B's ideal that would be made by B in accepting y, and (c) that equality of concession should govern fairness to the exclusion of any other principle of fairness. Figure 27 has been drawn as A would have us believe.

We reject the argument by A for retaining z because we reject all of the conditions just given. A discussion of interpersonally comparable utility and our reasons for rejecting it as a useful tool in conflict resolution was presented in Section 6.1.1. We reject the principle of equality of concession as an *exclusive* principle of fairness, in part because it depends on interpersonally comparable utility and in part because without a constraint on concession, escalation is invited, for reasons discussed shortly. The danger from escalation is that if an unacceptable level of concession is reached for either party, the conflict may become violent or may be converted into one of Type III, where the parties no longer attempt to reach agreement.

The fact that we reject the argument by A does not mean that A is convinced. We are not saying that A won't argue for the dominated option but that he or she should not. The apparent risk, that A or B might get stuck with more concession than necessary, is not the real risk, the real risk is escalation.

The frontier of preference is optimal in minimizing the concession of each party in the sense that if two parties agree on an option not on the frontier there is one on the frontier that would require less concession from at least one of them. The proof is trivial. Defining concession as the inverse of preference, it follows immediately that an option preferred by both parties to another option requires less concession from each.

Ideally, then, we are proposing a principle of optimally minimizing concession by both parties, a principle which is approximated, in the absence of interpersonally comparable utility, by the frontier of preference. Choosing an option not on this frontier requires an unnecessary additional concession from at least one of A and B.

With this principle of minimizing concession as a first principle, it is possible then to approximate a second principle of fairness in concession by creatively seeking other options between *a* and *b* which would be on the frontier and would permit finer ordinally discriminable degrees of concession.

This principle of optimally minimizing concession does not guarantee that the conflict will not become one of Type III. That depends on the restraint of the antagonists and on the creative development of options which push out the frontier and thereby lower the required concession to more acceptable levels.

The danger of failing to impose the first principle for the frontier of preference is that A's insistence on *z* could be perceived by B as a vindictive choice or as a threat to make B accept *x*, and so incite further misrepresentation and retaliation, leading to escalation.

Failing to impose this principle is not a positive step on the path to peaceful and rational conflict resolution. Deleting dominated options reduces the threat capability of both participants. Retaining dominated options and thereby violating the frontier of preference is perilous to the process of peaceful conflict resolution. It impedes rationality by exposing the process to unverifiable utility considerations, misinformation, and distrust.

The frontier of preference provides a solution to the first problem we just discussed, finding an optimal scale of options. The frontier is a total ordering of nondominated options which optimally minimizes the concessions that will be required. It focuses attention on the critical tradeoffs. We turn now to the second problem, that of selecting an option from this set.

9.2   The Second Problem: Choosing an Option

Given an efficient set of options, an individual in a Type I conflict can ensure that a decision function is single peaked by applying a proper preference function to make a choice. In a Type II conflict we cannot have an efficient set of options but the frontier of preference approximates it in that we have monotonicity of preference of each party over a set of options ordered between the ideals of the two parties, and the set of options is Pareto optimal from the point of view of the preferences of both parties.

In the absence of interpersonal conparability of preference (utility), a proper preference function cannot be applied. But there is a class of decision functions that are not proper preference functions but also ensure single peakedness in the presence of efficient sets. So they provide another route for approximating the conditions that ensure single peakedness of the decision function. In the next subsection we present and discuss the possible use of such decision functions in resolving Type II conflicts.

In the second subsection we discuss some of the difficulties that arise when the process of negotiation is multipeaked, rather than single peaked. In the succeeding subsections we discuss some aspects of a very common solution, the split-the-difference solution; some related literature on the selection of an option; the role of debate; and then an analysis of the process of negotiation by a well-known professional and a translation of his analysis into the language of the structure of Type II conflicts.

9.2.1   Some Alternative Composition Rules That Yield Single Peakedness

Much of this subsection is based on the paper by Aschenbrenner (1981) in which he shows that a wide variety of decision criteria — most of which have been observed in individual decision making (resolving Type I conflicts) — lead to SPF's in the presence of an efficient set. We review his paper first and then discuss its relevance to the problem of resolving a Type II conflict.

Aschenbrenner's work is based on a prior contribution by Tversky (1969) identifying two classes of information processing models of decision making: processing by option and processing by component (Aschenbrenner uses the terms alternative and attribute, respectively, which are the more commonly used terms in psychological literature, but we adopt these substitutes for greater compatibility with the literature on conflict).

These terms refer to the process of making a choice from a pair (or larger collection) of options. Processing by option refers to a class of models in which the information on each option is processed independently to arrive at a total assessment for each, and then the choice is made by comparing the total assessments (i.e., the information is processed an option at a time).

Processing by component refers to a class of models in which the information on a pair of options is processed a component at a time, and then the differences are combined over the components to determine which choice is made (i.e., the information is processed component-wise).

Tversky showed that the class of models by which differences are aggregated over components can lead to different choices than the former class. Indeed, it was Tversky's concern with intransitive preferential choice that motivated his study. He showed that processing information by options could lead to intransitivity only through random error, whereas processing information by component-wise differences could lead to systematic intransitivities, which he demonstrated empirically.

Aschenbrenner makes the point that the proper preference functions in our model of Type I conflict belong to the class of models in which information is processed by option. He shows that under certain conditions, component-wise information processing that does not satisfy the conditions for a proper preference function (cf. Section 2.4) will also lead to SPFs on efficient sets. Consequently, the class of models which lead to SPFs is expanded and offers new possibilities for models of equity, for the negotiation process, and for the choice of an option on the frontier. Some of these models do not require more than signed ordinal scales of utility, avoiding one of the most serious barriers to optimal choice in Type II conflict.

The component-wise models Tversky defined are called additive difference models (ADMs). They are defined as follows.

Definition. A preference structure is called an *additive difference model* (ADM) if and only if there exist real valued functions $u_1, \ldots, u_n$ and increasing real valued functions $w_1, \ldots, w_n$, such that $w_i(-d) = -w_i(d)$ and

$$x \succ y \text{ if and only if } \sum_i w_i(u_i(x_i) - u_i(y_i)) > 0,$$

where $\succ$ is the preference order.

A class of models in which information is processed an option at a time, called additive models, is defined as follows.

Definition. A preference structure is called an *additive model* if and only if there exist real valued functions $u_1, \ldots, u_n$ such that:

$$x \succ y \text{ if and only if } \sum_i u_i(x_i) > \sum_i u_i(y_i).$$

Clearly if the w_i are just multiplication by constant factors, then the ADM reduces to the additive model and cannot yield intransitive choices except by random error. The interesting cases, then, are those in which the w_i are functions other than multiplicative factors and intransitivities can occur. Among these cases are those in which the ADM yields SPFs. The conditions under which this occurs will clearly be more general than those under which the ADM becomes identical to the additive model.

The more general conditions do not require differentiability or even continuity. But a restriction is placed on pairs of "weighting" functions, w_i, w_j, called *quotient-order-preserving*: w_i and w_j are quotient-order-preserving if

$$\frac{a}{c} \leq \frac{c}{d} \quad \text{implies} \quad \frac{w_i(a)}{w_i(b)} \leq \frac{w_j(c)}{w_j(d)}.$$

This condition limits the weighting functions to power functions of the form:

$$w_k(d) = t_k \text{sign}(d)|d|^r,$$

with $t_k > 0$ for all k, $r > 0$, and $\text{sign}(d)$ is 1, 0, or -1 according as d is positive, zero, or negative.

This weighting function is closely related to the Minkowski r-metric, a distance function in which the difference between two options on a component is weighted by its absolute magnitude raised to the power r.

Aschenbrenner then defines a proper additive difference model (PADM) as one in which the u_i are either increasing or are decreasing, and are not positively accelerated, and the w_i are functions of the above form. Given these conditions, then, an efficient set is a necessary and sufficient condition for all PADM to be single peaked (cf. Appendix B).

This means that single peakedness will be achieved in a Type I conflict if the individual processes information about the options in an efficient set by substituting a proper additive difference model for the proper preference function defined in Section 2.4. What we are interested in, then, are the implications this may have for the process by which an option is chosen from the frontier of preference.

Here we have only two utility functions, the inner branches of the two opposing SPFs and we would like to know how information about the two adversaries' preferences could be processed so as not to prevent the possible existence of an SPF describing the search for an optimal solution.

Some examples of information processing models which are not proper preference functions but are additive difference models that are single peaked on efficient sets include May's (1954) majority rule, Huber's (1979a) weighted sets of dimensions rule, the lexicographic rule, and the greatest attractivity difference rule (Huber, 1979b).

May's (1954) majority rule states that in choosing between two options at a time, one should choose the one that is better on more components. This rule was designed by May to explain intransitive preference. However, if the options form an efficient set, the rule is single peaked. In the context of the frontier of preference, the most plausible generalization would be for each pair of options, x and y, to be compared by assessing the number of components in which x is better than y for A and, independently, for B, and the number of components in which y is better than x for A and, independently, for B. The choice between x and y would then be given by the sum of the number of components on which x exceeded y for either A or B or both. The larger sum determines the choice. Note that no cardinal utility measures are required but the prior prescription of components is required. In a Type I context this requirement would not be a serious issue, but in a Type II context there would have to be prior agreement on the number and definition of components and this might be difficult to achieve.

Huber's (1979a) weighted sets of dimensions rule calls for comparing the set of components on which x is preferred to y by either A or B or both with the set of components on which y is preferred to x by either A or B or both and judging which set is more important. The option chosen is the one preferred on the more important subset. As both A and B have contributed to both subsets, it is uncertain what effect this model would have on the negotiation process. Certainly it behooves each party to add components to which both parties agree, as these get doubly weighted.

In the lexicographic rule the components are ranked in order of importance and the options are compared component-wise, in decreasing order of importance, until a component is reached on which both adversaries agree that one option is superior to the other. This model, in the context of Type II conflict, requires agreement of the adversaries on the hierarchy of the components in the order of their importance; probably as difficult a condition to satisfy as agreement on the options in the first place. So this is not a promising model for this purpose in general.

The greatest attractivity difference model requires determining that component on which a pair of options differs most, and then uses the direction of that difference to decide which option is chosen.

This is subject to much the same criticism as the lexicographic rule as a potential model for the process of resolving a Type II conflict and is also dependent on interpersonally comparable utility.

There are two aspects of resolving a Type II conflict that make Aschenbrenner's work relevant: One is the fact that during some stages of the process of negotiation the interaction between antagonists is over the components of what will become parts of "whole" options. The other is the advantage of single peakedness over multipeakedness in all stages of negotiation, whether over components or over "whole" options.

These aspects are important because his analysis reveals that there are other ways that components can be combined in the course of negotiation than by proper preference functions and still ensuring single peakedness over an efficient set.

The next section clarifies the consequences of violating single peakedness.

9.2.2   The Problem with Multipeaked Functions in Negotiation

The importance of the distinction between multipeaked and single peaked decision functions is greater in Type II conflicts than in Type I for two reasons. One is that the options on the frontier of preference do not form an efficient set (see Section 9.3) and so multipeakedness of the decision function is virtually assured, and the other is that the severity of this effect on the search for a solution is greater in a Type II than a Type I. The greater severity of this effect is due to the fact that the utility functions are in different heads. When they are in one head, as in a Type I conflict, an exhaustive search is relatively feasible because comparing the values of the decision function appears to be a simple process for an individual. This process within an individual is popularly known as "soul-searching." We call it "simple" here only in contrast to Type II conflict. When the utility functions are in different heads the path to a solution is inherently more difficult, and it is desirable to understand just how this purely structural effect comes about over and above any substantive considerations.

We discuss this with a numerical example, for simplicity, with given utility functions and with a decision function that is simply the sum of the utilities, but there is no loss of generality in that ordinal relations are what are critical. Of course, in the absence of intercomparable utility the numbers used in the example would not be known. Furthermore, no third party can be certain such numbers

Frontier of Preference:	a	x	y	z	b
A's inner branch:	100	60	40	20	-10
B's inner branch:	-20	-10	30	40	100
Decision Function:	80	50	70	60	90

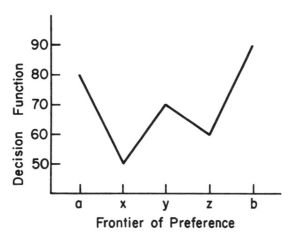

Figure 28: A multipeaked preference function

represent the truth because the sources are the parties involved and they are motivated to dissemble. But each party has a vague and inaccurate notion of the other's value structure and so has a feeling for relative gain and concession, and giving up more than one gets is resisted. Our arithmetic simplifies the discussion of these vague and inaccurate feelings of the disputants.

Let the frontier of preference consist of the ordered options $a\,x\,y\,z\,b$ and let the inner branches of A's and B's preference functions have the values shown in Figure 28 with the decision function illustrated. Note that the inner branches are both monotone preference functions, but the decision function is multipeaked. For concreteness, we point out that these options could be on a contract curve (cf. Section 9.3).

The argument that this unhappy situation is a consequence of the particular functions used is valid, but if the options do not constitute an efficient set for both parties then this situation can arise. In Figure 28, the cause of the multipeakedness of the decision function is that the options on the frontier do not constitute an efficient set (i.e., there does not exist a numerical representation for the frontier such that it is an efficient set and the preference functions of both parties are proper utility functions).

Consider the effect as the options on the frontier are traversed in order from a to b. From a to x there is a 40-unit concession by A and a 10-unit gain by B. From x to y and then to z is a 20-unit concession each time for A where B gets a 40-unit gain and a 10-unit gain. Then from z to b there is a 30-unit concession for A and a 60-unit gain by B.

In brief, the relative tradeoffs of concessions and gains are irregular. From a to x, for example, A's concession is four times B's gain; from x to y it is half as great; and from y to z, it is twice as great. From z to b, it is half as great again.

This irregularity in relative tradeoffs of concessions and gains reflects multipeakedness which may arise on the frontier. One peak will favor one party, the other peak will favor the other party, and the decision function dips between them. Such irregularity is inevitable in the absence of single peakedness, and it is a serious impediment to negotiation.

Let us modify the example to form an efficient set. As before, suppose the ordered options on the frontier are $a\,x\,y\,z\,b$ and the joint preference function is additive. However, this time the two monotone preference functions are as given in Figure 29.

From a to x, A's concession is 25 units and B's gain is 45 units. The relative concession to gain is 5/9 or 0.55. Traversing the frontier from a to b, the relative concession by A to gain by B at each step is 0.55, 0.71, 1.25, 1.75. That is, A's relative concession is increasing from left to right, and B's relative gain is decreasing. In going from right to left, the corresponding pattern holds, the degree of concession by B relative to A's gain is increasingly difficult for B to accept and the gain by A from B's concession becomes relatively less rewarding to A. It is easy to see the force of an SPF on seeking a compromise but it is also easy to see that the further apart two adversaries are the more difficult it must be to reach a compromise.

This last statement is a common truism, if not a tautology, but we can now break its circularity. Distance between options on an ordinal scale is meaningless so, for example, the number of options between the two ideal points is not a measure of distance. Indeed, empirical research may reveal that the density of options does not bear a simple relation to the difficulty of resolving a conflict; the relation may even be single peaked in that there is an optimal number!

It is the inversely related changes in the ambience of the options between the ideals of the two parties that makes compromise difficult.

Frontier of Preference:	a	x	y	z	b
A's inner branch:	100	75	50	25	-10
B's inner branch:	-20	25	60	80	100
Decision function:		80	100	110	105	90

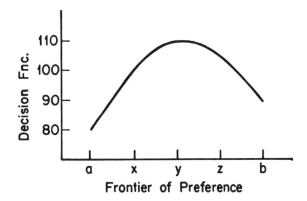

Figure 29: A single peaked preference function

This invariant and reversed monotonicity may also be accompanied by changes in sign between positive and negative ambience for each party, inducing changes between approach and avoidance processes, respectively. Looking ahead a little bit, these changes are exploited in the next chapter to provide a metric for the distance between adversaries, even in the absence of a metric on the scale of options.

This analysis also reveals another relation that can be important to negotiation strategy. In concession from a peak one always loses more than one gains because the preference function is monotonically decreasing. But from the status quo, or initial positions, one gains more than one loses if the options have positive ambience. It would seem that a mediator would be well advised, in general, to orient toward initial positions and improving the status quo, rather than ideal positions, in trying to find a mutually acceptable resolution.

In other words, the mediator would more easily bring the adversaries to a mutually acceptable agreement by emphasizing what each would be gaining relative to their respective status quos, rather than what each is conceding relative to their respective ideals.

In summary, in the presence of a decision function that is single peaked, the successive concessions by each party from its ideal are relatively small at first and become increasingly difficult to make. Equivalently, the successive gains by the other party are relatively large at first and become successively less as they continue, and this does not depend on interpersonal comparability of preference.

The regularity in the ratio of the respective gains and losses in ambience in the presence of a single peaked function is disrupted in the case of a multipeaked function, as has been shown. Such irregularity is inevitable on the frontier because the scale of options is not an efficient set. However, in the absence of interpersonal comparability of utility, the changes in ambience (i.e., preference or concession) for each party are somewhat ambiguous in that each party can only conjecture the magnitude of the other party's subjective changes in preference. This ambiguity is probably all to the good because the uncertainty blurs the distinction between single and multiple peakedness. This blurring effect should be less in a Type I conflict because the changes in the respective utility functions are in one head and it may still take some "soul-searching" to resolve the conflict.

In the case of a decision function that is multipeaked, this "smooth" tradeoff between concession and gain by both parties does not hold and barriers are thrown up which impede agreement on compromise. The greatest single source of this difficulty from a structural point of view is the absence of a common scale of options over which the opposing inner branches satisfy the conditions for proper utility functions.

The frontiers of preference for these two examples are displayed in Figure 30. The convexity of the efficient set relative to the origin reflects the increasing (relative) concession of one party that is associated with decreasing (relative) gain of the adversary. The irregularity in the inefficient frontier reveals the barriers that impede a smooth mediation process.

9.2.3   Which Option?

We have seen that if single peakedness describes the course of negotiation, it should be of some advantage to smoothing the process but that multipeakedness may not be as severe a hindrance as it could be in Type I conflict. But this still leaves the matter of which option should be selected as a resolution of the conflict.

We recognize that the nub of this problem in Type II revolves around fairness and justice, and there is little common agreement

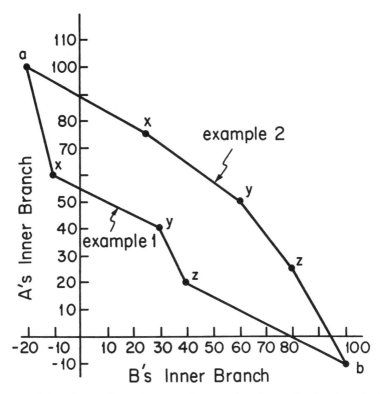

Figure 30: Frontiers of preference illustrating irregularity in relative concessions

on principles or on what is fair and/or just. Furthermore, and also important, there is no clearly satisfactory way to coordinate a function for distributive justice with the frontier of preference because the latter is an ordinal scale. A distribution function must compare the amounts of concession (i.e., changes in strength of preference) which are unknown, and to claim comparability is wishful thinking or fantasy. This leaves one with the ordinal scale, also an unhappy state of affairs, but for reasons of its inadequacy rather than arbitrariness.

If there is one principle, however, on which there is agreement, it is that individuals should share equally if their inputs are equal. Customarily, this means a split down the middle in the two-party case with a continuum of options between all and none. Consensus on distribution fades when the inputs are not equal.

An obvious, if crude, way to implement this principle, if the number of options is odd, is to choose the middle one. So on the frontiers of preference shown in Figure 30, this principle would pick option *y* in both.

Equality of distribution, splitting the difference, is often resorted to as a path of least resistance and so some discussion of the pros and cons of such an ordinal approximation is in order before we consider other methods. Our justification for the use of this principle is primarily negative: There are no sufficient grounds for anything else. On the one hand, there is no doubt that disparity in distribution may appear to be called for. On the other hand, there is no sufficient justification for any particular formula for the correspondence between the grounds for disparity and the amount of disparity. We may add to this that the evidence for disparity may be biased, untrustworthy, and differentially assessed by the antagonists.

There is no reason to believe that the midoption has equal utility for the antagonists or that they would have made equal concessions in accepting it or that it is even "fair." But we are of the opinion, and only that, that such a choice will generally be more acceptable as fair than almost any other except in the face of very (mutually) persuasive evidence to the contrary. Our negative justification is clearly a derivative of the principle of equal distribution of ignorance used as the basis for the Laplace criterion for decision making in games against nature (Milnor, 1954) and of James Bernoulli's principle of insufficient reason (Kasner & Newman, 1940). Both of these principles refer to the assignment of probabilities to events in the absence of information, but they seem relevant here also.

This system appears to have some built in defenses against self-serving strategies in which the antagonists misrepresent their preference orderings. Suppose, for example, that A's true preference ordering on the frontier of preference is $a\,c\,f\,p\,r\,s\,b$ and B's is the reverse. The midoption is p, and this would be an ordinal approximation to equalizing the concessions of the two parties.

If A misrepresented his or her preference ordering by depressing a more favored option with the intention of making it the midoption and thus getting a more favorable resolution, the effect would be to eliminate that option from the frontier, to A's disadvantage. For example, if A's pretended preference order were $a\,p\,f\,c\,r\,s\,b$ and B's preference order were unchanged, then we would have $p \succ_A f \succ_A c$ and $p \succ_B f \succ_B c$ so f and c would be eliminated, the frontier would be $a\,p\,r\,s\,b$ and the midoption would be r, nearer b than before, to A's disadvantage.

In general, if A's true preference order is misrepresented by advancing a less-preferred option and B's preference order remains unchanged, the effect is to eliminate from the frontier those options over which the less-preferred option has been advanced. If the options eliminated were predominantly on A's side of the midoption, then the effect is to make the new midoption more favorable to B, as in the example just given. Misrepresentation by B has a corresponding effect, mutatis mutandis.

This strategy, if exercised by both parties, can reduce the frontier to just the ideals, which puts a freeze on compromise, a confrontation in which each party seeks to impose its will on the other so that one party makes all the concession, and the confrontation runs the risk of escalation.

The strategy called the chilling effect, described by Pruitt and Rubin (1986), in which one party, say A, takes an extreme position in order that a split-the-difference solution will be more favorable, runs the risk of eliminating its ideal from the frontier of preference if the opponent concurs in preferring that extreme to A's ideal.

The best strategy for each party is to propose as many additional options favorable to itself as possible. A disparity in the number proposed would be to the advantage of the party with the greater number. The effect, however, would not be to widen the range between the ideal positions (see the concept of distance between adversaries, Section 10.2) and hence would not raise the ceiling on concession, but, rather, a larger number of options might tend to make the midoption a better estimate of a fair resolution based on the two parties meeting each other half way — or on any other split defined by a fairness function for concession.

The lack of options is probably the most serious handicap to the process of conflict resolution. This mechanism for choosing an option would tend to counteract this handicap by encouraging the construction of new options and would at the same time not increase the ceiling on concession but could decrease it. New options would be added to the frontier but only on the basis of the agreement of both parties (i.e., they are not dominated).

The value of numerous options is one more reason why, in negotiation, it is so important not to make statements which close out one's options. Though usually designed to reduce the options of an opponent, a threat makes one's own behavior more predictable and, hence, more vulnerable; threats put control of one's own behavior in the hands of the adversary. For example, a threat usually takes the form "if you do x I'll do y." So the opponent has control over whether the threatener does y.

If the procedure by which a resolution is arrived at is seen as assuring a fair and equitable choice (cf. Section 6.3), the acceptability of the resolution itself will be enhanced as compared with, say, a random device or a procedure vulnerable to sophisticated manipulation.

As a prescriptive principle, one should not entrust the resolution of a conflict to a procedure that depends on an adversary's altruism, good will, or benevolence. It is not a matter of a procedure being *usually* fair, it must *always* be fair, in the face of evil intent, to be acceptable and survive as a system. Although the frontier of preference and the midoption solution appear to have some desirable qualities, the question of how concession should be distributed between two parties when there is just claim for disparity is still open.

The issue is particularly difficult as such considerations may extend beyond their respective contributions. For example, a requirement for an optimal solution might be that it be mutually acceptable. Disparity in distribution, however, favors one party more than another and may incite strong reactions. The political realities of negotiation between sovereign states reveals that the abstract principle of symmetry, so common in formal theories of bargaining and so "obviously fair," is frequently violated.

The symmetry axiom imposes the condition that the identity of the antagonists is irrelevant as, for example, in our discussion of the conflict between husband and wife (Figures 14 and 15) either may be A.

If "it's a jungle out there," "might makes right," and "God is on the side of the bigger battalions," then symmetry is violated and national power decides. However, one of the things that tempers unrestricted use of raw power is the increasing importance of national image, which is fostered by a public forum like the UN. We return to this aspect of conflict resolution in Part III (see Schelling, 1960, for a critical review of the principle of symmetry and Lockhart, 1979, for an excellent analysis of international bargaining).

9.2.4   Some Related Literature

Specific procedures for resolving a Type II conflict are not the focus of this analysis of the structure of conflict, but there are some developments that should be mentioned.

Bartos (1977) uses the Nash model as a definition of fairness, making an even split of the difference between opening positions where the opening position is the best that each party could do that would still be acceptable to the other. Bartos also makes use of level of aspiration concepts. Although these ideas use cardinal utility, they are, with limitations, adaptable to a signed ordinal scale.

A useful reference on procedures for resolving conflict is Isard and Smith (1982) who discuss and classify many procedures for choosing an option. They classify these procedures in terms of certain relevant properties (e.g., whether the utility scales are ordinal, cardinal within individuals, or cardinally comparable between individuals, and whether the options are few or many, etc.). The methods covered are varied and suggestive, but there are some reservations to be kept in mind.

Measuring individual utility functions is not a matter to be taken lightly (see Section 6.1). The method they suggest for measuring utility is Stevens' method of ratio estimation (1958), designed for and used in the construction of ratio scales for measuring sensation. Its application to the development of a scale with both negative and positive values would require an individual to judge whether he likes something n times more than he dislikes something else. For this to be taken seriously as a valid representation of utility, quite aside from issues of strategic misrepresentation, requires justification (i.e., a representation theorem and empirical study of the testable postulates from which the theorem is derived). Isard and Smith suggest no method for assessing interpersonally comparable utility nor a defensible reason to believe it exists.

If we confine ourselves to ordinal preferences only, there are still a number of criteria for choice of an option and a number of methods for seeking it. Even in the domain of signed ordinal preferences, however, some of the criteria and procedures reviewed by Isard and Smith are subject to criticism.

A basic concept is what they call an "efficiency frontier of options," which is conceptually the same as Edgeworth's contract curve and so is not efficient in our sense of the term (cf. Section 9.3). However, the options are ordered if they are in not more than two dimensions; otherwise, they are not ordered. The frontier of preference, however, could be substituted.

Their criteria for solution include the median option on the contract curve or a weighting which may reflect "...more resources...more power...greater need...more inflexible or historically more committed to a position." In such cases "...then fairness suggests...a weighted average principle when participants agree on the weights" (p. 84-85). It would seem that direct bargaining on the contract curve would be more feasible than seeking agreement on each of those factors and then agreement on their aggregate. However, Isard and Smith's analysis has considerable value in bringing a variety of criteria and methods to mind for consideration.

Schelling's *Strategy of Conflict* (1960) is concerned entirely with conflicts that can be formulated as bargaining games and how best to play them (i.e., bargaining and negotiation).

Raiffa's work on the art and science of negotiation (1982) is also concerned with the structure of conflict as it affects the dynamics of bargaining and negotiation. Structural aspects he uses are whether there is only one issue at stake or whether there is multi-issue bargaining, whether there are only two parties involved or whether it is a multiparty conflict, whether there is a limited time frame for solution, etc. The book is an aid to thinking strategically about negotiation and is insightful and creative.

Pruitt and Rubin (1986) refer to problem solving as one of the principal strategies for resolving a conflict. By this is meant a concern on the part of both antagonists for the other's outcome as well as their own in the search for a mutually acceptable solution. Their discussion of problem solving ranges over the development of options, structuring the agenda, and tactics.

Very promising methods are developed under the rubric of alternative dispute resolution (Denenberg & Denenberg, 1981). These include a variety of new, more informal, hybrid processes including the mini-trial (Green, Marks, & Olson, 1978), innovative forms of arbitration such as "high-low, final offer" and "bracketed" arbitration (Perlman, 1979; Finz, 1976), and "rent-a-judge" (Green, 1984a). These are new models for dispute resolution with a playing down of the conventional role of judge and lawyers in the courtroom and replacing the adversarial relationship of the courtroom with the goal of seeking mutual agreement.

A solution is reached in a dispute resolution center by a process of mediation with a third party acting as buffer. The parties take responsibility themselves for concession and the solution reached is perhaps more likely to hold up than one imposed by the court with one's lawyers taking the responsibility.

As described by Green (1984b) in teaching the theory and practice of dispute resolution to third year law students:

> The purpose of this segment is to explore how the primary dispute resolution models [adjudication, arbitration, mediation, negotiation] can be taken apart and the components reformulated into new models that are better suited to particular kinds of disputes. (p. 254)

There are many dispute resolution centers across the country, supported by funds from government and private sources. The ordinary legal procedure is expensive, protracted, formal, and adversarial. These walk-in centers avoid all of these drawbacks, and as one legal scholar put it, dispute resolution "makes the forum fit the fuss" (Denenberg, 1981).

9.2.5 The Debate

The debate is a common and time-honored aid in the process of resolving Type II conflicts. It calls for some discussion because it has some disadvantages as well as advantages.

When there are two and only two options, as when the decision is to be guilty or not guilty or when there are only two candidates for office, the debate can clarify issues and distinctions. Also, as an exhibition of skill, it can be of interest in its own right, like a sport, in which case it is a Type III conflict (see Chap. 13).

But when options can exist between the two extremes, then the debate may be counterproductive. The two alternatives in a debate are formulated as extreme positions, diametrically opposite views, and all the talent and expertise is concentrated on the extremes. The debate is not a mechanism that focuses on tradeoffs, or "if/then" negotiation. It is not directed at creating intermediate options, or on seeking a compromise and mutual agreement. It is directed at seeking the better of two extreme positions. Hence, the debate polarizes, excluding compromise; it is an either/or confrontation between hard-edged positions.

In some ways, it is wasteful of talent. Individuals in a public role who become publicly identified with a position find it difficult to be flexible because that would make them vulnerable in other ways, for example, to being called opportunistic or being accused of lacking in principle. Experts who have participated in debate are also locked in. If they change their minds, they risk diminishing their credibility and status as experts.

The debate characterizes our judicial system. It tends to treat as adversaries people who outside the court may not be (e.g., neighbors, friends, lovers, etc.) and total victory for one may lead to reeruption of the conflict. The movement just discussed on alternative dispute resolution avoids litigation. Its techniques are borrowed from labor relations, mainly negotiation and arbitration. It seeks justice without the rigid formality of the courtroom and the roles that judges and lawyers normally play. They may serve as arbitrators instead, "neutrals" who render binding decisions, or as mediators, who serve as catalysts, helping the antagonists arrive at their own solutions.

A debate, although it does not itself resolve anything and may sacrifice half of the participants, does have the value of trying to bring together what is known about the best and worst of the two options. This effort is designed to influence those who will make a decision, such as a jury or the voters. The debate, by reducing the options to two, converts a multiparty conflict, one with large numbers

of individuals taking different positions, to a two-party conflict. This
has the virtue of making the resolution simple in a culture where
majority vote is accepted as a decision mechanism.

9.2.6   Negotiation: The View from Within and from Without

Playing the role of a third party, a "professional neutral," in the
process of dispute resolution, is both a science and an art. It requires
a blend of some general principles coupled with the personal skills
and creativity of the artist. Robben Fleming is a very experienced
and successful labor mediator who as Chancellor of the University of
Wisconsin and then President of the University of Michigan was in the
middle of disputes involving students, faculty, and Boards of Regents
and he is a past president of the National Academy of Arbitrators.

He describes himself (personal communication) as coming at conflict from a point of view different from ours, an experiential one, that
of a practitioner not a theorist, but generously provided us with an
introspective analysis of how he deals with and thinks about disputes.
We excerpt it here and then collate the two points of view.

> I have succeeded or failed to the extent that people trusted
> me and would work with me. I am conscious of how dif-
> ficult it is to apply terms like "fairness" and "equity" to
> disputes, yet I do it all the time. I suppose all I can say is
> that I apply my own standards, subject to such modifica-
> tion as I am willing to make after listening to arguments
> from the contestants. I tell them frankly that I won't at-
> tempt to help them reach an agreement that I think is
> unfair or inequitable. At that point they can retain me or
> let me go.
>
> If I try to break down the elements of what I do, I
> think I find five components. Perhaps I would find more
> or less if I thought about it more. The five are:
>
> 1. The first thing that I do on entering a dispute is to
>   immerse myself in the facts. I do this both by reading
>   all the available material on it, and then by talking
>   to the interested parties. I hope at the end of this
>   step to understand both the facts and the "flavor" of
>   the dispute.

2. I then make a deliberate effort to put myself in the place of each of the interested parties, hoping to understand how they reason out the situation, what their prejudices are, where the flexibility, if any, resides.

3. I then try in my own mind to "repackage" the dispute. That is, by the time most people are asking for the intervention of people like myself, they have a stake in the positions they have taken. If you want them to change you have to help them save face. One thing you can do is change the look of the dispute by coming at it from a different direction, using different key words to describe it, sometimes insisting with a straight face that it is now a new and different problem.

4. Throughout this effort I must, from my own point of view, establish my credibility. The parties must feel that I tell them the same things, that I do not violate confidences, that I am sympathetic if not always in agreement with the positions they take.

5. Finally, I insist that I cannot find solutions on my own. I tell them they know a great deal more about the problem than I do, and that while I will float possible solutions, they must take the responsibility for finding variations which will work. My theory is that they will more nearly accept a solution if they feel they have participated in designing it. In this process I, of course, use all the powers of persuasion which I have to get them into agreement.

I have frequently been asked why I think that I am regarded as successful in dispute situations. Assuming for the sake of argument that the conclusion is correct, I don't know the answer to the question. I believe that because I make it a point to know the facts in a case I sometimes give the parties the impression that I know more about a case than I really do. I may have a kind of built-in radar which helps me sense how people will react to situations and therefore where the points of flexibility are. I think integrity is a basic requirement, and I think imagination in doing what I call "repackaging" of disputes is very helpful. Perhaps some people are more persuasive than others.

We now compare his view with that of the structure of conflict and look for possible correspondences:

1. We see in his search for facts and "flavor" a search for the components of the dispute, not the elemental components, perhaps, but the easily identified (and ambiguous) composites which are easily named, like safety, security, comfort, rewards, recognition, perks, and other generally positive components. Such variables mediate the concepts of ambience and the distance between adversaries depending on how relatively important they are and whether they have a positive or negative sense.

2. Putting himself in the place of the interested parties, a role-playing posture, is, in our terms, directed at assessing the respective preference functions of the parties to the dispute and estimating ideal points and initial positions. The extent to which the expressed values of components are merely strategic positions assumed for bargaining strength and their relative susceptibility to concession are all part of what is sought in this role-playing stance.

3. "Repackaging" is crucial. It controls and directs the attention of the disputants in a new direction. It changes the preferences of the disputants, and may lead to the development of new options and change the frontier of preference. Restructuring (e.g., reframing) is one way to save an adversary's face — the dilemma is by-passed — a way out is provided. "Key words" and appropriate labels tied to the frontier can assist in giving the dispute a new direction. Forming the frontier of preference can literally make the dispute a "new and different problem" (see, also, Section 13.3).

4. We see here the importance of trust, credibility, impartiality, and empathy. Although not a part of the formal structure of conflict because credibility is the judgment of an intangible and is imperfectly understood, it is universally recognized by every scholar and practioner as a prerequisite for an effective professional neutral.

5. Solutions are to be found among the options on the frontier and here Fleming exploits the knowledge and understanding of the antagonists to select the variations in tradeoffs that generate new options. Their participation in the contruction of options is psychologically imperative, because even if the ultimate resolution were known beforehand and offered at the beginning, it

would almost certainly be rejected out of hand. Participating in the construction of an option creates a vested interest and makes agreement easier to achieve.

Of course, in neither view are these components of the negotiations process to be thought of as a sequential series of discrete stages, but rather as intermittently overlapping and interacting.

Fleming's view is only partially captured in our translation of it. There is a richness to his open-ended account that is compatible with but not explicit in our more formal structure. His reference to the flavor of a dispute, for example, can mean much more than estimating the sign and strength of the ambience and searching for the components about which the dispute revolves. The personalities of the participants, the history of previous confrontations, the relation of the participants to their constituencies, are among a host of aspects that are part of the flavor and have an enormous impact on the course of negotiation.

His use of the term "restructuring" can encompass more than the search for the frontier of preference; it could involve framing options differently, redistributing the emphasis on the component dimensions of the options, and thereby their relative weights. His reference to saving face is totally outside our structure.

Nevertheless, overall and within the limitations of our framework, we perceive a substantial compatibility between these two views. A coordination between them should be helpful to one seeking to sharpen his skills as a negotiator and to those to whom the art of negotiation does not come naturally. It could provide a deeper understanding for the experienced and the expert.

9.3 Construction of the Contract Curve

The procedure for constructing the frontier of preference can be shown to converge on the contract curve in Edgeworth's economical calculus (cf. Section 7.1). Consider an arbitrary option and the indifference curves through it as, for example, is illustrated in Figure 31 by the point labeled a and the curves labeled L and M for Labor and Management, respectively. The indifference curves generate a "canoe" shaped region, labeled x, with the point for the option being either at the bow or stern unless the two indifference curves are tangent, in which case the option a is on the contract curve. The curves also generate other regions making five in all, labeled v, w, x, y, and z.

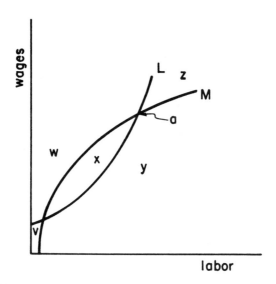

Figure 31: Regions generated by an option a

If we label an option in a region by the label of the region, then the preference orders of Labor and of Management are, respectively:

$$(x, w) \succ_L a \succ_L (v, y, z) \text{ and}$$

$$(y, x) \succ_M a \succ_M (v, w, z),$$

where the parentheses signify that any preference order on the options in those regions is possible depending on their precise locus.

We see that both parties prefer x to a (i.e., any option within the canoe is preferred to the option that generated the canoe). Furthermore, outside the canoe there is no option both parties prefer to the option that generated the canoe.

In other words, to every option there corresponds a canoe and the contract curve must pass through every canoe. So if one option is preferred by both parties to a second option, then and only then is the canoe of the first option nested in the canoe of the second option. In the limit, nested canoes converge on the contract curve. This, of course, is exactly the process by which the frontier of preference is constructed, so we see that the frontier of preference converges on the contract curve and in the finite case is an approximation.

It should be noted that the ends of the contract curve are not determined (i.e., the points ipL and ipM in Figure 20). A bargainer usually resists revealing a bottom line such as a seller's minimum price or a buyer's maximum price. Indeed professional negotiators are not usually told such things by the people who hire them for fear of a tendency to slack off in their negotiation when that point is reached, when perhaps more might be possible.

It is obvious that this method is applicable beyond the specific context of Edgeworth's formulation. This demonstration shows that the frontier of preference is a generalization of the contract curve to ordinal preferences and multiattribute options of any quantitative dimensionality and any qualitative complexity. The ideal conditions for its application are a two person Type II conflict with a moderately dense space of options.

For example, a couple with some substantial savings may consider buying a new car, taking an extended vacation, remodelling their home, having another child, or assisting a young relative to go to college. There are no common control variables running through these options and no natural ordering. Analysis into components and tradeoffs would be incredibly complex and not clearly useful.

The frontier can be useful, however, in providing guidance in the construction of new options. Any option preferred by both parties to another option provides cues as to the direction in which more acceptable options may be sought. Options are portfolios, clusters of piecemeal tradeoffs, and a careful content analysis of the binary relation of being doubly dominated may use the mutual preference to guide the construction of new options.

It should be emphasized that the preference relation being used here is the pairwise ordinal preference of each party and not an accept/reject stand on an option per se. It must be understood that a mutual preference for x over y does not imply a willingness to accept x but is merely a guide to the direction in which better options may be found.

We must further emphasize that this view of the dynamics of negotiation and mediation is in the context of a conflict in which there is a will on the part of both parties to find a mutually acceptable accommodation. This characterizes Type II conflict and distinguishes it from Type III.

Edgeworth's contract curve has also played a significant role in the game-theoretic analysis of bargaining: "An agreement is said to be 'efficient' (or 'Pareto-optimal,' ...) if it places the parties at some point on their 'utility frontier,' which is defined as the locus where, for any given attainable utility for one person, the other's utility is a maximum" (Bishop, 1963).

This is a version of the contract curve of Edgeworth based on cardinal utility, and it makes no distinction between a Pareto optimal set of options and an efficient set. The "negotiation-set" in game theory is a subset (which may be empty) of the utility frontier, and is discussed in Section 9.5.

9.4 An Extension of the Frontier of Preference to Type I Conflict

We may seek to extend the potential applicability of the frontier of preference in two directions — one is an extension to Type I conflict and the other is an extension to multiparty Type II conflicts such as may be resolved by a voting mechanism. We discuss here the extension to the intrapersonal conflict of Type I, and explore the extension to the multiparty conflict in Section 11.4.

The frontier of preference simplifies and focuses the resolution of a Type II conflict on an optimal set of options. Because of the close structural relation of Type I conflict to Type II conflict, the concept of the frontier should be transferable back to Type I. It is anticipated that the extension proposed here would be useful only in the case of complex multiattribute options in which the information to be considered taxes the individual's cognitive processing. In such a situation it would be advantageous to screen the options and focus the conflict on a totally ordered set.

The process we consider would require that the individual play the roles of two hypothetical antagonists of a Type II conflict in turn, constructing a preference order for each based on the inner branches of their respective SPFs.

The following steps are suggested, using the problem of selecting a new car or a place to go for a vacation as illustrations.

1. First, the individual is instructed to take a pessimistic point of view, that bad things that could reasonably be expected to happen will happen (e.g., the car develops all kinds of problems, the weather is bad, etc.). From this pessimistic orientation, the individual orders the options in preference and lets this ordering be the A ordering.

2. Then the individual is instructed to take an optimistic point of view, that everything will turn out for the best, imagine that good things that could reasonably be expected to happen will happen, that one could have it the way one wanted, (e.g., no repair problems, the weather will be great, etc.). From this optimistic orientation, the individual again orders the options in preference, and lets this be the B ordering.

3. The conjunction of these two orderings yields the frontier of preference for the individual. This screening process is intended to determine which options dominate which particular other options under both of the two orientations, points of view that are diametrically different but reasonably possible. This is a piecemeal process, each ordering done independently.

4. The next step, then, is an independent examination of these dominance relations to confirm or revise the piecemeal analysis. In this step, for every option not on the frontier as determined in step 3, there must exist an option on the frontier that the individual prefers to it. Any violation of this condition indicates inconsistency on the part of the individual and must be resolved, presumably by soul-searching. This consistency requirement provides a measure of control over the uncertainty and ambiguity that arises in constructing the preference orderings that represent the A and B orderings. Consistency must be reached before the frontier is acceptable.

Resolution of the Type I conflict on the frontier, choosing an option, does not involve the difficult problems that are aroused under Type II. In the Type I case the problem of interpersonally comparable utility does not arise because the two preference orderings are in one head, and the problem of fairness does not arise because the individual's preference function plays this role. Constructing the frontier in the Type I case, however, may be hard to do for the individual. Making use of the frontier has the advantage of being able to test for internal consistency, but this also puts cognitive strain on the individual.

The procedure makes use of a worst-case analysis about which there is great reservation (see Stech, 1980, for example), as well as a best-case analysis. Any decision based on an extreme case exclusively, whether a worst case or a best, is going to lead to a biased estimate. The method proposed here is a blend, a conjunction, which, indeed is just what a single peaked function is suited for and what Type I and Type II resolutions demand. The method proposed, however, is totally untested and its usefulness remains to be seen.

If the individual's proper preference function over the frontier is not single peaked, this is not a serious matter. The violation of single peakedness is readily detected in that for some $x < y < z$ on the frontier, $x \succ y$ and $z \succ y$. So we would have the ordered triple $x \, y \, z$ embedded in the total preference order with y last (i.e., either $x \succ z \succ y$ or $z \succ x \succ y$).

If the preference order on the triple is xzy but x is not first in the preference order over all the options, then the violation of single peakedness may be neglected as it cannot change the overall first choice which resolves the conflict optimally. If the preference order on the triple is zxy but z is not first in the preference order over all options, the same argument and conclusion apply.

If x is first in the preference ordering over all options, then the ideal, the peak of the SPF, may lie between x and z. Then the only issue is whether y can be modified (i.e., improved) so as to make it first choice, as it is nearer x than z is on the frontier. The same argument and conclusion follows if z is first, *mutatis mutandis*, because y is nearer z than x is on the frontier.

It is convenient to point out here the difference between the frontier of preference and the concept of Pareto optimality. Reducing a multidimensional space of options to a Pareto optimal subset yields a set of options more or less on the surface of that space and does not necessarily reduce the dimensionality. The frontier of preference simplifies that space further by selecting a one-dimensional piece of that surface (i.e., a line of ordered options on that surface) by replacing the possibly many components of the options by only two, those coming from the preference orders of the parties. This limits the resolution of the conflict to an option that is one of the best in the sense of minimizing the amount of tradeoff (concession) that needs to be made.

9.5   Game Theory

Game theory is concerned with conflict of interest and the resolution of such disputes. In this section we examine it from the perspective of the approach developed here. The first edition of von Neumann and Morgenstern's Theory of Games and Economic Behavior in 1944 gave new impetus to game theory, and there has been substantial growth since then. We will make no attempt to review or explicate this literature; the reader is referred to Luce and Raiffa (1957) for an account of game theory and the first 10 years of developments subsequent to the second edition of von Neumann and Morgenstern (1947), and to Jones (1980) for a more recent exposition.

We will begin with an instance of a type of game which is at the core of game theory. The analysis of it is relatively well developed and serves as a prototypical model for extensions, complications, and generalizations.

Consider the game shown in Figure 32 taken from Luce and Raiffa

$$\begin{array}{c}\quad\ \beta_1\ \ \beta_2\ \ \beta_3\ \ \beta_4\end{array}$$

	β_1	β_2	β_3	β_4
α_1	18	3	0	2
α_2	0	3	8	20
α_3	5	4	5	5
α_4	16	4	2	25
α_5	9	3	0	20

Figure 32: A strictly competitive game

(p. 61). This game is represented by a matrix in which one player chooses a row and the other player chooses a column and the entry in the corresponding cell is paid by the column player to the row player. This is called a strictly competitive (i.e., zero-sum) game because what one player gets the other loses. Suppose the row player chooses α_2 and the column player β_3, then the column player would pay the row player $8.

Note that if the row chosen is α_3 the row player will be assured of receiving at least $4 no matter what choice the column player makes. This is called the security level of that choice and a player is presumed to seek to maximize it. For the column player, these outcomes are all negative numbers, and so the maximum security level is to lose as little as possible. By choosing β_2 the most the column player can lose is $4, regardless of which course of action is chosen by the row player.

Game theory is concerned with an optimal strategy for each player, assuming each player is motivated by self-interest. If each player's strategy is to maximize the security level, the maximin strategy, then the entry in row 3 and column 2 would be the payoff, $4, from the column player to the row player. In this instance, these strategies are said to be in equilibrium because neither player is motivated to change. That is, it is assumed that each player knows the rules of the game and the other player's utility function and will assume that the other player will reason the same way. If each player reasons that the other player will search for the best course of action to maximize the security level, then the player's own best course of action is also to maximize his or her own security level and so neither party is motivated to move off $\alpha_3\beta_2$.

Not all strictly competitive games have such an equilibrium point, and if such points exist, they are not necessarily unique. For our purposes, however, we need not pursue these interesting questions and game theory's answers to them.

This simple example is sufficient to contrast game theory with our formulation of the structure of conflict. A Type II conflict that closely parallels this game is the following. Consider a worker seeking a raise. The range of options is from zero on up in a more or less discrete sequence of increments.

This differs from the game just described in that there would be communication and interaction between the worker and the employer and negotiation *which would seek agreement on an outcome.*

Game theory directs its attention to alternative courses of action which are once removed from the outcomes. There is no communication about outcomes; *no agreement* is sought. Each player makes a choice in the light of everything known about the game and expectations of what the other player will do. The conjunction of the choices of the players then determines the outcome. The decisions of the players are made separately, and then they live with the consequence. Each player's choice, a course of action, selects a subset of the total possible set of outcomes, a row and a column, and the intersection of the two sets determines the outcome for each player.

In our treatment of the problem, the outcomes themselves are the options, the participants are free to communicate, and we seek an optimal set of options to ensure that final agreement falls on one of the options in that set.

Pruitt and Rubin (1986) identify five different strategies for resolving a conflict. Of these, the one that characterizes classical game theory is "contending," by which is meant the player's primary concern is his or her own outcomes with little concern for the other's outcome. In contrast, the strategy for resolving a Type II conflict that characterizes our model for the structure of conflict is "problem solving," by which is meant both players are concerned for the other's outcome as well as their own.

This difference is illustrated by the Prisoner's Dilemma game, well known to social scientists and much studied both theoretically and experimentally (Rapoport & Chammah, 1965). This is a two-person non-zero-sum non-cooperative game. A non-cooperative game is one in which no preplay communication is permitted between the players. An example is presented in Figure 33, taken from Luce and Raiffa (p. 95).

The interpretation of the entries in this game matrix is as follows: $(-4, 6)$ in cell $\alpha_1\beta_2$ means that if player 1, the row player, chooses

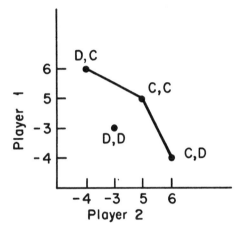

	β_1	β_2
α_1	5,5	-4,6
α_2	6,-4	-3,-3

Figure 33: A Prisoner's Dilemma game

Figure 34: The frontier of preference for the Prisoner's Dilemma game

α_1 and player 2, the column player, chooses β_2, then player 1 loses $4 and player 2 wins $6 (so the game is not zero-sum). Note that if the joint strategies are $\alpha_1\beta_1$, then each player gets $5. This joint strategy is referred to in the literature on Prisoner's Dilemma as the players cooperating, (C,C). If either player is tempted to defect by the outcome of $6, the other player, if he continues to cooperate, would lose $4. If both players defect, (D,D), then both lose $3.

The game matrix is plotted in Figure 34 with player 1's utilities, assuming utility for money is linear for simplicity, on the vertical axis and player 2's utilities on the horizontal axis. A line has been drawn connecting the points (D,C), (C,C), (C,D). This line of options is called, in game theory, the *negotiation set* (Luce & Raiffa, 1957). This set of options bears some resemblance to the frontier of preference but the concepts are not the same, so we digress here briefly to clarify the distinction.

Without dwelling on the technical details, the principal differences between the negotiation set and the frontier of preference are that the negotiation set is based on cardinal utilities; it is the convex closure of Pareto optimal options and so is an efficient set if there are only two players (efficiency is stronger than convexity in general but in two dimensions they are equivalent); it is bounded by each player's "maximin" strategy (which puts a lower bound on the amount of utility a player can guarantee himself or herself regardless of what the other player does, and which also, incidently, places an upper bound on the amount of utility the other player can achieve); it is a set of options that constitutes an approach/approach conflict but in a slightly different sense from ours.

The frontier of preference is based on a signed ordinal scale of preference for each player; it is Pareto optimal but almost certainly not an efficient set; it may be finite; it is bounded by the peaks of the two preference functions; and, as we shall see in the next chapter, it may have segments that are approach/avoidance and/or either approach/approach or avoidance/avoidance but not both.

There are some other more subtle differences. If the players were presented with the cells of the game matrix (the space of options in a Type II conflict) and sought to come to mutual agreement on one, it is possible that the frontier of preference would reveal the option (C,C) to dominate all others. These differences could arise with the ability to communicate and the intent to seek agreement because of being motivated by a common interest. We discuss these differences later in this section and further in Section 13.2.2 in the context of Type III conflict. Here we continue with the game-theoretic analysis.

One might anticipate that different numerical values in the cells of the game matrix (but still preserving the ordinal properties that characterize the Prisoner's Dilemma) would affect the player's behavior. Axelrod (1967, 1970) developed a measure of the degree of conflict of interest and used it to make a number of predictions of behavior in repeated play. These predictions were testable using data reported by Rapoport and Chammah (1965).

In a given game that has been played many times by pairs of players, eight numbers can be computed. These are the probabilities that Player A will defect after a move on which the following happened:

1. Player B cooperated

2. Player A cooperated

3. Player A defected

4. Player B defected

5. Both cooperated

6. Player A cooperated and Player B defected

7. Player A defected and Player B cooperated

8. Both defected

The predictions were that the more conflict of interest there is in a game, the larger each of these probabilities will be. Using the data of Rapoport and Chammah, the lowest rank order correlation coefficient reported was .61.

The nature of this measure of the degree of conflict of interest is discussed in more detail below.

The types of games discussed so far are all non-cooperative games, by which is meant there is no preplay communication. They are games in which there is a prescribed set of courses of action available to each player, each player has full knowledge of the set available to every other player and has full knowledge of the joint (social) consequences (i.e., the outcome for each player of every conjunction of courses of action). The theory is concerned with determining the best choices for players acting in their own self-interest.

These are instances in which the consequences of an individual's behavior are partially dependent on the behavior of others, a very common state of affairs in individual choice. In our terms, these are Type I conflicts, a conflict within the individual torn between incompatible goals, essentially greed and fear.

Another class of games, called cooperative games, involve negotiation as in bargaining. In these games von Neumann and Morgenstern introduced the notion of the negotiation set, as the set of non-dominated options. On such options the players are guaranteed at least as much as they can secure without cooperating (e.g., the status quo obtains). The negotiation set corresponds to our frontier of preference except the negotiation set is obtained from cardinal utilities and our frontier is obtained from a holistic preference comparison. von Neumann and Morgenstern stop there, they do not propose a solution to such games.

> They [von Neumann & Morgenstern] have argued that the actual selection of an outcome from the multiplicity of points in the negotiation set N, depends upon certain psychological aspects of the players which are relevant to the bargaining context. They acknowledge that the actual selection of a point from N is a most intriguing problem, but they contend that further speculation in this direction is not of a mathematical nature — at least, not with the present mathematical abstraction. (Luce & Raiffa, 1957, pp. 118-119)

Game theorists since, however, have not stopped there, and some important work has been done on the problem of selecting an option from the negotiation set (Jones, 1980). Game theorists have been aggressive in seeking "solutions," a strategy which we would not discourage. Of course, the same problems arise which were discussed in Chapter 6 and Section 9.2, the problem of interpersonal comparability of utility and the problem of fairness in the face of power and threat capability. The work of Nash, Harsanyi, and others, discussed in Luce and Raiffa, are examples of the top-down approach to fairness mentioned in Section 6.3.

We will make no attempt to review this work but merely indicate that, typically, some "reasonable" conditions (axioms) that a "fair" solution should satisfy are proposed and then a solution is derived involving the measurement of utility on an interval scale for an individual but not, in all solutions, requiring comparability across individuals. The Nash solution to the bargaining problem, for example, is that point in the negotiation set in which the relative marginal concessions in utility are equal, having set the status quo equal to zero. So this solution requires measuring utility but does not require comparability across individuals.

Although the solutions offered are not satisfactory to social scientists, nor, indeed, to mathematicians, they are logical consequences of precisely stated axioms about proposed desirable properties that a solution should satisfy. More satisfactory solutions depend on the construction of alternative axioms that can be operationalized and that capture what are still only imprecise behavioral and social science notions.

It is in this spirit that Axelrod (1970) developed his measure of the intensity of conflict of interest. The development was patterned on the development of Shannon's measure of information (Shannon & Weaver, 1949) and was constructed in the context of bargaining games and then generalized to the Prisoner's Dilemma and other complex games.

In brief the measure is derived from a set of five precisely specified desirable properties. They are:

1. Symmetry: invariance with respect to interchange of the labels of the players (anonymity).

2. Independence: independence with respect to linear transformations of player's utility schedules (not dependent on comparability of utility).

3. Continuity: for a given game, G, and an infinite sequence of games, G_i, all with the same "no agreement" point, if the region

of G is the limit of the regions of G_i then the conflict of interest of G is the limit of the conflicts of interest of the games G_i. (This is a technical condition. The region of G is the space of all feasible agreements including the no agreement point. It is convex because probability mixtures of feasible agreements are allowed, for example, coin tossing. In Figure 35 the region of all feasible agreements for the conflict between husband and wife discussed in Section 5.2 is bounded by the heavy line connecting the points 0, 1, 2, 3, and 4 children. If two games are similar, this property requires that they should have similar amounts of conflict of interest if they also have the same no agreement point.)

4. Boundedness: the bargaining game with the most conflict of interest has conflict of interest equal to one-half (a scale property).

5. Additivity: in normalized games, if the cost to one player of meeting a demand by the other is the sum of the costs of meeting the same demand divided between two other games, then the conflict of interest of that game is the sum of the conflicts of interest of the other two games (a strong and very important condition).

To measure conflict of interest, the game is normalized by transforming each player's utilities to the interval zero to one, with zero the utility of the worst that can happen and one the utility of the best that can happen. Then the area in the unit square above and to the right of the region of feasible outcomes is a measure of the degree of conflict of interest.

What Axelrod shows is that this conflict of interest measure satisfies all five properties and is the only measure that can.

As an illustration, we present in Figure 35 the way in which the conflict of interest would be calculated for the conflict shown between husband and wife over number of children, which was displayed as a Type II conflict in Figure 14. For purposes of illustration, the utilities used in Figure 35 are taken from Figure 14 as if they were known and true. The origin or zero point of utility is what each player can guarantee himself or herself unilaterally, which in this case is to have no children. The unit of utility is the best a player can do in the light of the fact that the other player is sure to veto any agreement that was not at least as good as the no agreement value.

The best for A is to have one child as that is A's most preferred outcome and it is regarded positively by B so would not be vetoed.

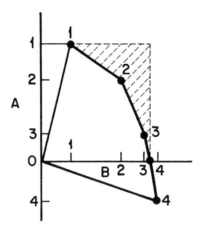

Figure 35: The conflict of interest measure for conflict between husband and wife

The best for B is to have three children, *mutatis mutandis*, so the rectangle that contains the conflict is completed by the dotted lines. Here the measure is 19.8%.

In Figure 36 we show the calculation of the conflict measure for the Prisoner's Dilemma game from Figure 33. The measure here is 12.3%, assuming linear utility for the outcomes of the game.

Clearly, the conflict of interest measure requires the measurement of utility of each party on an interval scale, but neither interpersonal comparability of differences in utility nor normalization is required.

Given cardinal utility, the measure is promising for comparing the degree of conflict of interest for the same pair of individuals playing a set of games which are alike in certain ways (e.g., the same demand area and the same social and psychological context). The relative degree of conflict is maximal, equal to one-half, when the negotiation set lies on the diagonal from upper left to lower right. As the line of the negotiation set bulges up and out toward the upper right corner both players can increasingly get what they want and the conflict of interest is said to diminish.

But, of course, if the limits of the demand space are changed, or if the social or psychological context of the game is changed, for example, by changing the players, or by repetitive play, or by changing the payoffs to approach/approach, approach/avoidance, or avoidance/avoidance conflicts without changing the relative space of infeasible outcomes, then comparisons are not justified. Such changes constitute perhaps one reason that the relations observed using Rapoport

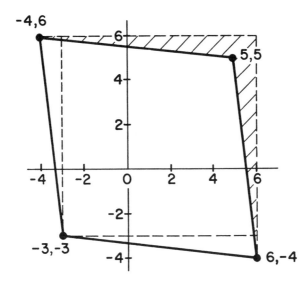

Figure 36: The conflict of interest measure in the Prisoner's Dilemma game

and Chammah's data on the Prisoners' Dilemma game were not better than they are. That they were as high as they are perhaps reflects the structural similarity of their conflicts and the effectiveness of the measure in capturing this similarity.

In an iterated Prisoner's Dilemma if players believe their own behavior can influence the other player then the game is no longer a dilemma (Am. Rapoport, 1967) and a "tit-for-tat" strategy is the best in securing cooperation (Axelrod, 1984).

Attempts to apply game theory to some dozen real conflict situations, ex post facto, by Snyder and Diesing (1977) bring out its value in clarifying options and issues but also its inadequacies due to its restrictive assumptions. The limitations of game theory in its classical form as a model for conflict situations are widely recognized, and there have been a number of modifications and extensions suggested. But when one leaves the domain of two-person zero sum games with saddle points, then rational choice becomes encumbered with psychological issues like self-interest versus collective interest, trust and suspicion, and broader issues like social norms and ethical principles.

In comparison with the theory of the structure of conflict developed here, classical game theory gets stronger results from stronger assumptions that are unrealistic beyond a very limited domain of conflicts. In that domain, players are driven by self-interest, choose a course of action independently of each other, and must accept the collective consequence of their separate decisions — a normative approach to maximizing self-interest.

The theory of the structure of conflict makes weaker assumptions and gets weaker results applicable to a broad domain of conflict. Players are assumed to be driven by self-interest but, in the case of Type II conflicts, *must* seek agreement on the outcomes of their joint action, a collective interest.

The development of what is called higher game theory consists of extending the classical theory either by relaxing restrictive assumptions to increase the relevance and applicability of the theory or by narrowing the domain by changing the assumptions and adding others to make the theory more relevant to particular conflicts. Examples include: relaxation of the restriction on the quantification of utility (e.g., Rapoport, An., Guyer, & Gordon, 1976; Howard, 1971; Brams, 1975); the exhaustiveness of information on options and outcomes of both parties (Harsanyi, 1967-1968); substitution of satisficing for the maximization of utility (Simon, 1955, 1957); and the introduction of metagames in which sequentially conditional choices are introduced (Howard, 1971). Such efforts can go far to increase the relevance of game theory to real conflicts but usually at considerable cost to the strength and power of the theory, and the assumptions made have been frequently criticised (see e.g., Brams, 1976, for a review of the controversy aroused by metagame theory). See Section 13.2.2 for further discussion of the role of higher game theory in the context of Type III conflict.

Chapter 10

The Classification and the Difficulty of Resolving Type II Conflicts

10.1   The Variety of Type II Conflicts

An approach/approach Type II conflict, as we defined it in Section 5.3, is over a pair of options each of which has positive ambience for both parties; that is, both options represent an improvement on the status quo of both parties. One option represents a greater gain than the other option does on the status quo of one party, and the reverse is true for the other party or there would be no conflict. The conflict pertains to which party should get the greater gain.

What one party gains is not what the other party loses, either qualitatively or quantitatively. A choice of one option over the other may be a greater gain in preference for one party than for the other party, but for each party, that choice is a gain from its respective initial position. The gain of either party is a composite of the gains and losses on the components that the party regards as relevant, as evaluated through the party's utility functions for these components, and, finally, the party's preference function which aggregates them. None of these are observables in an authentically verifiable sense.

Of course, some of the components seen by one party as a gain in the choice of one option over another may also be seen by the other party as gains; for example, what to one party is a gain in employee morale may be valued by the other party as a gain in employee safety or working conditions. Thus, it is not only misleading but also false to say that one party's gain is the other party's loss. Each party gains something and loses something in resolving an approach/approach conflict, and what one party gains may be part of the other party's gain or loss and what one party loses may be part of the other party's gain or loss. It may be said, however, that each party has gained more than it has lost.

The preceding discussion was cast in terms of resolving an approach/approach conflict, but a parallel scenario may be written for an avoidance/avoidance conflict in which the resolution involves deciding which party should take the greater relative loss, as both options represent reductions from the initial positions of both parties.

In an approach/avoidance conflict one party favors an option that the other party opposes, relative to their respective initial positions. It would seem that this is not an attractive situation in which to seek mutual agreement. This type of conflict, however, is quite common and almost as commonly resolved easily (e.g., an employee asking for a raise, or a spouse wanting to go on a fishing trip or to the ballet), where the resolution is simplified by the need or desire to preserve the relationship.

These considerations bear on the interpretation of substantive differences in the classification of Type II conflicts and, of course, bear on the difficulty of resolving them. These substantive differences, however, do not lend themselves in any obvious systematic way to the question of the relative difficulty of resolving the different classes of Type II conflicts. In addition to the substantive character of a conflict, however, its structural characteristics may also be expected to affect the difficulty of resolving it. In which case, if it is easier to resolve one kind than another, then it may be worthwhile in the course of negotiation to direct attention to peaks and initial positions to change the conflict, not substantively, but structurally.

We turn, then, to more general structural properties of Type II conflicts which will permit the construction of a scale of difficulty independent of context. By means of the frontier of preference any two-person Type II conflict can, in principle, be structured in terms of a totally ordered scale of viable options, those between the two peaks, and covered by the inner branches of two adversarial preference functions, each monotone over the scale and with slopes of opposite sign. The relation of these preference functions to the scale of options may have profound effects on the relative difficulty of resolving Type II conflicts for structural reasons alone, as we will now suggest.

For this purpose, the simple classification of Type II conflicts as approach/approach, approach/avoidance, and avoidance/avoidance will be augmented by taking ordinal strength of preference into ac-

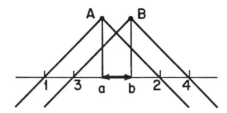

Figure 37: Viable options bounded by a–b

count. The result will yield as many as nine varieties of Type II conflicts and a metricized concept of distance between adversaries that will bear on the difficulty of resolving their conflicts.

We introduce this discussion with Figure 37 showing two SPFs labeled A and B with peaks at a and b, respectively, with a to the left of b on the scale of options. For simplicity and clarity we have adopted some notational conventions for this discussion. The SPFs are drawn with straight lines and pointed peaks and each SPF intersects the scale of options on the left and on the right of its peak reflecting the effects of status quo and background variables. These initial positions for A are labeled 1 and 2, to the left and right of a, respectively, and the intercepts for B are labeled 3 and 4 to the left and right of b, respectively.

The peaks and intercepts partition the scale of options into segments, and the figure is drawn with the boundaries of segments equally spaced. The reader is reminded, however, that the scale of options is only ordinal.

The range of viable options is bounded by the peaks of the two SPFs and this segment of the scale of options is indicated by a heavy line with arrows designating the boundaries. We see from the figure that in the range a-b all options have positive sign for both parties. We also note that the entire range of viable options is covered by the highest portion of the preference functions, their "upper ends," so we will refer to the strength of the ambience as "high" for each party (precise definitions of the ratings of strength are given below). It is to be understood, of course, that this reference to strength does not imply anything about comparability between parties but only relative strength of preference for each party separately (i.e., an ordinal scale of strength and strictly intrapersonal).

Note that the intercepts 1 and 3 could be in either order and the intercepts 2 and 4 could be in either order without affecting the bounds on the viable options. Because the viable options are an intact segment, not partitioned by initial positions, the ideals are in

Row	Ease of Resolution (1 = Easiest)	Segment	Ambience		Illustration	Distance Apart
			Sign (A/B)	Strength (A/B)		
1	1	a-b	app/app	high/high	Fig. 37	1
2		3-b	app/app	intermediate/-	Fig. 38(a)	2
3	2	3-2	app/app	low/low	Fig. 38(b)	3
4		a-2	app/app	-/intermediate	Fig. 39(a)	2
5	3	a-3	app/av	high/-	Fig. 38(a), Fig. 38(b)	2, 3
6		2-b	av/app	-/high	Fig. 39(a), Fig. 39(b)	2, 3
7	4	a-2	app/av	-/high	Fig. 39(b)	4
8		3-b	av/app	high/-	Fig. 39(b)	4
9	5	2-3	av/av	low/low	Fig. 39(b)	4

Table 3: Conjectured relation of the ambience of segments of options to ease of conflict resolution

some sense "closer"; the two parties are not far apart. Also, because these viable options have positive ambience and for each party the ambience is high, one might anticipate that on the basis of these structural characteristics only, conflicts of this variety might be the easiest of all to resolve.

This information is summarized in the first row of Table 3, as follows. We have an intact segment of viable options between the two peaks, *a-b*. The ambience is positive for both A and B so it is an approach/approach conflict; the ambience is at the highest positive end of the preference function for A and B, so it is indicated as high/high for A and B respectively. The conflict is displayed in Figure 37. It is conjectured to be the easiest of all varieties of Type II conflicts to resolve, so is rated "one" in the first column of Table 3.

Initial positions, however, can partition the scale of options between the peaks. In this case, different segments within the range of viable options represent conflicts with ambiences that differ in sign and strength and hence may differ in ease of resolution.

The strengths of the approach tendencies are rated high, low, -, or intermediate, defined as follows:

high: the range includes the peak but not the initial position.
low: the range includes the initial position but not the peak.
-:   the range includes the peak and the initial position.
intermediate: otherwise.

The strengths of avoidance tendencies are rated high, low, or -, defined as follows:

(a) a-3-b

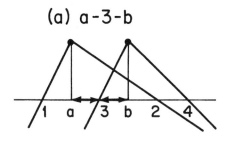

(b) a-3-2-b

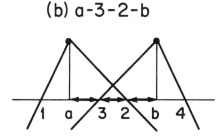

Figure 38: Viable options bounded by *a–3–b* and *a–3–2–b*

high: the range does not include the initial position.
low: the range includes the initial position and is cut off.
−: the range includes the initial position and is not cut off.

All further varieties of Type II conflicts are displayed in Figures 38 and 39 and are summarized in the remaining rows of Table 3. We will discuss rows 2 and 8 of the table to complete the notational conventions and to show how qualitative changes in conflicts may come about from structural changes alone.

In row 2, we are informed that a segment of viable options bounded by 3 and *b* (the bounds indicated by arrow heads) gives rise to an approach/approach conflict; that the strength of the ambience of the conflict over this segment is rated intermediate/− for A and B respectively; and that the conflict is illustrated in Figure 38(a). The last column of the table is explained in the next section.

In row 8 of the table we have another instance of a segment of viable options bounded by 3 and *b*. In this case, the segment is found in Figure 39(b), where we see that the ambience for A has become negative, so the conflict has changed radically and is qualitatively different. A's initial position 2 intersects the range of viable options

(a) a-2-b

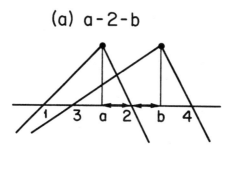

(b) a-2-3-b

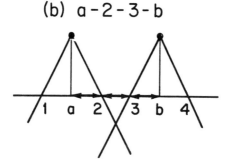

Figure 39: Viable options bounded by *a–2–b* and *a–2–3–b*

to the left of 3, so that A's preference function over the segment bounded by 3 and *b* is highly negative, and so indicated in the table. For B the ambience is positive and the range includes the peak and initial position so the strength is indicated by a – after the slash.

Each of the remaining rows of Table 3 corresponds to a segment of the scale of options of Figure 38 or 39 as indicated in the table and the reader can verify the summary offered in the table.

It might be pointed out that Figures 38(a) and 39(a) are essentially symmetrical structurally in that the conflict over the segment 3-*b* in Figure 38(a) is equivalent to that over *a*-2 in Figure 39(a) if the A and B labels are interchanged. Similarly the conflict over 2-*b* in Figure 39(a) and that over *a*-3 in Figure 38(a) are equivalent. This symmetry, however, is formal and not independent of the identity of A and B in substantive cases. See, for example, Schelling's (1960) criticism of Nash's symmetry condition in his bargaining solution.

It is interesting to note that high negative ambience when it occurs is always associated with positive ambience for the other party, see Figure 39(b), segments 3-*b* and *a*-2. These conflicts could be reminiscent of examples of seeking a raise or reducing wages, respectively.

The figures and the table reveal that there can be as many as nine varieties of Type II conflicts, conjecturally distributed over five levels of difficulty. This classification depends only on ordinal properties but takes into account the sign and strength of the ambience and the identification of the parties as A and B. There are four varieties of approach/approach, two varieties of approach/avoidance, two of avoidance/approach, and only one of avoidance/avoidance, the latter being one in which the ambience for both parties though negative is relatively low in strength for both of them.

High negative ambience only occurs associated with positive ambience for the other party, as already noted. This is an example of an interaction that could easily be interpreted as a psychological one whereas it is entirely structural in its origin.

We have seen that these nine varieties are conjectured to fall into five levels of difficulty indicated by the ranking in Table 3. There are really two things we are doing here and they should be distinguished: One is to point out structural features that might be related to the difficulty of reaching mutual agreement on an option and so are fertile areas for research; and the second is to conjecture what the relations between the structural features and the difficulty of reaching agreement might be. We hold no particular brief for these conjectures, as there are counter arguments. For example, the avoidance/avoidance conflict in row 9 of Table 3 we have rated as ninth, most difficult to resolve. However, the options in that segment are the most intermediate between the ideals and *both* parties are unhappy whereas a resolution in a segment on either side will have positive ambience for one party and be strongly negative for the other. The equity literature suggests that people don't like large disparities in outcomes. So this argument suggests that the resolution is most apt to be in the middle segment, but not that it would be easily reached. These conjectures are all empirical questions to be settled experimentally.

These nine varieties arise because we are examining segments of the viable options between two peaks as the viable options become partitioned by initial positions and we take no advantage of possible symmetries. We will next develop another approach to measuring the structural difficulty of resolving Type II conflicts by introducing a metric for the distance between peaks and we do take advantage of symmetries. This new concept is related to the development in this section but is a function of the entire range of viable options and not of each segment separately.

10.2   Distance Between Adversaries

Rhetorically it is not uncommon to speak of how far apart two adversaries are and of trying to bring them closer together. Although
our level of analysis of the structure of conflict does not lend itself
to a metric for distance *between options*, a metric is possible for the
distance *between adversaries*. The idea was introduced in the discussion of Figure 37 in which the viable options bounded by the ideals of
the two parties is an intact segment and hence an approach/approach
conflict with relatively high ambience was a basis for judging the two
parties to be "close" together. Let us pursue this reasoning further.

Suppose, for example, one were to visualize moving A and B further apart by changing A's ideal to an option on the left past B's
intercept 3, as in Figure 38(a).

Alternatively, we could have done the symmetric thing by changing B's ideal to an option on the right of A's intercept 2, as in Figure
39(a).

If we did both of these things, thereby moving A and B still further
apart, we would have Figure 38(b).

Finally, we could take one more step, and move A and B still
further apart until the order of the intercepts 3 and 2 was reversed to
form Figure 39(b).

The purpose of this "visualizing" is merely to convey the notion
that there is a useful sense, then, in which the adversaries may be
said to be closest together in the conflict portrayed in Figure 37;
next closest together in those conflicts portrayed by Figure 38(a) and
Figure 39(a). They may be said to be further apart in Figure 38(b)
and furthest apart in Figure 39(b).

It would be not unreasonable to anticipate that this order on the
distance between two parties would be related to the relative difficulty
of resolving their conflict, insofar as only structural characteristics
introduced here are considered. These results are in conformity with
common sense expectations that approach processes make resolution
easier and avoidance processes make it more difficult.

There are observations, however, which would degrade these distinctions between conflicts. In the language of game theory an ap-
proach/approach conflict is a variable but positive sum game, an
avoidance/avoidance conflict a negative sum game, and a zero sum
game would be an approach/avoidance conflict. Cooper (1985) remarks

> there is typical disagreement on the distribution of gains
> from cooperation. ... I was surprised to find that at its

core every negotiation is a zero sum game. Even when
there are substantial mutual gains to be had by all the
parties engaged in the negotiations, there is great disagreement over the distribution of gains or the sharing
of the costs. If the mutual gains are obvious, the negotiators quickly take them for granted and the bargaining
immediately focuses on the distribution of gains or costs.
(p. 30)

In our terms, this adaptation reflects the volatility of initial positions, which are less immune to misrepresentation than preference
orders and are more adaptable to circumstances.

That our concept of distance is a strictly subjective one and not
a metric on the scale of options may be seen as follows. Instead of
translating A's (or B's) ideals to make them further apart on the
scale of options, one could imagine the inner branches of their SPFs
having steeper slopes, reflecting a more rapid decay of preference,
and thereby transforming one figure into another. Figure 37 is transformed into Figure 38(a) if the inner branch of B's SPF reflects a
sufficiently rapid decay in preference over the viable options, so that
B's intercept labeled 3 is an option between a and b. In a very real
sense the options to the left of b are farther apart, from the point
of view of B's preference function, the steeper the slope of B's inner
branch. In a relative sense, the options in Figure 38(a) are farther
apart for B than they are for A.

Similarly, Figure 37 is transformed into Figure 39(a) if the slope
of the inner branch of A's SPF were increased so that A's intercept
labeled 2 is an option between a and b. Again, the adversaries have
not been moved farther apart with respect to their ideal options, a and
b, but only with respect to the decay of their preference functions over
the options between their ideals. Equivalently, it becomes relatively
more difficult to make concessions the steeper the slope of the inner
branch.

If the slopes of both inner branches have become steeper we get
Figure 38(b) first and then, finally, Figure 39(b).

This makes it clear that this concept of a distance between parties
in conflict has nothing to do with distance between their ideals on
the scale of options, which is only an ordinal scale in the first place,
but rather reflects an increasing "reluctance" to depart from their
respective ideals, a subjective metric.

It is possible to put a metric on the distance between parties in
a Type II conflict without any reference to distance on the scale of
options by taking advantage of the Kemeny metric on orderings. Ke-

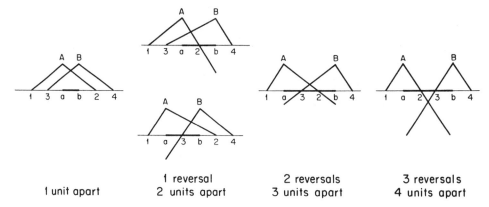

Figure 40: Distance between adversaries

Kemeny (1959) showed that the minimum number of interchanges of two adjacent elements required to transform one ordering into another satisfies the metric axioms. For example, the two orderings $a\,b\,c\,d\,e$ and $a\,b\,d\,c\,e$ are one unit apart because exactly one adjacent pair are reversed. The orderings $a\,b\,c\,d\,e$ and $a\,b\,e\,d\,c$ are three units apart because it takes three such permutations to convert one into the other. (A slightly different metric is used if ties are allowed.)

Figure 40 illustrates the four levels of Type II conflict using the Kemeny metric. On the left is the approach/approach conflict which we define to be one unit apart. Next are the two conflicts illustrated by Figures 38(a) and 39(a). They each require one pairwise reversal to reduce them to the approach/approach conflict so they are each one more unit apart (i.e., two units in all).

Adversaries three units apart are shown next and correspond to Figure 38(b); and finally, adversaries four units apart are as far apart as they can get and the figure corresponds to Figure 39(b).

Note that only reversals under the inner branches are relevant, as they cover the viable options. In other words, the ordering of intercepts to the left of a and to the right of b are irrelevant to this index of distance between adversaries. We have entered in the last column of Table 3 the distances between adversaries bounding the scale of viable options to which each row (a segment of the scale of options) belongs. The five levels in Column 1 of Table 3 pertain to *segments* of the scale of options, and the four levels indicated in the last column pertain to the *entire* scale of viable options. That these concepts are closely related appears obvious, and indicates a rich opportunity for empirical exploration.

This metric is technically an absolute scale having a natural zero point and counting a natural unit, pairwise permutations, that is indivisible. One must avoid, however, getting an exaggerated impression of its generality. Given distances between adversaries in different conflicts or between different adversaries in the same conflict are almost certainly not equally easy to traverse, any more than a given distance between cities is always equally difficult to traverse. If, however, one can shorten the distance in any particular instance it certainly becomes easier to traverse. So also must it be in resolving a conflict.

The context of a conflict introduces many factors besides these structural characteristics that affect the difficulty of resolving it, so across different conflicts these ratings of difficulty would not apply. But in any particular substantive instance, shifting initial positions by changes in the status quo and/or background variables can be as effective as changing ideal points in reducing the rating of the difficulty of resolving any particular conflict. One effect may be easier to induce than another.

One might push this speculation on the difficulty of resolution a bit further. Consider Figure 38(a). The viable options, those between the two peaks, a and b, are divided into segments, a-3 and 3-b, an approach/avoidance segment, and an approach/approach segment, respectively. One might expect, then, that the resolution would tend to be in the segment 3-b rather than in the segment a-3, especially if failure to agree means retaining the status quo, for B will refuse to accept an option worse than the status quo. *Mutatis mutandis* for Figure 39(a).

In Figure 38(b) we have a low approach/approach conflict between two approach/avoidance conflicts, and one would suspect that the resolution would tend to be an option in the central approach/approach segment.

Figure 39(b) presents a particularly recalcitrant conflict; it is a low avoidance/avoidance conflict embedded between two approach/avoidance conflicts in which the avoidance component in each case is high. It is a case in which somebody is going to be awfully unhappy or else neither will be satisfied with the outcome but probably glad to have it over with.

What this discussion reveals is that the zero point on the signed ordinal scale of each party is a significant step toward interpersonally comparable utility and is vulnerable to strategic manipulation and outside intervention due to its relation to the status quo and initial positions.

It must be recognized that the locus of a peak and of the intercepts are inherently independent except for their rank order, and the conjunction of two SPFs over a common total ordering of options forms an ordering of the six points as shown in Table 3. There is no possible monotone rescaling of the options that can change the joint ordering of peaks and intercepts.

It is obvious that a procedure for resolving conflict which requires that the opposing parties reveal their preference orderings is going to be resisted, in the first place, and if that is overcome, is going to entice misrepresentation in one way or another (i.e., by exaggeration and by dissembling). We speculate here on the pros and cons of misrepresentation.

Consider the following two scenarios:

1. Suppose that B dissembles by insisting that intercept number 3 is between a and b, as in Figure 38(a), so the approach/approach options are between 3 and b, and a solution in that interval is to B's advantage.

2. Alternatively, suppose that A dissembles by exaggerating A's ideal to make it appear to the left of the number 3 intercept.

Either of these two scenarios would transform the conflict from that displayed in Figure 37 to that displayed in Figure 38(a). That is, B's misrepresentation of B's initial position, which would seem to be to B's advantage, would also be achieved by A's misrepresentation of A's ideal. The argument, of course, is symmetric, so if the roles were reversed the effect would be represented by the transformation from Figure 37 to that of Figure 39(a).

This argument leads to the conclusion that neither party should dissemble by exaggerating its ideal, as this would work to the other party's advantage. The argument, however, is fragile. The two scenarios are different even though they lead to the same formal structure. B's involves the decay of B's inner branch, protesting that any compromise beyond (to the left of) intercept 3 is out of bounds. A's involves exaggerating the ideal, moving further away from B's ideal in a different sense, by "asking for the moon." So although the formal structure is the same, the psychological environments of the two scenarios are different and may well affect the assessment and behavior of a mediator or the decision of an adjudicator differently.

If the strategies are perceived by the adversaries as we have initially put them, then the conclusion is that it would be better for A to dissemble with respect to the number 2 intercept instead of with respect to the ideal. In which case, with both parties misrepresenting their accept/reject threshhold, the conflict becomes that represented by Figure 38(b) or that represented by Figure 39(b).

In other words, both parties are driven to appear as far apart as possible but it is better to do so by exaggerating their unwillingness to concede rather than by exaggerating their ideals. The further implication is that mediation would be more effectively directed at changing initial positions rather than at changing ideals.

These same effects may occur in a natural way in the case of a strike. As the reserves of the strikers and the company deteriorate over time, the initial positions move from the avoidance/avoidance pattern of Figure 39(b) toward that of Figure 38(b) and the strike can be settled.

We would like to emphasize that these are gratuitous speculations and there are good arguments for alternative scenarios and conclusions. We mention these only to provide stimulation and guidance on what seem to us empirically researchable problems that are of some significance.

The best resolution of a Type II conflict is one which is mutually acceptable to both parties (i.e., at least as good as the status quo), and this implies an approach/approach conflict. Thus, for example, the very difficult conflict portrayed in Figure 39(b) requires reversing the order of intercepts 2 and 3. Reversing the order of this pair of intercepts excludes avoidance/avoidance conflicts and transforms the situation into that of one of the other figures, in each of which there is one segment of viable options with positive ambience for both parties. This transformation can be accomplished by shifting the ideal points or, independently, manipulating the status quo and hence, the initial positions. Such transformations are not only a structural matter but a substantive one, and there are more possibilities than there are individuals in conflict. This raises the question of the generality of empirical research on these problems, and to what extent the conclusions are context bound. The question is too open and further speculation does not seem profitable at this time.

Chapter 11

Multiparty Conflicts and Election Systems

When there are more than two parties involved in a conflict and one option to be chosen, a common final step in making a decision is a voting procedure. It may be preceded by debate and discussion, but after that some sense of consensus is sought — usually by means of a vote.

11.1 Majority Vote and Intransitivity

There is one voting mechanism (set of rules) for the resolution of multiparty conflicts in a democracy that is readily available and highly approved. That is decision by majority choice, which as a mechanism, weights individuals equally by giving one vote to each. Unfortunately, this mechanism turns out to have some serious defects except in the simple case of exactly two options or two candidates. When there are three or more options, the natural extension of majority choice to a pairwise elimination procedure can be intransitive, as was pointed out by Condorcet (1785). A consequence of this is that the outcome may be strategically manipulated by controlling the order in which comparisons are made.

Suppose, for example, that we have three options, a, b, and c, and two-thirds of the electorate prefer a over b, two-thirds prefer b over c, and two-thirds prefer c over a.

These pairwise majority choices are intransitive and could arise from individual preferences which are themselves transitive. For example, if one-third of the electorate had the preference ordering $a\,b\,c$, another one-third had the preference ordering $b\,c\,a$, and the rest had the preference ordering $c\,a\,b$, the pairwise majority choices above would arise if all voters expressed their true preference.

This intransitivity is a matter of serious concern because the consequence is that a pairwise elimination procedure by majority choice (a common procedure in legislatures) will end up with a different winner depending on which pair is tested first. For example, if a and b were tested first, b would be eliminated and a tested against c would yield c as the winner. If the elimination procedure began with the pair b and c, then a would win, and if it began with a and c, then b would win.

The source of the concern is that this procedure provides an opportunity to play strategic games by manipulating the agenda. Such manipulation is clearly undesirable in a system intended to express the will of the majority. Consequently, a number of election systems have been proposed in which the voter provides a complete preference ordering on the three or more options, and then the set of preference orderings are aggregated according to some rule. A familiar one is Plurality which uses only the first choice of each voter; another, the Borda system, averages the ranks of each candidate; a third, sometimes called the Hare system, is a sequential elimination procedure that may use the entire preference ordering of each voter to arrive at a winner.

Arrow (1963) showed that no such system can be without fault, so choosing a system is a matter of the seriousness of different faults and the sensitivity of a system to each. This is an area with a substantial theoretical literature which it is inappropriate to review here in greater detail; the reader is referred to Fishburn (1973) and to Sen (1970) for further reading.

11.2   Effect of Single Peakedness

Single peakedness enters into the aggregation of preference orders in the following manner. Note that, in the previous example, the three preference orderings $a\,b\,c$, $b\,c\,a$, and $c\,a\,b$ cannot be generated by single peaked functions over the same ordering because they end in three different options. If there were a common ordering underlying the three preference functions, then the preference orderings could only end in one of two different options (a necessary but not sufficient condition).

However, if all individual preferences are single peaked over the same ordered set of options, majority choice will also be single peaked.

This is a well-known result (see Luce & Raiffa, 1957) and may be easily shown as follows. Assume there are three ordered options, $a <$ $b < c$ and that all individual preference orderings are single peaked. If we suppose the contrary, that majority choice is not single peaked, then a majority would prefer a to b and a majority would prefer c to b, thereby violating single peakedness. But the two majorities must have at least one individual in common who, then, must prefer a to b and prefer c to b, contradicting the hypothesis that all preference orderings are single peaked.

Under this condition, that all voters' preference functions be single peaked, majority choice would have the certainty of optimally matching the will of the people in the same sense that single peakedness does for an individual. It would be invulnerable to strategic manipulation and voters could not gain an advantage by misrepresenting their preferences. There is empirical evidence from some substantial election data, however, which indicates that even in the absence of individual SPFs, the occurrence of intransitive majority choice may not be as likely as feared (Chamberlin, Cohen, & Coombs, 1984; Coombs, Cohen, & Chamberlin, 1984; Fishburn, 1986).

A constraint necessary to ensure that every voter will have a single peaked preference function under the other assumptions of Type I theory, is, as we have seen, that the options constitute an efficient set. This is certainly not a condition that can be imposed on political candidates freely chosen, nor can they even be required to constitute a Pareto optimal set! We may note, however, that each candidate is to some degree a portfolio of decisions (tradeoffs) on a number of issues and so may be regarded as analogous to the end product of a single negotiable text (see Chapter 8). If the concept of the frontier of preference could be generalized to multiparty conflict, then the desirable properties of majority choice would be more nearly assured (see Section 11.4).

A voting system is not the only mechanism for resolving multiparty conflicts, of course. A most complex example is the multinational agreement on the Law of the Sea (Borgese, 1983), a natural extension of procedures already discussed, like negotiation, but with greater complexities (see also Section 14.2). Also, resolution of a multiparty conflict may be imposed, as when a President issues a decree in the public interest, or a manager or a judge or an administrator interprets a rule or principle. Any conflict of any type can be resolved by a third party with sufficient power to enforce the decision.

11.3   The Jury System

There are some special circumstances in which single peakedness is achievable in the voting process. Our jury system is a case in point. This differs from other voting systems in that it requires unanimity of first choice. When there are three or more options, as in deciding between first and second degree murder, manslaughter, or not guilty, or in deciding on the amount of damages to be awarded a plaintiff, each juror could have a single peaked preference function over the options because the options have a common ordering. If the foreman of the jury merely took a vote, then majority decision would be transitive and would yield an optimal decision in the sense of averaging the will of the jurors.

The search for certainty "beyond a reasonable doubt" is presumed to be more closely approached by requiring unanimity of the 12 jurors than a majority choice. It would seem that justice is better served. In the late 14th century, when unanimity of a jury of 12 was first universally required, it was not always easily achieved. Deprivation of food was sometimes resorted to by judges to coerce unanimity (Encyl. Brit., 1973, 13, p. 160).

Unanimity ceased to be required of United Kingdom juries several years ago. The argument was that requiring unanimity made it easier to secure improper acquittals because only a single juror had to be corrupted. An analysis in terms of signal detectability theory might be relevant here; the higher the level of agreement required of a jury the lower the hit rate (fewer of the guilty convicted) and the lower the false alarm rate (more of the innocent set free). The question is whether the ratio of hits to false alarms changes systematically with the level of agreement required of a jury and what the optimal level is for a just society, as both kinds of errors are inevitable in a "noisy" environment. This, of course, assumes a criterion of guilty/not guilty other than the legal one.

11.4   An Extension of the Frontier of Preference to Election Data

In the study of Type II conflicts in previous chapters, the conflicts were between just two parties, or, if they involved many individuals, could essentially be reduced to two parties such as Labor and Management.

In the case of conflicts involving many individuals who do not coalesce into two polarized parties, a common mechanism for making a decision is to run an election.

If, in pairwise comparisons, one option is chosen over each of the others by a majority choice, it is called a Condorcet winner. A Condorcet winner, if one exists, is generally regarded as a "fair" or "best" choice. But when there are more than two options, a Condorcet winner may not exist and for an election system to be decisive (i.e., not end up in a draw) some other system must be used. None of these other systems is regarded as superior in all instances.

With more than two options, the frontier of preference would go a long way toward ensuring a Condorcet winner, particularly if the options are as complex as candidates. Candidates necessarily have different positions; each is a bundle of "positions" forged in the image of a constituency. A set of candidates, then, are far from the ordered set of optimal options that would constitute the frontier of preference.

An advantage of a two party system is that if both parties prefer some option to another, the latter is dominated and neglected or, in the case of a candidate, may withdraw, leading to a frontier of preference. With more than two parties, the options that survive, even if Pareto optimal in the sense of *some* party preferring each member of a pair, are not necessarily totally ordered, and reaching an acceptable resolution is made more difficult.

In order to help make majority choice an effective decision mechanism for a multiparty conflict, we propose for further investigation a filtering procedure for constructing a frontier of preference for a multiparty conflict with multiple options (e.g., candidates). The procedure involves polarizing the many preference orderings to form a polarized conflict and construct a frontier of preference by filtering the candidates.

We seek two preference orderings to represent hypothetical parties, A and B. The following procedure is proposed.

1. Let $S = a, b, \ldots$ be a set of candidates (options). The data needed are the pairwise preferences of each voter. If the original observations are complete rank orders they must be decomposed into pairwise preferences.

2. Aggregate the pairwise preferences to determine the pairwise percentages for the electorate as a whole.

3. Let x, y in S be the pair of candidates for which the proportion preferring x over y is as close as possible to .50 but no smaller than .50. Select the subset of voters who have preferred x to z for all z in S, call them the A group; and select the subset

of voters who prefer y to z for all z in S, and call them the B group. If either of these subgroups is empty pass on to the next pair for which the proportion choosing x over y, $p(x, y)$, is nearest .50.

4. Taking x as the ideal point for the A group, calculate the pairwise proportions $p(x, z)$ for all z in S, and rank order these proportions from .5 to 1.0. This yields the preference order for A.

5. Taking y as the ideal point for the B group, construct the preference order for B using the proportions $p(y, z)$ for all z in S and order them from .5 to 1.0.

6. Following the algorithm described in Section 9.1, construct the frontier of preference. This will yield a totally ordered subset of candidates and the possibility that majority choice would be transitive is enhanced.

7. Over the subset of options on this frontier, determine the majority choice using the total electorate. If majority choice is not transitive or there is a violation of single peakedness, the choice of a winner is not affected unless the first three candidates in the majority choice ordering are the culprits. The treatment of this case is discussed in Section 9.4 in the extension of the frontier to Type I conflict.

A $p(x, y)$ close to .50 could be a consequence of either of two states of affairs: the pair x and y may be nearly indistinguishable or the electorate is split nearly equally between them. The correlation between A's and B's preference ordering can distinguish these two states of affairs. If the correlation is positive, then x and y are similar and $p(x, y)$ close to .50 merely indicates a difficult discrimination. If the correlation is negative, then they are discriminated and the electorate is almost evenly split between them.

By reducing all preference orderings to only those options on the frontier of preference between A and B, the distribution of first place votes can be used to determine the median voter whose first choice would correspond to the majority choice.

If there are different solutions given by different pairs x, y, then a choice among these may be made using the pairwise preferences of the entire electorate.

We explored this procedure empirically using election data for five separate elections of the American Psychological Association (APA). The data are described in some detail in Coombs, Cohen, and Chamberlin (1984), so will only be briefly summarized here. The data are

Ordering By Majority Choice: dabec

Complete Ballots: 5,168
Total Ballots: 11,560
Membership: 42,028

Pair	$p(x,y)$	A	B	F/P	$\tau(A,B)$	Condorcet Winner
be	.507	984 bdcea	956 ebcda	be	+.2	No
ec	.525	ebcda	611 cdbea	ebc	0	No
bc	.546	bdcea	cdbea	bdc	+.4	Yes
ab	.556	1389 adceb	bdcea	adb	−.4	Yes
da	.562	1308 dabce	ebcda	da	+.4	Yes
ae	.562	adceb	cdbea	adce	−.8	Yes
ac	.588	adceb	cdbea	adc	−.2	Yes
db	.617	dabce	bdcea	db	+.2	Yes
de	.633	dabce	ebcda	dbe	−.6	Yes
dc	.644	dabce	cdbea	dc	0	Yes

Table 4: 1976 Election

from five annual elections for President-elect of the American Psychological Association run in 1976, 1978, 1979, 1980, and 1981. Members of the association ranked as many of the candidates as they wished; the election was run according to the Hare system, that is, at each cycle the candidates were ranked on the basis of the number of first place votes they had received. If no candidate had a majority of the votes, then the candidate with the fewest first place votes was eliminated, the candidates below the eliminated one in each voter's preference ranking were raised one notch, and another cycle was run. Cycling was continued until one candidate had a majority. Over the five elections there was an average of 14,010 ballots returned with an average of 5,831 complete rank orders of the five candidates. Only the complete ballots were used in this analysis.

In Table 4 we report the analysis for the 1976 election and in Table 5 we summarize the analyses of the five elections. The heading of Table 4 indicates the ordering by majority choice, the number of complete ballots, the total number of ballets returned, and the total membership of the association that year. The candidates are labeled a, b, c, d, e. In none of the five elections was there an intransitive cycle by majority choice.

We followed the procedure outlined above for extending the frontier of preference to an election except that we took every pair instead of preselecting.

The first column on the left of the table indicates a pair of candidates and the second column the proportion of pairwise preferences for the one on the left over the one on the right. Beginning with the proportion nearest .50 in the first row, the pair is b and e and the proportion choosing b over e is .507. In the column labeled A is the preference order determined by the majority choice of all and only those voters whose preference order began with candidate b. In this case their preference order is $b\,d\,c\,e\,a$. In column B the preference order is given that is obtained by majority choice of all and only those voters whose preference orders began with candidate e. In this case their preference order is $e\,b\,c\,d\,a$.

In each election all 120 possible preference orderings occurred, and over the five elections the highest frequency is 201, the lowest 6. In the 1976 election the cumulative frequency over the 20 preference orders that have b as first choice is 984 and for those that begin with e it is 956.

The only candidates that survive the screening for the frontier of preference are b and e, shown in the column headed F/P.

The rank order correlation between the two opposed preference orders is $+.2$ and, as the Condorcet winner for the total election is d, we see that the frontier based on the orderings provided by the pair be does not contain the Condorcet winner.

The intent of the procedure is to make a solution by majority choice emerge when one does not exist in the total election, and we are making this analysis to test the proposed criteria for guiding the procedure. If, in some instance, the procedure fails to yield the Condorcet winner when one is known to exist, then the criteria are not adequate. We have here two criteria, a $p(x,y)$ of .507 and a $\tau(A,B) = +.2$. The evidence so far is that these are suspect.

In Table 4 for the year 1976, we see that the Condorcet winner appears on eight of the 10 instances: all those in which $\tau(A,B)$ is negative (four times), one instance in which $\tau(A,B)$ is zero, and three in which $\tau(A,B)$ is positive. These numbers are reported as ratios in the first row of Table 5, which reports the ratios for all elections.

In the more detailed analysis of which Table 5 is a summary, no relation was observed between $p(x,y)$, which ranged from .501 to .647, and the appearance of the Condorcet winner on the frontier.

We see from Table 5 that out of the 50 tests, 26 had negative

	$\tau(A, B)$		
	-	0	+
1976	4/4	1/2	3/4
1978	4/5	1/2	1/3
1979	5/5	2/2	2/3
1980	6/6	0/0	1/4
1981	6/6	0/1	1/3
Overall	25/26	4/7	8/17

Table 5: Proportion of Condorcet winners on frontier of preference as a function of $\tau(A, B)$

τ's and in 25 of these 26 the Condorcet winner in the total election appeared on the frontier. In the other 24 instances τ is zero or positive and in only half of these cases was the Condorcet winner present.

In the one instance in which τ is negative and the Condorcet winner did not appear, $\tau(A, B) = -.2$.

In conclusion it would appear that $p(x, y)$ is not very relevant, but that a negative $\tau(A, B)$ is critical.

These results, however, are not conclusive. What we find here is that if a Condorcet winner exists, these screenings to obtain a total ordering of options will include the Condorcet winner with high probability. What one does not know is whether, if a Condorcet winner does not exist in the total election, one would appear on the frontier of preference? While it is the case that a Condorcet winner is not assured, it seems that the total ordering of the frontier greatly increases its likelihood.

In the absence of a Condorcet winner, then, the procedure that is recommended is that the frontier of preference be constructed for some (highly) negative $\tau(A, B)$ and then either of two procedures be followed:

1. rerun the election using the totally ordered slate that constitutes the frontier, or, if economy is critical,

2. reprocess the original profile of preference orderings, deleting those candidates not on the frontier.

Chapter 12

A Summary, Some Correspondences, and a Transition

12.1   Summary of Part II

This summary emphasizes continuity, and is essentially integrative. It is not a detailed review of the content of Part II. Only what we consider the more important elements in the development of the structure of conflict are included.

There is some underlying order to the sequence of the first 7 chapters of Part II that should be made explicit. Chapters 5, 7, 9, and 11 are concerned with Type II conflicts of increasing complexity from the point of view of structure. Chapters 5, 7, and 9 deal with increasingly complex options but all are two-party conflicts. Then chapter 11 increases complexity by considering conflicts between more than two parties.

In Chapter 5, the minimum level of the complexity of the options is due to the natural and unique ordering on the options, the number of children. In Chapter 7, the options are in exactly two dimensions and so have no natural ordering. In Chapter 9, the options may be of any dimensionality and of any qualitative complexity. In Chapter 11, the options may be as complex as those considered in Chapter 9, such as candidates for office might be, and increased complexity is introduced by there being more than two opposing preference orderings.

Chapters 6, 8, and 10 are "interstitial connectives" that pursue related problems and developments of interest and concern in their own

177

right. Chapter 6 discusses the measurement of utility, interpersonal comparability of utility, the role of power, and the complex problems of fairness and justice.

Chapter 8 discusses the construction of options when there are multiple criteria or multiple conflicting goals and options need to be contrived, fashioned by knowledgeable experts immersed in the issues. This is the complex reality for which the frontier of preference provides structure. The frontier effectively simplifies the environment by reducing the candidates for choice by focusing attention on those that are not dominated by any others. Further structure is provided by their being ordered between the adversaries. The value of the frontier of preference lies in providing an optimal set of options in the sense of minimizing concession, its weakness lies in that it calls for some rationality in what is usually a highly charged atmosphere.

The variety of Type II conflicts is discussed in Chapter 10 in terms of the motivational processes induced by the conjunction of the SPFs with the scale of options. Using ordinal relations on the strength of the motivational processes, the three conventional varieties of conflict, approach/approach, approach/avoidance, and avoidance/avoidance, can be further divided to provide as many as nine varieties. We conjecture a weak ordering on their difficulty of resolution based only on structure. This conjecture provides some guidance to strategies that could facilitate resolution. We then take a further step and introduce a metric for the conventional notion of distance between adversaries. Using the Kemeny metric, there may be from one to four units of distance between adversaries with SPFs over a common totally ordered set of options. We show how these are related to the nine varieties of Type II conflict, and how they might bear on strategies for resolving conflict.

The discussion of multiparty conflicts, in Chapter 11, is primarily focused on their resolution by voting processes. Some of the problems with such systems are discussed, including the jury system. Again, a most serious source of difficulty in resolving the conflict is the structure, or lack of it, on the options; so an ad hoc procedure for seeking a frontier of preference for multiparty conflicts is suggested and explored empirically.

We may characterize the Type II conflict as one in which the process of resolution involves seeking a compromise which all parties will accept, even if reluctantly, just as an individual must accept a compromise when torn between incompatible goals. The only rational alternative in either case is to seek or create more acceptable alternatives. But the goals may still remain incompatible and so a compromise remains inevitable.

The differences between Type I and Type II conflict arise from the fact that each party brings only part of the structure to a Type II conflict that the single individual brings to a Type I. Fitting together the separate contributions from two parties gives rise to difficult and interesting problems, some of which are amenable to rational solution.

12.2 Correspondences Between Type I and Type II Conflict

The correspondences between Type I and Type II conflict may be summarized in terms of three conditions: proper utility functions, a proper preference function, and an efficient set of options. This structure from Type I conflict was used to model the Type II conflict with the following correspondences and consequences:

1. In a Type I conflict the opposing proper utility functions, representing incompatible goals, are replaced in a Type II conflict with the inner branches of two SPFs, one from each of the opposing parties. The inner branches correspond to monotone preference functions over the viable options but do not satisfy the definition of proper utility functions unless the individuals' proper preference functions are restricted (e.g., to additivity).

2. In a Type I conflict the proper preference function is a generalization of a rule for combining component-wise utility functions to form a total preference. In a Type II conflict, its role is played by a decision function, a rule, formula, or procedure for choosing the option which is to hold for both adversaries. Problems of interpersonal comparability of utility arise. Even if these were solved, and they are not, there remain the ethical problems of equity, fairness, justice, morality, and the role of power. All of these are normative issues and matters of judgment and opinion. That this decision function would satisfy the conditions of a proper preference function (or a proper additive difference function) is seriously open to doubt.

3. A necessary and sufficient condition for the existence of SPFs in a Type I conflict, given a proper preference function is the

existence of an efficient set of options. The existence of an efficient set in a Type I conflict is not a naturally occurring phenomenon and, in general, can only be contrived in the laboratory. The individual, by neglecting dominated alternatives, can screen them to select a Pareto optimal set, but such a set is not, in general, efficient, and not, in general, even totally ordered. This is probably the principal reason for the infrequent occurrence of SPFs in Type I conflict, a totally ordered set of options being a necessary condition for the existence of an efficient set which will ensure that proper preference functions and proper additive difference models will be single peaked.

In a Type II conflict the space of options is screened to form the frontier of preference. This frontier is a totally ordered set of options that are optimal in that the choice of any option not on the frontier requires unnecessary concessions from one or both parties. But this frontier is not an efficient set, and hence multi-peakedness in traversing the frontier of preference is inevitable. As a consequence, there are local maxima which seem more fair to one of the parties than others in the neighborhood and hence are barriers to further concession. A true or global maximum is undefined and hence unrecognizable in the absence of a decision function, and probably based on some comparison of utilities. Hence, the search for a solution is along a bumpy road and not even an exhaustive search can ensure a *best* solution but only a nondominated one.

In comparison with Type I conflict, however, the frontier of preference provides a totally ordered set of options which is not generally the case in a Type I conflict. So we are assured that the two parties have monotone preferences over the frontier, one increasing as the other is decreasing. In this respect, the structure of the options, no matter how complex they may be, is such that the resolution of a Type II conflict is made easier than in very complex Type I conflicts. On the other hand, in other respects the inner branches and their aggregation are more difficult to work with in Type II than in Type I, and so the resolution of Type II conflicts can face difficulties for structural reasons, as we have seen, even in the absence of ill-will or evil intent. It is not unusual, then, to turn to a third party for assistance in resolving such conflicts (e.g., a mediator, negotiator, arbitrator, or adjudicator, depending on the degree of power allocated). We discuss this further in Chapter 13 under the topic transformations of type.

12.3 Relation Between Type II and Type III Conflict

Let us return for the moment to the general problem of the classification of types of conflict. In Part I we discussed the theory of individual preferential choice and we reinterpreted preferential choice as the resolution of a conflict within an individual torn between incompatible goals.

In Part II we discussed a type of social conflict which occurs between individuals because they want different things and must settle for the same thing. It was most important, here, to recognize the parallel between the structures of Type I and Type II conflict. Each serves as a metaphor for the other, but the differences give rise to unique problems which constitute much of the content of Part II.

Now, if conflict may occur between individuals because they want different things and must settle for the same thing, then there must logically be another type of social conflict, conflict that occurs between individuals because they want the same thing and must settle for different things. We call this third type, Type III, and these three types must exhaust the domain of conflict.

In the preceding section we emphasized the differences between Type I and Type II that bear upon the relative difficulty of resolving them. Now, however, we want to emphasize something they have in common that distinguishes them both from Type III.

The source of the commonality in the structure of Type I and Type II conflict lies in the fact that in both cases a single entity exists and an acceptable resolution is one which preserves it. In a Type I conflict this entity is the individual. In a Type II conflict the entity is anything that creates a bond, a relationship, a sense of community or solidarity. In our examples, the entity was a family, a business corporation, and a political entity. Individuals are components, members of, the entity, and a resolution is sought which will preserve the bond, the relationship, so compromise is usually involved.

In a Type III conflict, to which we turn next, no entity exists or the intent to preserve it is abandoned (e.g., the couple decides to get a divorce, the company is driven out of business, two countries war over an island).

The distinction between Type II and Type III conflict is closely related to the distinction between internal and external conflict recognized in sociological literature since Simmel (1904), see for example, Bernard (1957). It is Bernard's theory that conflict arises because there are mutually exclusive goals espoused by different parties; an internal conflict is between segments of a total system and, in an external conflict, one whole system expects to benefit at the expense of the other if it wins.

Part III

Type III Conflict

conflict that arises between individuals who want the same thing and have to settle for different things

Preview

The parties in a Type III conflict are not restrained by seeking to preserve an entity of which they are both a part or to gain some common goal. We discuss the structure of such conflicts and their resolution, with emphasis on the transformation of Type III conflicts into Type II or Type I. Some developments in higher game theory are interpreted in this light and as efforts to contain escalation.

A major part of our analysis involved the distinction between those aspects of conflict that reflect what is brought to the conflict by the individuals involved and those aspects that reflect the characteristics of the options available. In the final chapter, we briefly review the ideas that provide the foundation for this distinction and review its consequences for the various types of conflict. We point out the sense in which Type II and Type III are extreme characterizations of a continuum generated by the relation between the self-interest and the mutual interest within each of the parties involved. In a final section we offer some more personal conclusions which have emerged in the course of our study of conflict.

Chapter 13

Type III Conflict

13.1 The Nature of Type III Conflict

In Section 12.3 the principal contrast between Type II and Type III conflict was discussed, this being the existence, in Type II, of a compelling need to seek agreement whereas, in Type III, self-interest dominates. The options in a Type III conflict are courses of action, available to each party separately, which jointly result in an outcome. In a Type III conflict the parties do not negotiate over outcomes; there is no process in which the parties seek agreement on an outcome which will hold for both, the parties are unilaterally choosing between courses of action which are once removed from their outcomes.

There are two cases that we will use to illustrate the range and characteristics of Type III conflicts. One is competitive sports and the other is conflict between sovereign states. In the former case, both antagonists want to win, to be champion. In the latter case, two countries are seeking hegemony over a target, one over the other or each over the same territory. In each case they want the same thing but can't both have it. We pick these examples because of the difference between them in the extent to which third parties have the power to control escalation.

Competitive sports and, in particular, professional sports of all kinds, illustrate some of the essential characteristics of Type III conflict. Each party seeks to impose its will on the other. The typical pattern of a Type III conflict consists of a sequence of actions and reactions sequentially selected by each party. The posture is aggressive, and persuasion is subordinated to power.

It may seem facetious but these distinctions are well illustrated by a tennis match. The options are not the final score, as they could be if the match were an exhibition in which the parties reached an agreement beforehand (i.e., a Type II conflict). Instead, the options are the actions available in the repertoire of each player, and the outcome is uncertain. The courses of action available to one party may not be known in full to the other party and the outcome of a sequence of choices can only be conjectured.

In the case of competitive sports, sportsmanship, courtesy, altruism, morality, etc., are deterrents to escalation but are less reliable deterrents the more there is at stake. There is little that makes losing attractive and increasing the reward of the winner makes losing even less so. So in competitive sports there are umpires to enforce rules and impose penalties. In professional sports, where more is at stake, escalation is more difficult to control and umpires sometimes need to be backed up by higher levels of authority with wider powers. But competitive sports are an acceptable form of Type III conflict for the obvious reasons of being of benefit to many and because escalation is controlled. The options available to the opponents are relatively well specified and predictable, so they are highly practiced and the quality and effectiveness of execution contribute to the entertainment value of such Type III conflicts.

A more extreme form of Type III conflict is that between sovereign states seeking an objective that can only be possessed by one. Usually, there is no third party with power to control escalation nor is there a higher entity creating a bond strong enough to overcome self-interest or impose restraint. The sequence of unilateral actions and reactions may only be controlled by the parties themselves and by their fear of consequences.

13.1.1   Conflict Resolution in the Animal Kingdom

Type III conflicts are found in nature, both within and between species. Trivers (1985), discussing parent-offspring conflict, describes the course of parental attitude in pigeons as passing from early solicitude to avoiding their chicks when they are nearly fully fledged, when the chicks often attack their parents, crowding them into corners and begging for food. Among langur monkeys and baboons conflict over weaning occurs. "The infant utters a series of piercing cries in its efforts to beg milk from mother and may retaliate fiercely when rebuffed" (p.145).

Intraspecies Type III conflicts are generally resolved by an established pecking order, a power hierarchy arrived at through play and bluster or ritualized aggression characterized by restraint with built-in submission signals (see Lorenz, 1966). Smith and Price (1973), using computer simulation of various styles of intraspecies conflict, concluded that being prepared to fight but not to the death, a style they called limited war, was the most conducive to species survival.

Gilbert (1987) seems to come to the same conclusion:

> Zoological evidence strongly suggests that for virtually all creatures, direct win-lose contests are risky and inefficient last-resort options for getting things, and are therefore best avoided. To this end many species have developed communicative, social and territorial behaviors aimed at forestalling head-to-head brawls. (p. 78)

Interspecies Type III conflicts are reduced by the principle of competitive exclusion (Hardin, 1960; Mayr, 1970), which asserts that two competitive species cannot coexist in a single ecological niche, and generally seem to have little relevance for the study of social conflict between humans. The conflict between a predator and its prey, which might be regarded as the most escalated form of Type III conflict, seems to be even less relevant.

There is at least some evidence, however, that some cases of intraspecies Type III conflict are relevant to the human one. Desmond Morris, perhaps indulging in a little hyperbole, writes in the introduction to *Chimpanzee Politics* (de Waal, 1982) that:

> The apes, when carefully studied, reveal themselves to be adept at subtle political maneuvers. Their social life is full of take-overs, dominance networks, power struggles, alliance, divide-and-rule, strategies, coalitions, arbitration, collective leadership, privileges and bargaining. There is hardly anything that occurs in the corridors of power of the human world that cannot be found in embryo in the social life of a chimpanzee colony. (p. 14)

We will see, before we're through, that there is a kind of continuum between Type II and Type III that is a function of a willingness to concede some self-interest to preserve a relationship, on the one hand, and the dominance of self-interest over a common interest, on the other. Type II and Type III conflicts are characterized by volatile states of mind in different heads. Type II lends itself to compromise, but if self-interest is dominant in either head then Type III results, and that lends itself to escalation.

What is of interest to us in the case of the great apes is that they manage Type III conflicts, and resolve them, without serious escalation. For example, reconciliation of two males by an adult female as mediator (but never one with sexual swelling) is described by de Waal as varying from subtle to more or less forced contact between the males. In one instance it reduced the tension but the conflict continued for a period of over 2 months but never escalated beyond a few bites on limbs.

There is litle in the summary by Morris, just quoted, or in the interesting and more detailed account by de Waal in the book itself, that diverges far from a struggle for power with the exception of the reference to bargaining. Inasmuch as the issue revolves around what is in the minds of the apes, and their very intelligence encourages anthropomorphism, hard and convincing evidence is still lacking, although it is difficult to imagine what that evidence might be.

As an aside, debatable and not central to our thesis, it seems to us that Type I and Type III conflicts predominate in nature. Bonds of communality, as in Type II conflicts, in which self-interest is subordinated to mutual interest and adversaries seek a mutually acceptable outcome through a process of negotiation, seems a primarily human characteristic. So one cannot hope to learn how to resolve Type II conflicts from nature. But perhaps of even greater importance, is the light such study might throw on controlling the escalation of Type III conflict.

13.2   Resolving Type III Conflict

"Trial by combat" is the characteristic mode of resolving Type III conflict. The two extreme forms differ in whether or not there is an umpire who limits escalation. There are three problems which concern us: the availability of courses of action, selecting a course of action, and getting out of a Type III in the first place. We discuss the first two here as subsections and take up the third in the next section under the heading Transformations of Type.

13.2.1   The Availability of Courses of Action

The courses of action available to sovereign states are much less restricted than in competitive sports and are less predictable. Some courses of action are obvious to most adversaries, but others are conceived and created by each party in reaction to courses of action chosen by the other party.

Expertise in the area of constructing courses of action springs from wisdom and experience. There is no more adequate theory for constructing courses of action than there is for constructing options for mutual agreement in Type II conflict, discussed in Chapter 8. Of course, the two have a great deal in common and Lockhart (1979) discusses some important factors and procedures useful in generating alternative courses of action which are equally useful for generating options for mutual agreement in Type II conflicts.

He suggests a brain-storming process, one-on-one or in groups. An atmosphere of tolerance, especially an openmindedness on the part of bureaucratic powers and decision makers, is essential to innovation and the development of unconventional approaches and the effective use of expert knowledge and talents. These seem obvious, but the tendency of leaders to select as advisors, supporters who have similar ideological backgrounds, may narrow severely the range and kind of options that are considered.

Of course, the encouragement of innovation can prolong the process of reaching a decision, to say nothing of making it more difficult and taxing a process. But tolerance for innovation is particularly important in Type III because conventional approaches are easily anticipated and so become easier to counter.

There is one aspect of contriving options for a Type II conflict that distinguishes it from the corresponding problem in a Type III conflict. Options in a Type II conflict are designed for mutual agreement, so joint participation in their design, as in the process followed in pursuing a single negotiable text (Chapter 8), is an asset.

In contrast, courses of action may be designed with either of two objectives in mind: to overcome the adversary's will to resist or to reduce tension and control escalation. With the former objective, courses of action are best developed in secrecy and sprung as a complete surprise. In the latter case a more subtle psychological process is invoked. This process is illustrated by a proposal of Osgood's (1962) that involved triggering a sequence of actions and reactions by unilaterally taking the initiative with an action designed to reduce tension. This is really a mechanism for creating an atmosphere of trust, an effective preliminary for a transfer from Type III to Type II. One is essentially trying to induce the opponent to create courses of action with a similar objective.

Etzioni (1967) reports a study of arms negotiation between Kennedy and Khrushchev in which a series of small reciprocating initiatives were instrumental in bringing about bilateral agreements. It appears that even small initiatives can have substantial psychological impact.

With the inevitable changes in leadership, however, they are difficult to sustain.

Thompson (1985), in a monograph sponsored by the British Psychological Society on psychological aspects of nuclear war, discusses Osgood's proposal of graduated tension reduction and other contributions from psychological research. They include crisis analysis and conference process analysis of the negotiation process. There are a number of studies, briefly reviewed by Thompson, in which research findings provide guidance in creating a spiral of trust, a psychological environment which fosters motivation to achieve a solution that can lead to successful negotiation and bargaining rather than escalation.

Scoville (1985) refers to essentially the same approach as Osgood's as "reciprocal national restraint" and emphasizes its possible usefulness as an alternative path to arms control in place of negotiating. It continues as long as the other side reciprocates, and arms control at some achievable level becomes a fait accompli. He makes the point that restraint is just the reverse philosophy of the bargaining chip theory, in which one builds weapons in order to discard them. Instead of tension spiralling down, applying bargaining chip theory would tend to spiral tension up.

Both reciprocal national restraint and bargaining chip theory constitute changes in the status quo, but in opposite directions, the former in a direction conducive to a Type II resolution of the conflict, the latter in a direction conducive to a Type III resolution. A policy of reciprocal national restrain is a move closer to an agreement that reduces armaments, a move toward a Type II resolution; the bargaining chip policy is a move further away from an agreement to reduce armaments. It is a move closer to a Type III resolution, one in which power replaces persuasion.

13.2.2   Selecting a Course of Action: Higher Game Theory

Higher game theory is the most extensive and substantial theory of the sequence of actions and reactions in a Type III conflict between sovereign entities. Implicit in the conduct of a sequence of interactions is the absence of trustworthy communication between the adversaries. Words and actions are all there are, and the latter are said to be the more trusted. Clearly, this approach to conflict is in the spirit of game theory except that neither the courses of action available to the other party nor the outcomes are known.

Our earlier discussion of game theory (Section 9.5) was limited mostly to what has been called classical game theory, which is generally regarded as too restricted to be directly applicable to the resolution of real conflicts. The particular limitations relevant here are the lack of communication assumed in classical game theory, the presumed knowledge of each adversary of all the courses of action available to the other party, and the presumed knowledge of each adversary of the utilities of all consequences to all parties of their joint courses of action. Classical game theory is, at best, most applicable to a single choice by each player, a sort of what-to-do-next theory; after each choice and its consequences are revealed, a total reassessment has to be made.

Here we will summarize some advanced developments in game theory which are in directions more relevant to the resolution of Type III conflicts. In anticipation of a later section, we add that in our opinion, the peaceful resolution of Type III conflicts is best accomplished by transforming them into Type II conflicts. That leads to more direct communication between adversaries and a shift of attention from unilateral choices of courses of action to mutual agreement on joint outcomes. So our interest in higher game theory is its movement in that direction.

An instructive example is the Prisoner's Dilemma game discussed in Section 9.5. In a single play of this game the conflict is a Type I for each party as each is torn between cooperating and defecting. In the absence of any communication each player assesses the alternative courses of action as best he or she can, then each makes a unilateral decision in his or her own best interests, as he or she sees them, with the outcome in an ambiguous future.

In multiple plays of this game, the interaction in the sequence of plays provides an implicit line of communication between the players, and the game ceases to be a Type I. There is now social interaction, and whether the game becomes a Type II or Type III conflict is, in part, dependent on its parameters.

For example, using the Prisoner's Dilemma game portrayed in Figures 33 and 34, we see that as a Type II game, the outcome $(5,5)$ is a likely point of agreement in iterated play. The outcome $(5,5)$, however, may be varied in a sequence of experiments, so that the frontier varies from a relatively straight line to one that "bulges" up and to the right, and the area representing the intensity of conflict would decrease. As the bulge decreases and the frontier approaches a "straight" line, the intensity of conflict increases and the players are increasingly attracted to their extreme preferences at their respective ideal ends of the frontier (Defection) and the outcome $(-3,-3)$ is increasingly likely, as was found in the data of Rapoport and Chammah

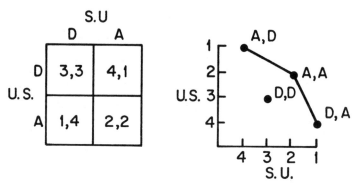

Figure 41: The Leader's game

(cf. Section 9.5). In defecting, the parties do not seek to preserve an entity (partnership) and a Type III conflict is created — a quantitative change becomes qualitative.

The Prisoner's Dilemma has been given a lot of attention as a model of the superpower nuclear arms race, particularly as an iterated game. Hardin (1983) says "I am convinced that this game represents the preference ordering of virtually all articulate policy makers and policy analysts in the United States and presumably also in the Soviet Union" (p. 248).

He examines some six other 2 × 2 games as models of the nuclear arms competition, including one he calls the Leader's game and another game known as Chicken.

The game matrix for the Leader's game is displayed in Figure 41 along with its frontier of preference, where A signifies armament, D signifies disarmament, and SU signifies the Soviet Union. The cell entries are the rank order preferences of the players with 1 representing highest preference. Thus, in the cell (A,D) the entry (1,4) signifies it is the most preferred outcome for the US and the least preferred by the SU. We see that armament is preferred to disarmament regardless of the adversary's preference, with the result that mutual armament, (A,A), dominates mutual disarmament, (D,D). Such a hawkish preference on the part of national leaders is presumed to hold for domestic political reasons, hegemony over allies, and other reasons that may or may not be justified.

The game of Chicken, shown in Figure 42 with the same notation as used in Figure 41, is another modification of the Prisoner's Dilemma game in which the last two preferences of each party are reversed. The game matrix and the resulting frontier are shown in the

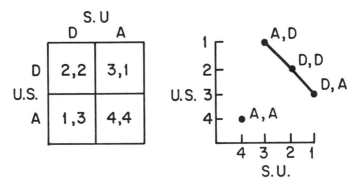

Figure 42: Chicken

figure. In contrast to the Leader's game, armament no longer dominates disarmament for either player. Hardin remarks that this game
was one considered by many analysts to be the best representation
of the nuclear arms competition. It is interesting that in this game,
compared with the Prisoner's Dilemma, all options on the frontier
dominate mutual armament.

Brams (1985) models deterrence as a supergame, one in which
there are repeated plays of a component game. In this case he argues
persuasively for Chicken as the component game. Seeking a rational
solution to such a confrontation he uses Schelling's (1960) notion of
a probabilistic threat and carries it further. A probabilistic threat
introduces uncertainty as to whether or not the threat will be carried
out, thereby making a threat divisible in the sense of there being
degrees of it. Equivalently, the threshold for carrying out the threat
might be flexible, making it a weaker threat if the likelihood of it
being carried out is low, or a stronger threat if the contrary is true.

Brams suggests that the two important parameters of a threat are
its credibility (that it might really be carried out) and its effectiveness
(how damaging it would be). He measures the first as a function of the
cost to the threatener and the second as a function of the cost to the
threatened. Credibility and effectiveness vary inversely. Increasing
the probability of carrying out a threat increases the measure of its
effectiveness as a threat in terms of the harm it causes the threatened
party, but makes it more incredible that it would be carried out in
terms of the harm it causes the threatener. He uses Ellsberg's (1975)
concept of critical risk to calculate the probability at which the payoff
to the threatener is the same whether the threat is or is not carried
out. For the arms race, Brams uses the Prisoner's Dilemma to which

he adds the requirement that each participant can predict cooperation on the part of the other player with a specified probability.

These developments of the 2×2 game are of more interest to academicians, perhaps, than to those directly involved in the negotiations. It is not appropriate here to pursue the technical details of such developments but rather to put them in perspective with our theory of the structure of conflict.

Countries choosing a course of action are acting in their own self-interest. In our terms, their choices represent resolutions of a Type I conflict for each of them. The 2×2 games used to model such conflicts yield a Type III confrontation for which the collective outcome may be abhorrent and even disastrous. In the classical theory of these 2×2 models, each party must choose one of only two courses of action. Not only is this an extreme oversimplification but there is no role for communication and for sequential acts by which each party may display its attitude toward risk and compromise, its trust, and its trustworthiness. The result is that the models appear to condone the irrationality of superpower conflict. Game theory is a normative approach to maximizing self-interest.

Assuming that this irrationality may stem from the limited variety of courses of action available in the models rather than from such uncontrollable aggressive tendencies in the parties involved that they cease to be prudent and rational, these extensions seek to overcome this limitation. Probabilistic threats are one way to make available a dense range of options between the two extremes of cooperate or defect.

Another extension is found in the work of Howard (1971) on metagames. These are sequential games, repeated plays of the same game, in which successive choices by players are conditional on preceding choices.

The motivation behind such extensions would appear to be tacit communication, to introduce ways of exchanging information about such things as attitudes, values, and intentions in a credible way. An adversary's selection of courses of action provides a way of gauging strength of will, intentions, and capabilities, not unambiguously and not with perfect accuracy, but in a fashion generally regarded as more reliable than words.

This is not easy to do, of course, and the extensions are easily criticized. It is hardly credible, for example, that a random device is going to be used to decide whether nuclear weapons will be released or that cardinal utilities of both parties are known to each party or that repetitive play will be converging when the actors change even though the countries remain the same. So there is much that is unsatisfactory but these extensions reveal issues and clarify tradeoffs that must be made.

Unfortunately, courses of action and outcomes, seen in their respective roles as means and ends, are too separated, the relation between them is not, and cannot, be clear.

13.3 Transformations of Type: Getting Out of a Type III Conflict

There are essentially two general ways of resolving Type III conflicts. The first is by the parties themselves, they "fight it out" with or without third-party control of escalation; the second is to transform the conflict into a Type II, in which the adversaries are brought to a negotiating posture and can be helped to reach an agreement with less likelihood of escalation.

Letting the parties resolve a Type III conflict themselves has been discussed here. Competitive sports, professional or otherwise, provide an illustration in which escalation is controlled by a third party but the adversaries still settle the conflict themselves. Game theory was used to illustrate a normative approach to the resolution of a Type III conflict when no third party exists with power to control escalation.

From time to time, we have used the term transformation of type and have now come to the point where the process needs to be examined in more detail and discussed in terms of what is gained and lost by transformation. The initiatives suggested by Osgood and others, and the use of higher game theory, may be seen as an approach to inducing a transformation of a Type III conflict into a Type II. Credible communication between adversaries is a central facet of Type II conflict and we see in the previously discussed approaches to resolving Type III conflict that tacit communication is being given more attention. The intent, presumably, is to emphasize outcomes, mutual interests, and cooperation.

Our analysis of the structure of conflict classifies conflicts into three types, which are exhaustive but not mutually exclusive. This means that a conflict is not uniquely a particular type but depends on who is looking at it or how it is looked at. Two men courting the same woman may see it as a Type III conflict, they want the same thing but will have to settle for different things; but to the woman it is a Type I conflict if she is torn between incompatible goals, perhaps security or excitement, long-term or short-term benefits.

A revolution, for example, may be formulated in terms of two parties wanting the same thing (i.e., control of the State), a Type III conflict, and then it will tend to be resolved violently. Or, a revolution may be formulated as two parties wanting different things (i.e., a different head of government), a Type II conflict, and then it may be resolved by voting. The importance of transformations is that from one point of view a conflict may appear intractable but from another it may appear less so, and hence the steps proposed to resolve the conflict may be different and perhaps more or less successful. One is forcefully reminded here of Fleming's description of "repackaging" a dispute (Section 9.2.6).

As another example, suppose one party wants compensation from another party for an alleged injury. If it is left to the parties involved and the injured party takes things into its own hands, "an eye for an eye ... ," it is a Type III conflict. Alternatively, our society provides a legal recourse to settle such a dispute by turning it over to a jury to decide. This transforms the conflict into a Type II conflict in that the jury members have to resolve their differences and their decision resolves the conflict by virtue of the power to enforce it.

If the conflict had been turned over to a judge instead of a jury, it would have become a Type I conflict in that the judge, torn between the incompatible goals of the belligerents, as assessed by the judge, makes the tradeoff he or she considers fair for the parties involved. A divorce settlement by a judge is an example of a Type III conflict transformed into Type I.

As is evident, this process of transformation is analogous in some ways to the process of framing a decision problem, shown by Tversky and Kahneman (1981) to be so important in individual decision making (see Section 3.2). How far this analogy may be pursued needs further study, but it is evident that transforming a conflict is sometimes no more than an exercise in semantics. This is not to be despised. Any experienced diplomat or negotiator is extremely aware of and sensitive to the importance of semantics. Face-saving of the actors in a negotiation may be a prerequisite to resolving a conflict.

For rhetorical convenience we shall refer to transformations III→II, III→I, II→I, as transformations *down*. Transformations down require the consent of the parties involved or power of a third party to impose them and neither may be easy to come by. Disputes between sovereign states tend to be of Type III as the conflicts arise because they each want the same thing and they have to settle for different things and there is no entity to be preserved. Transforming these into conflicts of Type II by turning such a dispute over to the International Court of Justice, for example, may be unacceptable. Adjudication seeks a winner (and a loser) and is not conducive to political compromise, so it tends to be avoided by states unwilling to put their vital interests, as they perceive them, at risk. For this reason alone, the International Court of Justice may never be the primary method for conflict resolution between powerful adversaries with vital interests at stake, although its opinions can be influential (see Claude, 1971, for a detailed analysis). The International Court of Justice has had only one contentious case per year, on the average, over its first 33 years of existence, and one advisory opinion every other year.

Transformations may occur in the other direction, too, which we will call transformations *up*. If the woman with a Type I conflict deciding between two suitors, asks her parents for advice it may become a Type II conflict between them, and it is not beyond the bounds of possibilities that it becomes a Type III conflict between them if they are unable to agree and each wants to control their daughter's decision!

Jervis (1976) discusses a number of incidents in the history of international diplomacy in which decision makers were faced with a choice between firmness or conciliation. He discusses some hypotheses and some relevant empirical literature indicating when threat or concession, as courses of action, will induce the same or opposite responses. These are examples of Type I decisions, each party choosing a course of action. The sequence may lead to a Type II or a Type III conflict depending on whether the process leads to cooperation or competition.

Transformations up are common. The American revolution is an example. It started out as a sequence of Type I decisions, spiralling up in escalation. Neither party succeeded in transforming the conflict into a Type II, trying to preserve the entity of which they were a part. The unwillingness of the two parties to compromise transformed the conflict into a Type III, and the colonies revolted. The American Civil War is another example.

One aspect of the transformation of a conflict between Type II and Type III is that conflict over principle is much more difficult to reconcile than conflict over issues. Conflict between parties over principle is likely to lead to a Type III conflict because neither party wants to compromise on principle. Escalation to Type III of a conflict over principle may reflect the effect of the number of options on the scale between the peaks. With principles there are fewer intermediate options; principles don't lend themselves to compromise. This suggests that resolution may be facilitated if options can be formulated in terms of issues rather than in terms of principles, the latter should be suppressed and the conflict "repackaged" (see Section 9.2.6) as a conflict over issues if it can be, and not rights, religion, or principles.

Issues that are intrinsically unimportant can be blown up into serious confrontations when perceived as setting undesirable precedents in the absence of a policy of firm resistance. Such occurences illustrate the danger of escalation from interpreting conflict over issues into conflict over principles.

It only takes one party to transform a conflict into a Type III; when one party wants to impose its will on another, resistance is almost a moral obligation and escalation is almost inevitable. It takes both parties to transform conflict from a Type III to a Type II so, unfortunately, transformations up are easier than transformations down and are more dangerous.

It also only takes one party to start a Type III conflict. If one party wants what another party has and initiates an attack to get it, or wants to impose its will on another at most any cost, resistance is again almost a moral obligation and escalation is almost inevitable. History is replete with instances. The only restraint on escalation in such a Type III conflict is fear of consequences, as in the case of nuclear war.

Motivated by fear of consequences, as in the case of an overwhelmingly superior adversary, one recourse of the target of aggression is to seek to transform the conflict into a Type II by unilaterally adjusting its own goals and objectives, to create a line of options, a frontier of preference, along which negotiation (compromise or, more likely in this case, appeasement) can take place. This is a very delicate transition to bring about.

Transformations of Type III down are particularly important because Type III conflicts are difficult for the parties to resolve nonviolently by themselves; their resolution tends to be a destructive process. A Type II conflict, in contrast, lends itself more readily to compromise, a constructive resolution. Persuasion preserves, power divides.

There is some relevant and valuable experimental evidence on transforming a Type III conflict into a Type II in the studies of Muzafer Sherif (1966) at a boys' camp. He created a situation in which an intergroup conflict of Type III was formed. He then found that intergroup conflict receded when a new situation was created in which their wider identity as members of the camp superseded their subgroup identification. This was done by inducing a common predicament which created a broader framework for their actions. Their intergroup conflicts became Type II, intragroup, and compromise solutions could be sought rather than extreme solutions.

These results are supported by some recent psychological research on ingroup-outgroup biases and intergroup conflict (see Brewer, 1979;

Komorita & Lapworth, 1982) which suggests that dividing groups into smaller units may enhance intragroup cooperation but with the side effect of decreased intergroup cooperation (Samuelson, Messick, Allison, & Beggan, 1986).

Dawes, Alphons, van de Kragt, & Orbell (1987), in related research draw the conclusion from 10 years of experimental work on social dilemmas, that group identity (i.e., solidarity) can enhance cooperative responding and diminish the rate of defecting, even in the absence of any expectation of future reciprocity, current rewards, punishment, or even reputational consequences among other group members. Moreover, this identity operates independently of the dictates of conscience. In other words, their experiments indicate that group solidarity increases cooperation independently of the side payments — either internal or external — often associated with such identity. In our terms, creating a common identity can transform a conflict from Type III to Type II, an intergroup conflict becomes an intragroup conflict, and accommodation can replace confrontation.

Not all Type III conflicts should be transformed, however (see Coser, 1956, 1957, for a review of functions that social conflict fulfills). Such conflicts are characterized by competition, and competition can promote excellence, whether the context is a Wimbledon tournament or the America's Cup. Corporate business is another example of Type III conflict that is indistinguishable in structure from professional sports. In this case, the government is the umpire, preventing such things as restraint of trade and monopolies (i.e., escalation).

One of the dangers in the resolution of a Type III conflict with no third-party constraint is that it will be resolved solely to the satisfaction of one party. Such a resolution merely sows the seeds of further Type III conflicts, although their effects may not be observed until much later, witness the Treaty of Versailles after WWI.

On the level of serious international conflicts one might interpret the course of the Type III conflict as a jockeying for positions of strength when the conflict is finally resolved around a peace table. Lockhart (1979), in discussing such conflicts, conceptualizes them in terms of four phases: an intolerable violation, an act of resistance, a confrontation, and an accommodation. These phases are each discussed in terms of their characteristic patterns of information interpretation, decision foci, strategy search, resourcefulness, and strategy dilemmas, with many historical examples. Sources of difficulties that arise and ways in which they have been handled are illustrated.

These phases are offered as a chronology of what, in our terms, is a Type III conflict. The final phase, accommodation, occurs after the coercive probing of the confrontation phase and has much in common with the negotiation process as it occurs in resolving Type II conflict. Lockhart's detailed analysis, with a number of instructive examples, is equally relevant to both types of conflict.

The further one goes in transforming conflicts down from Type III to Type II or Type I by introducing a third party, the easier it is for that party to arrive at a decision but the more third-party power is required to put it in place. It's a lot easier to propose a solution than to impose it. The latter takes power, as in backing up the decision of a court. Yielding to third-party power is associated with some loss of sovereignty on the part of the parties in conflict. A referee, for example, places a constraint on the options available to the competitors, they have lost some freedom of choice.

The United Nations, if it had the power, could eliminate war, and a world dictator could do it even more easily, in the sense of reaching a decision, but that would take enormous power to put into effect. But, understandably, the sovereignty of states is their most precious possession and domestic political wisdom also militates against a politician proposing any concession of sovereignty. Power is the politician's most precious possession and such a move would expose the perpetrator to inflammatory rhetoric and loss of votes.

The formal adversarial structure of the law does not appear to be a promising approach to the resolution of Type III conflicts between sovereign states because of the threat to sovereignty and to the domestic political power structure.

> It took over fifty years to get the states of the Union to accept the decisions of the Supreme Court of the United States on boundary questions; it was over eighty years before any other question of importance [between states] was submitted for its decision! (Warren, 1941, p. 20)

The growth of international jurisdiction cannot be much faster (Lissitzyn, 1972), or, indeed, as fast!

There is, however, another kind of initiative that has promise. This is one similar in concept to the dispute resolution centers (cf. Section 9.2.4) but on a level more appropriate to international disputes. There is little question that dispute resolution centers are effective and this is in no small part due to the fact that when two parties enter upon it they are not conceding any sovereignty, as they do in a court of law or in recognizing the authority of any third power. The problem of finding a solution is not delegated to a third party. If either of the antagonists doesn't like the outcome, that party may withdraw and seek some other alternative. The important things are the preservation of sovereignty and the domestic power structure. To be acceptable, a resolution of a conflict must pass muster with those who stayed at home. This is reminiscent of Carter, Begin, and Sadat at Camp David, as well as of the dispute resolution centers.

Relations between sovereign states are inherently anarchical. Any recognition of third-party power is a loss of sovereignty. Public images, public opinion, and norms, are substitutes, precursors of law, and they can counteract anarchy. A trusted world figure in the role of mediator, with no formal power, appears to be a promising ingredient for resolving Type III conflicts in danger of escalation. Such a figure offers no threat to sovereignty and is face-saving.

13.4 Summary

The following are characteristics of Type III conflict which distinguish it from others:

- The options consist of alternative courses of action, rather than their consequences, and both are unpredictable;
- The course of a Type III conflict consists of a sequence of actions and reactions taken by the antagonists unilaterally;
- Communication is limited and untrustworthy, words and actions may not be compatible;
- Power dominates persuasion;
- Self-interest dominates common interest;
- It is highly susceptible to escalation;
- It may be resolved by the parties themselves by "playing it out" (e.g., combat) or by transformation into Type II with reduced likelihood of escalation, a defusing process, at the price of some loss of sovereignty;
- Controlled by loss of sovereignty;
- There is always a loser.

A Type III conflict is intrinsically one in which the parties resolve the conflict themselves. In its milder form it proceeds under the supervision of a referee to control escalation. In a more severe form, as between sovereign states, there is no third-party power that can control escalation, although the parties may be influenced by attempted mediation or by world opinion.

The fact that the three types of conflict are exhaustive but not mutually exclusive permits transformation from one type to another. The classification of a conflict is in the eyes of the beholder and may be differently classified by the antagonists and by observers.

Type III conflict is the "game" for which game theory was introduced and which higher game theory moves away from. We reviewed some of the applications of game theory to international issues.

We reviewed some psychological contributions, as well as others, to the resolution of international conflicts, and point out a direction that is a blend of dispute resolution centers and a single negotiable text. Such a blend does not jeopardize sovereignty, one of the major obstacles to resolving a Type III conflict.

Chapter 14

Perspective and Conclusions

14.1 An Overall Perspective

The particular character of this analysis of the structure of conflict is formed by the confluence of three lines of thought: (a) some behavioral (descriptive) principles which account for certain general regularities in choice behavior, (b) certain ethical (prescriptive) principles which are matters of judgment and opinion, and (c) the conviction that only ordinal preferences with a threshold that serves as a zero point between approach and avoidance processes provide a structural framework of sufficient generality and with some freedom from strategic misrepresentation.

In summary form, the following notions provide the foundation supporting the formal basis of the structure of conflict: (a) good things satiate, (b) bad things escalate, (c) dominated options are neglected, (d) there is motivation to improve the status quo, (e) there is motivation to avoid worsening it, (f) in seeking compromise it is desirable to minimize concession in a certain precise sense, (g) equal participants with equal claims should share equally in any gains or losses, (h) utility may be justifiably measured on a signed ordinal scale with the status quo set equal to zero and not subject to transformation.

The first five ideas are descriptive behavioral principles of some generality but not without exception and not universal. The sixth is a principle governing the screening of options for resolving conflict. The seventh is a limited ethical principle for selecting an option. Severe normative issues arise when the parties are not equal in power or have unequal claims. These issues are not resolved. The eighth specifies the level of measurement required for this analysis, which is more than an interval scale in the sense that it has a nonarbitrary zero point, and less than an interval scale in the sense that it has no unit of measurement. These ideas provide the basis for the formal mathematical assumptions from which the structure is derived.

We first described the decision mechanism within an individual for making a choice that involves a tradeoff across "good" things, or across "bad" things, or between good and bad things, a Type I conflict. We find that the effectiveness of the mechanism is assured when the options available also have a certain structure, but that the individual, in general, has limited control over the conditions that ensure that structure.

We generalized this mechanism to describe the structure of a certain type of conflict between individuals, Type II. We sought to expose those characteristics of the structure of Type II conflict that are particularly relevant to the difficulty of finding and accepting an optimum solution. Certain of these characteristics are properties of the individuals and certain of them are properties of the options. We sought ways to modify both classes of properties so as to simplify the search for solutions and to ensure that a solution is optimal in a certain sense. The answers are neither as satisfying nor as complete as we would like, but they reveal some pitfalls and stumbling blocks to conflict resolution that are due to characteristics that are solely structural and not substantive.

In the course of this study of conflict, we have come to the realization that the structural complexity of Type I conflict in its less favorable aspects is not due to what people bring to the conflict situation. Insofar as people are concerned, the logical structure is very simple: they have preference functions, initial positions, a modest amount of rationality, are hedonistic, and that's about it.

What makes the resolution of conflict within an individual complex or difficult is the structure on the alternatives, or better put, perhaps, the lack of structure. The most effective and efficient process for resolving conflict optimally is described by a single peaked function over an ordered set of optimal options. What people bring to the choice situation lends itself readily to that objective, but the requirements also include a certain structure on the options that does not occur naturally except in rare instances. The absence of single peakedness over an ordered set of options makes the process of seeking a resolution more difficult, and a resolution may be less than optimal.

Of course, resolutions may be less then optimal due to misperceptions, inconsistent assessments, conation, affect, cognitive overload, etc. These effects are important because they increase the decision maker's vulnerability to inconsistency. But these effects do not displace the underlying logic of the decision process, rather it is due to the underlying logic that the decision maker is vulnerable. Our attention in this monograph has been concentrated on the underlying structure.

In contrast to Type I, what makes the resolution of Type II conflict between individuals complex is not so much the structure on the options, because the frontier of preference screens options to select a totally ordered set that is optimal. Instead the difficulty lies in the arousal of interpersonal processes not present in Type I conflict, particularly the compelling necessity to make concessions and the impact of such little understood issues as fairness, justice, and the political reality of power. Underlying the resolution of a Type II conflict is the further acceptance of a loss of sovereignty on the part of the antagonists, implicit in concession.

A Type III conflict lacks this process of concession. Instead it is characterized by the intent to impose one's will on the other party, and so is vulnerable to escalation. This is why we emphasized the transformation of types, in the last chapter, as a first step in seeking to resolve a Type III conflict.

A Type II conflict has a problem-solving orientation toward conflict resolution, Type III has a competitive orientation. A problem-solving orientation encourages accommodation and a competitive orientation encourages coercion.

We provide with Figure 43 an overall summary of the interrelatedness of the three types of conflict. In this 2×2 table are contrasted what individuals want, which may be the same or different things, corresponding to the two rows of the table, and what individuals may get, which may be the same or different things, corresponding to the two columns of the table.

If individuals want the same thing and may have the same thing, there is no conflict; a prior condition, of course is that there be adequate resources. This case is illustrated in the cell in the upper left of the figure.

If individuals want different things and may have different things there are, again, no grounds for conflict. This case is dependent on freedom of choice as well as adequate resources and is illustrated in the cell on the lower right.

The cell on the lower left is the case of wanting different things but having to settle for the same thing. If the conflict is within an individual, a Type I conflict, the individual has competing goals which cannot be fully satisfied by any single option. So the option that is

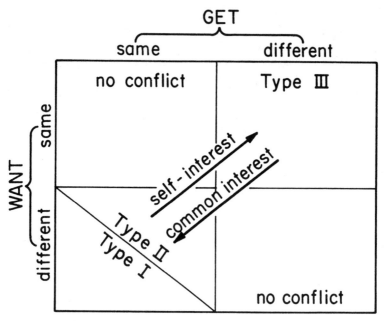

Figure 43: Transformations of type

chosen holds for both goals and is the individual's compromise between them. If the conflict is between individuals, a Type II conflict,
both their goals cannot be fully satisfied by any single option, so the
option that is chosen is a compromise.

The cell on the upper right is the case of two or more parties
having the same goal but it being possible for at most one to achieve
it. The diagonal arrows in the figure indicate the flow between Type
II and Type III conflict (i.e., the transformation of type driven by
self-interest in the direction from Type II to Type III and by mutual
interest in the direction from Type III to Type II, leading to a decision
by each party to cooperate or compete, cooperate or defect). The
arrow from Type II to Type III puts escalation at risk and the arrow
in the other direction puts sovereignty at risk.

Of course, in any conflict between individuals there is both self-
interest and common interest on the part of each party to some degree,
which each party assesses for itself. So one may imagine a range of
degrees between two extremes, from common interest that is maximal and self-interest negligible at one extreme, to the other extreme,
where self-interest is maximal and common interest is negligible. Each
party could be represented by a separate point in this range, reflecting
the relative strengths of these opposed tendencies for each. If mutual

interest dominates self-interest in both parties then they each see the conflict as a Type II, otherwise it is a Type III.

One may see, then, how it is that the classification of a conflict as Type II or Type III may be differently perceived by the parties themselves or by third parties. The classification of a conflict as Type II or III is not an inherent structural property but a characterization of it by the observer, a description of the psychological environment as the observer perceives it. This characterization is important because it substantially effects the direction and kinds of efforts that are taken to transform and ultimately to resolve the conflict.

It is useful to recognize a duality between the notion of goals and the notion of options. It is customary to refer to competing goals as giving rise to conflict. But goals do not compete. The conflict is over options, not goals. Each option satisfies one or more goals better than another option, otherwise it would be dominated. Conflict arises, then, because a choice has to be made between options. And the conflict is resolved by the decision that makes the tradeoff, that is, which (or whose) goals will be favored.

This directs attention to creating options as much as trying to modify the goals of the adversaries, and it is another route to resolving conflict. The frontier of preference provides a method for the analysis of options to provide cues to the construction of dominating options and thereby reduce the intensity of the conflict. There is, however, nothing that will ensure that a *single* dominating option exists. On the other hand, there is nothing that ensures one does not, except limited resources and lack of creativity.

The role played by this structure of conflict in the varied and immense task of resolving conflicts may be placed in perspective by an analogy. A theory such as this about the logical structure of conflict is to the resolution of conflict, as anatomy is to curing disease. Anatomy does not, in itself, cure anything, but it is basic, necessary information, and the practicing physician is the better for knowing it.

14.2 Some Conclusions

It is exceedingly difficult, if not impossible, to build such a theory as this free of personal values and judgments about some aspects of society. We have tried to be explicit about our assumptions and distinguish what is essentially descriptive of structure and what is prescriptive for resolving a conflict optimally. In the course of this analysis we have come to certain conclusions, and we would like to take the liberty of expressing them without the readers' judgment of the preceding chapters being affected by their assessment of these conclusions. We feel that this final section is as completely independent of the preceding chapters as the objective analysis can be free of subjective coloration.

We have been much impressed by the conclusions of others, particularly by Michael Howard's writings as compiled in his *Causes of Wars* (1983). From his perspective as a military historian he arrives at the conclusion that a supranational authority enforcing a universal rule of law is the only system under which there can be peace and freedom from all fear of uncontrolled violence.

Another author reaching the same conclusion is Lissitzyn (1972):

> Effective adjudication of international disputes on an obligatory basis ... must be supported by the development of a sentiment of world community and a determination to uphold the rule of law in relations between states. (p. 101)

Supporting views are found in Angell (1957, 1979) and Parsons (1962) and a host of others. But this is pie in the sky, a goal but not a path.

If a nation wants to maintain total and complete sovereignty, and acknowledges no higher authority, it is almost inevitable that it will go to war. Expanding world population and higher standards of living place greater demands on limited resources. So there will always be parties who want the same thing and will have to settle for different things. It is understandable that situations may arise in which war is the lesser evil, for example, compared with genocide. The problem is to prevent such an avoidance/avoidance conflict from arising. The solution to this problem may not depend on political insight and brilliance so much as on political courage and self-restraint, which are scarce and hard to come by.

Furthermore, there are contexts in which Type III conflict is desirable because it promotes excellence, as for example, the America's Cup. So the problem is not to eliminate Type III conflict, which we are convinced is futile and not even desirable, but to contain its inherent tendency to escalate.

One possible way to accomplish this is to establish third-party power that can put a ceiling on escalation, such as the umpire in a professional sport, or that can transform the Type III conflict down into one of Type II or even Type I (e.g., turning the power of resolution over to a court, a commission, or an individual).

Doing this successfully, however, requires third-party power, and the price of this is some loss of freedom of choice, of sovereignty, for the parties involved. This is generally distasteful. But freedom of choice is already compromised when people have to live together. Law is required and law is ineffective without power. In this case, avoiding one evil is at the price of accepting another evil, an avoidance/avoidance conflict, the most difficult of all to resolve.

None of the above is very helpful without a feasible course of action which offers some promise of controlling escalation. There is evidence from social science, particularly anthropology and sociology, that a promising path lies in multiple group networks, through relations that cut across boundaries of all kinds. Many already exist, such as the Olympic games, international scientific meetings, cultural and student exchanges, and tourism. An international business network is another promising means for controlling escalation through common goals.

These are stabilizing influences, generating cohesion through a common core within otherwise diverse peoples. The integrative role of personal mobility and overlapping group membership and its effectiveness in reducing tension and militancy is discussed in Alger (1965), who brings together some of the findings that provide supporting evidence.

Other ways also exist for controlling escalation. These include extensive interaction if it creates a sense of community, a state of mind. The United Nations, the Law of the Sea, and the European Economic Community are cases in point.

The United Nations provides a forum for the presentation and discussion of international disputes. The imperative public defense of international violence by offending parties is salutary. Even though the record of the International Court of Justice and the Security Council of the United Nations on the control of international violence has not come up to expectations, there has been steady progress in the emergence of restraint and consensus (Murphy, 1982). Its value is long range.

The United Nations Convention on Law of the Sea is the culmination of many years of labor (Borgese, 1983). It is a constitution for the oceans, replacing the laissez faire system of freedom of the seas. The Third United Nations Conference on the Law of the Sea began in 1973 and engaged as many as 3,000 delegates representing more than 150 nations in 11 long sessions totaling 585 days. In December, 1982, it was signed by 119 nations (not including the United States). It is a monument to rational resolution of international disputes.

Economic integration, as in the European Economic Community, involves give and take. Over a period of time a state of mind can emerge in which escalation of conflict is simply not an acceptable route to resolve differences. Such a global sense of community is a long time building and is easily set back. It is most easily achieved by eliminating differences but it is by preserving these very differences that interaction derives its pleasure and spice.

The only way to eliminate conflict is to eliminate freedom of choice. We assume that that is unacceptable. So conflict is inevitable. But war is not. We know what it takes to contain Type III conflict, accepting a lesser evil. Postponing confrontation permits the cultivation of a more global sense of community.

Appendix A

On Proper Preference Functions

We give here a proof of the theorem stated in Section 2.4.3, that a proper preference function is single peaked on an efficient set. This presentation essentially follows that of our 1977 paper (Coombs & Avrunin, 1977a) but has been modified slightly to reflect some changes in approach and terminology inspired by the structure of conflict of Type II.

For the rest of this discussion, we assume that those elementary components of options relevant to the decision are fixed, and we choose a representation of options as points in $\mathbb{R}^n$ such that dimensions 1 through m correspond to increasingly desirable components and dimensions $m + 1$ through n correspond to increasingly undesirable components. We recall the following definitions, which depend on the chosen representation of options.

Definition. We say that $F : \mathbb{R}^n \to \mathbb{R}$ is a *proper preference function* if

(i) all its first-order partial derivatives, F_i, exist,

(ii) $x_j \leq y_j$ for all j and $x_i < y_i$ for some $i \leq m$ implies that $F_i(x_1, \ldots, x_n) \geq F_i(y_1, \ldots, y_n) \geq 0$, and

(iii) $x_j \leq y_j$ for all j and $x_i < y_i$ for some $i > m$ implies that $0 \geq F_i(x_1, \ldots, x_n) \geq F_i(y_1, \ldots, y_n)$.

Definition. A set $S \subseteq \mathbb{R}^n$ is an *efficient set* if the following conditions are satisfied:

213

(i) for any pair of points $(x_1, \ldots, x_n)$ and $(y_1, \ldots, y_n)$ in S, we have $x_i \leq y_i$ for some i if and only if $x_j \leq y_j$ for all j, and $x_i < y_i$ for some $i \leq m$ if and only if $x_j < y_j$ for some $j > m$, and

(ii) for each triple $(x_1, \ldots, x_n), (y_1, \ldots, y_n), (z_1, \ldots, z_n)$ in S with $x_1 < y_1 < z_1$, there exists a positive real number c such that

$$c(y_i - x_i) \geq z_i - y_i \quad \text{for all } i \leq m, \text{ and}$$
$$c(y_j - x_j) \leq x_j - y_j \quad \text{for all } j > m.$$

Theorem. *Let S be an efficient set and suppose that $G : \mathbb{R}^n \to \mathbb{R}$ is a function such that, for some strictly increasing $g : \mathbb{R} \to \mathbb{R}$, the function $F = g \circ G$ is a proper preference function. Then G is single peaked on S with respect to the ordering induced by the natural order on any component.*

Proof. Since g and g^{-1} preserve order, it suffices to prove that F is single peaked on S. Suppose that $(x_1, \ldots, x_n)$, $(y_1, \ldots, y_n)$, and $(z_1, \ldots, z_n)$ are points in S with $x_1 < y_1 < z_1$ (and hence $x_i \leq y_i \leq z_i$ for all i), and that $F(x_1, \ldots, x_n) > F(y_1, \ldots, y_n)$. We need to show that $F(y_1, \ldots, y_n) > F(z_1, \ldots, z_n)$.

By repeated application of the mean value theorem, we have

$$F(y_1, \ldots, y_n) =$$
$$F(x_1, \ldots, x_n) + \sum_{i=1}^{n} F_i(y_1, \ldots, y_{i-1}, a_i, x_{i+1} \ldots, x_n)(y_i - x_i),$$

where a_i is some number between x_i and y_i. Similarly,

$$F(z_1, \ldots, z_n) =$$
$$F(y_1, \ldots, y_n) + \sum_{i=1}^{n} F_i(z_1, \ldots, z_{i-1}, b_i, y_{i+1} \ldots, y_n)(z_i - y_i),$$

where b_i is some number between y_i and z_i.

Since there is a positive number c with $c(y_i - x_i) \geq (z_i - y_i)$ for $i \leq m$, and F is a proper preference function, we have

$$c \sum_{i=1}^{m} F_i(y_1, \ldots, y_{i-1}, a_i, x_{i+1}, \ldots, x_n)(y_i - x_i) \geq$$
$$\sum_{i=1}^{m} F_i(z_1, \ldots, z_{i-1}, b_i, y_{i+1} \ldots, y_n)(z_i - y_i) \geq 0.$$

Similarly,

$$0 \geq c \sum_{i=m+1}^{n} F_i(y_1, \ldots, y_{i-1}, a_i, x_{i+1}, \ldots, x_n)(y_i - x_i) \geq$$

$$\sum_{i=m+1}^{n} F_i(z_1, \ldots, z_{i-1}, b_i, y_{i+1} \ldots, y_n)(z_i - y_i).$$

Since $F(x_1, \ldots, x_n) > F(y_1, \ldots, y_n)$, we have

$$\sum_{i=1}^{n} F_i(y_1, \ldots, y_{i-1}, a_i, x_{i+1}, \ldots, x_n)(y_i - x_i) < 0,$$

and it then follows that

$$\sum_{i=1}^{n} F_i(z_1, \ldots, z_{i-1}, b_i, y_{i+1}, \ldots, y_n)(z_i - y_i) < 0.$$

Thus, $F(y_1, \ldots, y_n) > F(z_1, \ldots, z_n)$, and F is single peaked on S.

Appendix B

On Proper Additive Difference Models as Preference Functions

For the reader's convenience, we give here Aschenbrenner's proof (Aschenbrenner, 1981) that all proper additive difference models are single peaked on a set of options S if and only if S is an efficient set (see Section 9.2.1). As usual, we will regard S as a subset of n-dimensional Euclidean space $\mathbb{R}^n$, and let I_1 and I_2 be, respectively, the sets of indices corresponding to increasingly desirable and increasingly undesirable components of the options.

Definition. A monotone function v is *not positively accelerated* if, for any $x < y < z$,

$$\frac{v(y) - v(x)}{y - x} \geq \frac{v(z) - v(y)}{z - y}.$$

Definition. A preference structure on S is an *additive difference model* if and only if there exist real-valued functions $v_1, \ldots, v_n$ and increasing real-valued functions $w_1, \ldots, w_n$ such that $w_i(d) = -w_i(d)$ for all i and

$$x \succ y \quad \text{if and only if} \quad \sum_{k=1}^{n} w_k(v_i(x_i) - v_i(y_i)) \geq 0,$$

where $\succ$ is the preference ordering.

An additive difference model is *proper* (with respect to S) if *(i)* v_i is increasing if $i \in I_1$, and decreasing if $i \in I_2$,

(ii) all v_i are not positively accelerated, and

(iii) each w_i is of the form $w_i(d) = t_i \mathrm{sign}(d)|d|^r$ for some fixed $r \geq 0$, where $t_i > 0$ and $\mathrm{sign}(d)$ equals 1, 0, or -1 according as d is positive, zero, or negative.

The third condition in the definition of a proper additive difference model reflects the fact, proved by Aschenbrenner, that only functions of this form satisfy a property he calls *quotient-order-preserving*.

Theorem. (S, I_1, I_2) *is an efficient set if and only if all proper additive difference models are single peaked on S.*

Proof. Assume first that (S, I_1, I_2) is efficient, and consider a proper additive difference model with functions $v_1, \ldots, v_n$ and $w_1, \ldots, w_n$ as in the definition.

Suppose $x = (x_1, \ldots, x_n)$, $y = (y_1, \ldots, y_n)$, and $z = (z_1, \ldots, z_n)$ are distinct points in S with $x_k \leq y_k \leq z_k$ for some (and hence all) k. The fact that the v_k are not positively accelerated implies that, for all k,

$$(v_k(z_k) - v_k(y_k))(y_k - x_k) \leq (v_k(y_k) - v_k(x_k))(z_k - y_k).$$

If $k \in I_1$, both sides of this inequality are nonnegative, since v_k is an increasing function. If $k \in I_2$, both sides are nonpositive. For convenience, we write d_{krs} for $v_k(r_k) - v_k(s_k)$.

Choose $i \in I_1$ and $j \in I_2$. Then we have

$$0 \geq d_{izy} d_{jyx} (y_i - x_i)(z_j - y_j) \geq d_{iyx} d_{jzy} (z_i - y_i)(y_j - x_j).$$

Since S is efficient, $0 \leq (z_i - y_i)(y_j - x_j) \leq (z_j - y_j)(y_i - x_i)$. If $z_i = y_i$ or $y_j = x_j$, then we have d_{izy} or d_{jyx} equal to 0. If $y_i = x_i$, the definition of efficiency forces $z_i = y_i$, and then both d_{izy} and d_{jyx} vanish. Similarly, if $z_j = y_j$, we have $d_{jyz} = d_{jxy} = 0$. We may thus conclude that

$$0 \geq d_{izy} d_{jyx} \geq d_{iyx} d_{jzy}.$$

Since each w_k has the form $w_k(d) = t_k \mathrm{sign}(d)|d|^r$ with $t_k > 0$, we see that, for i and j as above,

$$0 \geq w_i(d_{izy}) w_j(d_{jyx}) \geq w_i(d_{iyx}) w_j(d_{jzy}).$$

Summing over $i \in I_1$ and $j \in I_2$ yields

$$\left(\sum_{i \in I_1} w_i(d_{izy})\right)\left(\sum_{j \in I_2} w_j(d_{iyx})\right) \geq \left(\sum_{i \in I_1} w_i(d_{iyx})\right)\left(\sum_{j \in I_2} w_j(d_{izy})\right),$$

where both sides of the inequality are nonpositive.

Suppose that $x \succ y$. Then we have $\sum_k w_k(d_{kyx}) < 0$, so

$$0 < \sum_{i \in I_1} w_i(d_{iyx}) \leq -\sum_{j \in I_2} w_j(d_{jyx}).$$

Combining this with the preceding inequality involving products of sums, we get

$$0 < \sum_{i \in I_1} w_i(d_{izy}) \leq -\sum_{j \in I_2} w_j(d_{jzy}),$$

so $y \succ z$. If $z \succ y$, a similar argument gives $y \succ x$, and we see that all proper additive difference models are single peaked on S.

To prove the converse, suppose that S is not efficient. If the points in S are not ordered the same on all components, single peakedness of S is not even well-defined, so we will assume that the points of S are ordered the same on all components.

If S is not efficient, there must exist distint points $x = (x_1, \ldots, x_n)$, $y = (y_1, \ldots, y_n)$, $z = (z_1, \ldots, z_n) \in S$ and indices $i \in I_1$, $j \in I_2$ such that

$$(z_j - y_j)(y_i - x_i) < (z_i - y_i)(y_j - x_j),$$

with $z_i > x_i$. We may assume that $i = 1$ and $j = 2$.

In order to produce a proper additive difference model that is not single peaked on S, it is sufficient to construct one that is not single peaked on (S', I_1', I_2'), where S' is the projection of S on the first two components, $I_1' = \{1\}$, and $I_2' = \{2\}$. This is because we can choose the t_k, for $k > 2$, to be sufficiently small that preference on S is determined entirely by the first two components.

Now set $v_1(a_1) = a_1$, $v_2(a_2) = -a_2$, $w_1(d_1) = d_1(z_2 - x_2)/(z_1 - x_1)$, and $w_2(d_2) = d_2$. We then have

$$w_i\Big(v_1(y_1) - v_1(x_1)\Big) + w_2\Big(v_2(y_2) - v_2(x_2)\Big) =$$
$$\frac{(y_1 - x_1)(z_2 - x_2)}{z_1 - x_1} - (y_2 - x_2).$$

Since $(z_2 - y_2)(y_1 - x_1) < (z_1 - y_1)(y_2 - x_2)$, we see that

$$(z_2 - y_2)(y_1 - x_1) + (y_2 - x_2)(y_1 - x_1) < (z_1 - y_1)(y_2 - x_2) + (y_1 - x_1)(y_2 - x_2),$$

so

$$(y_1 - x_1)(z_2 - x_2) - (z_1 - x_1)(y_2 - x_2) < 0.$$

We conclude that $(x_1, x_2) \succ (y_1, y_2)$.

A similar argument shows that $(z_1, z_2) \succ (y_1, y_2)$. We have thus constructed a proper additive difference model that is not single peaked on S'. It follows, as previously noted, that there is a proper additive difference model that is not single peaked on S. This completes the proof.

Glossary

ambience: With reference to an option, it indicates the sign of the preference function, which is positive when the option is preferred to the status quo and negative when the status quo is preferred to the option. With reference to a conflict, see approach/approach, approach/avoidance, avoidance/avoidance.

approach/approach conflict: In the Type I case, a conflict in which all options have positive ambience and the individual must trade off more of one good for less of another. In the Type II case, a conflict in which the options have positive ambience for both parties, so each option other than the status quo represents a gain for both parties and both can be better off than before. The conflict is defined to have positive ambience.

approach/avoidance conflict: In the Type I case, a conflict in which one option has positive ambience and the other has negative or zero ambience; typically one option is the status quo and the other option must be accepted or rejected. In the Type II case, a conflict in which the options have positive ambience for one party and negative ambience for the other party, so every option other than the status quo represents a gain for one party and a loss for the other. The conflict is defined to have negative ambience.

avoidance/avoidance conflict: In the Type I case, a conflict in which all options have negative ambience and the individual must trade off more of one evil against less of another. In the Type II case, a conflict in which the options have negative ambience for both parties, so every option other than the status quo represents a loss for both parties. The conflict is defined to have negative ambience.

approach process: A motivational process induced by positive ambience.

avoidance process: A motivational process induced by negative ambience.

bad: With reference to an option, it indicates that the preference function is negative and the status quo is preferred to the option (i.e., the option has negative ambience). With reference to a component, it indicates that the utility function is decreasing. Has no moral implication.

conflict: A situation in which a choice must be made in the absence of dominance (i.e., a decision must be made that requires a tradeoff).

dominance: A relation between a pair of options such that one is as good as the other on every component and better on at least one.

efficient set: A set of options that are ordered the same or reversed on every elemental component and such that the relative increments in any good component never increase in proportion to the decrements in any bad component. See Section 2.4.2 for the formal definition.

elemental component: A primitive term, undefined. An indecomposable attribute characterized by a utility function that only decreases or only increases and is negatively accelerated (concave down) over an interval scale.

good: With reference to an option, it indicates that the preference function is positive and the option is preferred to the status quo (i.e., the option has positive ambience). With reference to a component, it indicates that the utility function is increasing. Has no moral implication.

interval scale: A numerical representation in which the origin and the unit of measurement are arbitrary. The representation is subject to any affine transformation (i.e., $y = ax + b$ with $a > 0$); these are scales in which the ratio of differences between scale values is a meaningful quantity and is preserved under admissible transformation. The Celsius and Fahrenheit temperature scales are typical examples.

monotonicity: A property of a function that never decreases or never increases. An increasing monotone function may level off, but never actually decrease. Similarly, a decreasing monotone function may level off but never actually increase.

ordinal scale: A numerical representation subject to any positive monotone transformation, that is, $a > b$ if and only if $f(a) > f(b)$. (A positive monotone transformation is one which preserves the ordering; a negative monotone transformation would reverse the ordering.) Moh's hardness scale and a preference for colors are typical examples.

option: An alternative, used in the most general sense.

Pareto optimal set: A set of options such that no one is dominated by another. In any pair of options, each option is better than the other in some respect. See Section 2.4.2 for the formal definition.

preference function: A function giving the degree of preference for options. We often regard it as a composite of utility functions. See Section 2.4.1 for the formal definiton of a proper preference function.

signed ordinal scale: An ordinal scale with a zero point not subject to any transformation (i.e., an ordinal scale subject to any monotone transformation that preserves sign).

single peaked function: A function defined over an ordered set with the property that, given any three points, the value of the function at the intermediate point is not less than the value at either of the other two.

status quo: The current state. Defined to have zero ambience.

utility: Degree of preference measured on at least an ordinal scale.

viable options: The options in a Type II conflict between the two peaks and covered by the inner branches of the two SPFs.

variance: A measure of the dispersion or spread of values of some variable. It is the sum of the squared deviations from the mean.

References

Adams, S. J. (1965). Inequity in social exchange. In L. Berkowitz (Ed.), *Advances in experimental social psychology* (Vol. 2). New York: Academic Press.

Alger, C. F. (1965). Decision-making theory and human conflict. In E. B. McNeil (Ed.), *The nature of human conflict.* Englewood Cliffs, NJ: Prentice-Hall.

Anderson, N. H. (1976). Equity judgments as information integration. *Journal of Personality and Social Psychology, 33,* 291–299.

Angell, R. C. (1957). Discovering paths to peace. In International Sociological Association, *The nature of conflict: Studies of the sociological aspects of international tensions.* Paris: UNESCO.

Angell, R. C. (1965). The sociology of human conflict. In E. B. McNeil (Ed.), *The nature of human conflict.* Englewood Cliffs, NJ: Prentice-Hall.

Angell, R. C. (1979). *The quest for world order.* Ann Arbor, MI: University of Michigan Press.

Arrow, K. (1963). *Social choice and individual values* (2nd ed.). New York: Wiley.

Aschenbrenner, K. M. (1981). Efficient sets, decision heuristics, and single peaked preferences. *Journal of Mathematical Psychology, 23,* 227–256.

Axelrod, R. (1967). Conflict of interest: An axiomatic approach. *Journal of Conflict Resolution, 11,* 87–99.

Axelrod, R. (1970). *Conflict of interest. A theory of divergent goals with applications to politics.* Chicago: Markham Publishing.

Axelrod, R. (1984). *The evolution of cooperation.* New York: Basic Books.

Bartos, O. J. (1977). Simple model of negotiation: A sociological point of view. *Journal of Conflict Resolution, 21,* 565–579.

Bazerman, M. H., & Neale, M. A. (1983). Heuristics in negotiation: Limitations to effective dispute resolution. In M. H. Bazerman & R. J. Lewicki (Eds.), *Negotiating in organizations.* Beverly Hills, CA: Sage.

Bernard, J. (1950). Where is the modern sociology of conflict? *American Journal of Sociology, 56,* 11-16.

Bernard, J. (1957). The sociological study of conflict. In International Sociological Association, *The nature of conflict: Studies of the sociological aspects of international tensions.* Paris: UNESCO.

Bishop, R. L. (1963). A game-theoretic analysis of bargaining. *Quarterly Journal of Economics, 77,* 559–602.

Boasson, C. (1958). A review of Jessie Bernard, T. H. Pear, Raymond Aron, and Robert C. Angell, *The nature of conflict: Studies of the sociological aspects of international tensions. Journal of Conflict Resolution, 2,* 194–198.

Borgese, E. M. (1983). The law of the sea. *Scientific American, 248,* 42–49.

Boulding, K. E. (1965). The economics of human conflict. In E. B. McNeil (Ed.), *The nature of human conflict.* Englewood Cliffs, NJ: Prentice-Hall.

Brams, S. J. (1975). *Game theory and politics.* New York: The Free Press.

Brams, S. J. (1976). *Paradoxes in politics: An introduction to the nonobvious in political science.* New York: The Free Press.

Brams, S. J. (1985). *Superpower games.* New Haven, CT: Yale University Press.

Brewer, M. B. (1979). In-group bias in the minimal intergroup situation: A cognitive-motivational analysis. *Psychological Bulletin, 86,* 307–324.

Calero, H. H. (1979). *Winning the negotiation.* New York: Hawthorne Books.

Camerer, C. T., & MacCrimmon, K. R. (1983). Underground and overpaid: Equity theory in practice. In D. M. Messick & K. S. Cook (Eds.), *Equity theory: Psychological and sociological perspectives.* New York: Praeger.

Chamberlin, J. R., Cohen, J. L., & Coombs, C. H. (1984). Social choice observed: Five presidential elections of the American Psychological Association. *The Journal of Politics, 46,* 479–502.

Claude, I. L., Jr. (1971). *Swords into plowshares* (4th ed.). New York: Random House.

Condorcet, M. (1785). *Essai sur l'application de l'analyse a la probabilite des decisions rendues a la pluralite des voix.* Paris.

Coombs, C. H. (1958). On the use of inconsistency of preferences in psychological measurement. *Journal of Experimental Psychology, 55,* 1–7.

Coombs, C. H. (1976). *A theory of data.* Ann Arbor, MI: Mathesis Press. (Originally published, 1964.)

Coombs, C. H. (1983). *Psychology and mathematics.* Ann Arbor, MI: University of Michigan Press.

Coombs, C. H., & Avrunin, G. S. (1977a). A theorem on single peaked preference functions in one dimension. *Journal of Mathematical Psychology, 16,* 261–266.

Coombs, C. H., & Avrunin, G. S. (1977b). Single peaked functions and the theory of preference. *Psychological Review, 84,* 216–230.

Coombs, C. H., Coombs, L. C., & McClelland, G. H. (1975). Preference scales for number and sex of children. *Population Studies, 29,* 273–298.

Coombs, C. H., Cohen, J. L., & Chamberlin, J. R. (1984). An experimental study of some election systems. *American Psychologist, 39,* 140–157.

Coombs, L. C. (1976). *Are cross-cultural preference comparisons possible? A measurement-theoretic approach.* Liege, Belgium: International Union for the Scientific Study of Population Papers #5.

Cooper, R. N. (1985). International economic cooperation: Is it desirable? Is it likely? *Bulletin of American Academy of Arts and Sciences, 36*(2), 11–35.

Coser, L. A. (1956). *The functions of social conflict.* New York: The Free Press.

Coser, L. A. (1957). Social conflict and the theory of social change. *British Journal of Sociology, 8,* 197–207.

Dahrendorf, R. (1958). Toward a theory of social conflict. *Conflict Resolution, 2,* 170–183.

Dahrendorf, R. (1962). *Gesellschaft and Freiheit.* Munchen: R. Piper.

Daniel, T.E. (1978). Pitfalls in the theory of fairness. *Journal of Economic Theory, 19,* 561–64.

Dawes, R.M., Alphons, J.C., van de Kragt, J.C., & Orbell, J.M. (1987, August). Not me or thee but we: The importance of group identity in eliciting cooperation in dilemma situations: Experimental manipulations. To appear in the *Proceedings of the 11th International Conference on Subjective Probability, Utility, and Decision Making,* Cambridge, England.

de Waal, F. (1982). *Chimpanzee politics. Power and sex among apes.* New York: Harper & Row.

Denenberg, R. V. (1981). Third party to a quarrel. *The Dial, 2,* 42–45.

Denenberg, T. S., & Denenberg, R. V. (1981). *Dispute resolution: Settling conflicts without legal action.* New York: Public Affairs Committee.

Deutsch, M. (1954). Field theory in social psychology. In G. Lindzey (Ed.), *Handbook of social psychology Vol. I, theory and methods.* Reading, MA: Addison-Wesley.

Deutsch, M. (1973). *The resolution of conflict.* New Haven & London:

Yale University Press.

Deutsch, M. (1974). Awakening the sense of injustice. In M. Ross & M. Lerner (Eds.), *The quest for justice: Myth, reality, ideal.* New York: Holt, Rinehart & Winston.

Douglas, A. (1957). The peaceful settlement of industrial and intergroup disputes. *Conflict Resolution, 1,* 69–81.

Edgeworth, F. Y. (1881). *Mathematical psychics.* London: Kegan Paul.

Ellsberg, D. (1975). The theory and practice of blackmail. In O. R. Young (Ed.), *Bargaining: Formal theories of negotiation.* Urbana, IL: University of Illinois Press.

Encyclopedia Britannica (1973). Chicago: Encyclopedia Brittanica.

English, H. B., & English, A. C. (1958). *A comprehensive dictionary of psychological and psychoanalytic terms.* New York: Longmans, Green.

Etzioni, A. (1967). The Kennedy experiment. *Western Political Quarterly, 20,* 361–80.

Finz, L. L. (1976). The hi/lo contract. *New York State Bar Journal, 48,* 186.

Fishburn, P. C. (1973). *The theory of social choice.* Princeton, NJ: Princeton University Press.

Fishburn, P. C. (1986). Empirical comparisons of voting procedures. *Behavioral Science, 31,* 82–88.

Furby, L. (1986). Psychology and justice. In R. L. Cohen (Ed.), *Justice: Views from the social sciences.* New York: Plenum.

Gilbert, B. (1987). Lizards that take to the desert like ducks to water. *Smithsonian, 18(5),* 78–86.

Green, E. D. (1984a). *Avoiding the legal logjam—private justice, California style, in corporate dispute management.* In Center for Public Resource — CPR, *Corporate dispute management, 1982.* New York: Matthew Bender.

Green, E. D. (1984b). A comprehensive approach to the theory and practice of dispute resolution. *Journal of Legal Education, 34*, 245–258.

Green, E.D., Marks, J. B., & Olson, R. L. (1978). Settling large case litigation: An alternate approach, *Loyola of Los Angeles Law Review, 11*, 493.

Greenberg, M. G. (1961). *Response latency as a test of mathematical models for preference behavior.* Unpublished doctoral dissertation, University of Michigan.

Hardin, G. (1960). The competitive exclusion principle. *Science, 131*, 1292–1297.

Hardin, R. (1983). Unilateral versus mutual disarmament. *Philosophy and Public Affairs, 12*, 236–254.

Harris, R. J., & Joyce, M. A. (1980). What's fair: It depends on how you phrase the question. *Journal of Personality and Social Psychology, 38*, 165–179.

Harsanyi, J. C. (1967–1968). Games with incomplete information played by 'Bayesian' players. *Management Science, 14*, 159–182; 320–334; 486–502.

Howard, M. (1983). *The causes of wars.* London: Counterpoint, University Paperbacks.

Howard, N. (1971). *Paradoxes of rationality: Theory of metagames and political behavior.* Cambridge, MA: MIT Press.

Huber, O. (1979a). Intransitive Praferenzen und strategien fur multi-dimensionale entscheidungen: Gewichtete-preferenz-mengen- strategie und differenz-strategie. *Zeitschrift fur Experimentelle und Angewandte Psychologie, 26*, 72–93.

Huber, O. (1979b). Nontransitive multidimensional preferences: Theoretical analysis of a model. *Theory and Decision, 10*, 147–165.

Isard, W., & Smith, C. (1982). *Conflict analysis and practical conflict management procedures.* Cambridge, MA: Ballinger.

Jervis, R. (1976). *Perception and misperception in international politics.* Princeton, NJ: Princeton University Press.

Jones, A.J. (1980). *Game theory: mathematical models of conflict.*

Chichester: E. Harwood; New York: Halsted Press.

Kasner, E., & Newman, J. (1940). *Mathematics and the imagination.* New York: Simon & Schuster.

Kemeny, J. (1959). Mathematics without numbers. *Daedalus, 88,* 577–591.

Komorita, S. S., & Lapworth, C. W. (1982). Cooperative choice among individuals versus groups in an N-person dilemma situation. *Journal of Personality and Social Psychology, 42,* 487–496.

Krantz, D. H., & Tversky, A. (1965). *A critique of the applicability of cardinal utility theory* (Tech. Report MMPP65-4). University of Michigan, Michigan Mathematical Psychology Program.

Krantz, D. H., Luce, R. D., Suppes, P., & Tversky, A. (1971). *Foundations of measurement, (Vol. 1). Additive and polynomal representations.* New York: Academic Press.

Lewin, K. (1931). Environmental forces in child behavior and development. In C. Murchison (Ed.), *A handbook of child psychology.* Worcester, MA: Clark University Press.

Lewin, K. (1935). *A dynamic theory of personality.* New York: McGraw-Hill.

Lewin, K. (1951). *Field theory in social science.* New York: Harper & Brothers.

Lind, E. A., Lessik, R. I., & Conlon, D. E. (1983). Decision control and process control effects on procedural fairness judgments. *Journal of Applied Social Psychology, 13,* 338–350.

Lissitzyn, O. J. (1972). *The International Court of Justice: Its role in the maintenance of international peace and security.* New York: Octagon Books. (Originally published, 1951.)

Lockhart, C. (1979). *Bargaining in international conflicts.* New York: Columbia University Press.

Long, A. A. (1973). Psychological ideas in antiquity. In P. P. Wiener (Ed.), *A dictionary of the history of ideas* (Vol. IX). New York: Charles Scribner's Sons.

Lorenz, K. (1966). *On aggression.* New York: Harcourt, Brace, &

World.

Luce, R. D., & Raiffa, H. (1957). *Games and decisions.* New York: Wiley.

Maier, N. R. F. (1952). *Principles of human relations: Applications to management.* New York: Wiley.

May, K. O. (1954). Intransitivity, utility, and the aggregation of preference patterns. *Econometrica, 22,* 1–13.

Mayr, E. (1970). *Populations, species and evolution.* Cambridge: Harvard University Press.

Mellars, B. A. (1982). Equity judgment: A revision of Aristotelian views. *Journal of Experimental Psychology: General, 111*(2), 242–270.

Messick, D. M., & Cook, K. S. (1983). *Equity theory: Psychological and sociological perspectives.* New York: Praeger.

Messick, D. M., & Sentis, K. P. (1983). Fairness, preference, and fairness biases. In D. M. Messick & K. S. Cook (Eds.), *Equity theory: Psychological and sociological perspectives.* New York: Praeger.

Miller, N. E. (1944). Experimental studies of conflict. In J. M. V. Hunt (Ed.), *Personality and the behavior disorders* (Vol. 1). New York: The Ronald Press.

Milnor, J. (1954). Games against nature. In R. M. Thrall, C. H. Coombs, & R. L. Davis (Eds.), *Decision processes.* New York: Wiley.

Murphy, J. T. (1982). *The United Nations and the control of international violence.* Totowa, NJ: Allenhead, Osmun.

Narens, L., & Luce, R. D. (1983). How we may have been misled into believing in the interpersonal comparability of utility. *Theory and Decision, 15,* 247–60.

Nash, J. T. (1950). The bargaining problem. *Econometrica, 18,* 155–162.

Oliva, T. A., Peters, M. H., & Murthy, H. S. K. (1981). A preliminary empirical test of a cusp catastrophe model in the social sciences. *Behavioral Science, 26,* 153–162.

Osgood, C. E. (1962). *An alternative to war or surrender.* Urbana, IL: University of Illinois Press.

Parsons, T. (1962). Polarization of the world and international order. In Q. Wright, W. M. Evan, & M. Deutsch (Eds.), *Preventing World War III: Some proposals.* New York: Simon & Schuster.

Pazner, P. A. (1977). Pitfalls in the theory of fairness. *Journal of Economic Theory, 14,* 458–66.

Perlman, P. L. (1979). Final offer arbitration: A pre-trial settlement device. *Harvard Journal on Legislation, 16,* 513.

Pfanzagl, J. (1959). A general theory of measurement — applications to utility. *Naval Research Logistics Quarterly, 6,* 283–294.

Priestley, J. (1775). *Introductory essays to Hartley's theory of the human mind.* London: J. Johnson.

Pruitt, D. G. (1983). Achieving integrative agreements. In M. H. Bazerman & R. J. Lewicki (Eds.), *Negotiating in organizations.* Beverly Hills, CA: Sage.

Pruitt, D. G., & Rubin, J. Z. (1986). *Social conflict: Escalation, stalemate, and settlement.* New York: Random House.

Raiffa, H. (1982). *The art and science of negotiation.* Cambridge, MA: Harvard University Press.

Rapoport, Amnon (1967). Optimal policies for the Prisoner's Dilemma. *Psychological Review, 74,* 136–148.

Rapoport, Anatol. (1960). *Fights, games, and debates.* Ann Arbor, MI: University of Michigan Press.

Rapoport, Anatol, & Chammah, A. M. (1965). *Prisoner's dilemma, a study in conflict and cooperation.* Ann Arbor, MI: University of Michigan Press.

Rapoport, Anatol, Guyer, M. J., & Gordon, D. G. (1976). *The 2 × 2 game.* Ann Arbor, MI: University of Michigan Press.

Rawls, J. (1971). *The theory of justice.* Cambridge, MA: Harvard University Press.

Rescher, N. (1966). *Distributive justice: A constructive critique of the utilitarian theory of distribution.* New York: Bibbs-Merrill.

Reis, H. T. (1984). The multidimensionality of justice. In R. Folger (Ed.), *The sense of injustice: Social psychological perfections.* New York: Plenum.

Ross, W. D. (Ed.). (1966). *The works of Aristotle* (Vol. 9). London: Oxford University Press.

Samuelson, C.D., Messick, D.M., Allison, S.T., & Beggan, J.K. (1986). Utopia or Myopia? A reply to Fox. *American Psychologist, 41,* 227–229.

Schellenberg, J. A. (1982). *The science of conflict.* New York: Oxford University Press.

Schelling, T. C. (1960). *The strategy of conflict.* Cambridge, MA: Harvard University Press.

Schoemaker, P. J. H. (1982). The expected utility model: Its variants, purposes, evidence, and limitations. *Journal of Economic Literature, 20,* 529–563.

Scoville, H., Jr. (1985). Reciprocal national restraint: An alternative path to arms control. *Bulletin of American Academy of Arts and Sciences, 38,* 15–29.

Sen, A. (1970). *Collective choice and social welfare.* San Francisco: Holden-Day.

Shannon, C., & Weaver, W. (1949). *The mathematical theory of communication.* Urbana, IL: University of Illinois Press.

Sherif, M. (1966). *In common predicament.* Boston: Houghton Mifflin.

Simmel, G. (1904). The sociology of conflict. *American Journal of Sociology, 9,* 490–525; 672–689; 798–811.

Simon, H. A. (1955). A behavioral model of rational choice. *Quarterly Journal of Economics, 69,* 99–108.

Simon, H. A. (1957). *Models of man.* New York: Wiley.

Simon, H. A. (1969). *The sciences of the artificial.* Cambridge, MA: MIT Press.

Smith, J. M., & Price, G. R. (1973). The logic of animal conflict. *Nature, 246,* 15–18.

Snyder, G. H., & Diesing, P. (1977). *Conflict among nations.* Princeton, NJ: Princeton University Press.

Stagner, R., & Rosen, H. (1965). *Psychology of union management relations.* Belmont, CA: Wadsworth.

Stech, F. J. (1980). Self-deception: The other side of the coin. *The Washington Quarterly, 3,* 130–140.

Stevens, S. S. (1958). Problems and methods of psychophysics. *Psychological Bulletin, 55,* 177–196.

Suppes, P., & Zinnes, J. L. (1963). Basic measurement theory. In R. D. Luce, R. R. Bush, & E. Galanter (Eds.), *Handbook of mathematical psychology* (Vol. 1). New York: Wiley.

Thaler, R. H. (1980). Towards a positive theory of consumer choice. *Journal of Economic Behavior and Organization, 1,* 39–60.

Thibaut, J., & Walker, L. (1975). *Procedural justice: A psychological analysis.* Hillsdale, NJ: Lawrence Erlbaum Associates.

Thibaut, J., & Walker, L. (1978). *A theory of procedure.* California Law Review, 66, 541-566.

Thompson, J. (1985). *Psychological aspects of nuclear war.* New York: British Psychological Society and Wiley.

Trivers, R. (1985). *Principles of social evolution.* Menlo Park, CA: The Benjamin/Cummings Publishing Co., Inc.

Tversky, A. (1969). Intransitivity of preference. *Psychological Review, 76,* 31–48.

Tversky, A., & Kahneman, D. (1981). The framing of decisions and the psychology of choice. *Science, 211,* 453–458.

Tversky, A., & Kahneman, D. (1986). Rational choice and the framing of decisions. *The Journal of Business, 59*(4), Part 2, S251–S278.

van Avermaet, E. F. (1975). *Equity: A theoretical and experimental analysis.* Unpublished doctoral dissertation, University of California, Santa Barbara.

Varian, H. R. (1974). Equity, envy, and efficiency. *Journal of Economic Theory, 9,* 63–91.

Varian, H. R. (1976). Distributive justice, welfare economics, and the theory of fairness. *Philosophy of Public Affairs, 4,* 223–247.

von Neumann, J., & Morgenstern, O. (1947). *Theory of games and economic behavior* (2nd Ed.). Princeton, NJ: Princeton University Press.

Walster, E., Walster, G. W., & Berscheid, E. (1978). *Equity: Theory and research.* Boston, MA: Allyn & Bacon.

Walton, R. E., & McKersie, R. B. (1965). *A behavioral theory of labor negotiations: An analysis of a social interaction system.* New York: McGraw-Hill.

Warren, C. (1941, January). The Supreme Court and disputes between States. *International Conciliation,* No. 366.

Wernick, R. (1986). Summits of yore: Promises, promises, and a deal or two. *Smithsonian, 17*(6), 58–67.

Wundt, W. (1874). *Grundzuge der physiologischen psychologie.* Leipzig: Verlag von Wilhelm Engelmann.

Index

— T —

— U —

— V —

— W —

Walker, L., 94
Walster, E., 85, 88
Walster, G., 85, 88
Walton, R. E., 90
Warren, C., 202
Weaver, W., 148
weighted sets of dimensions
        rule, *see*
            • additive difference
              model, weighted sets
              of dimensions rule
Wernick, R., 67
worst-case analysis, 141
Wundt, W., 12

— Z —

zero point, 82
zero-sum game, *see*
            • strictly competitive
              game
Zinnes, J. L., 76